Transgressed

Intimate Partner Violence in Transgender Lives

Xavier L. Guadalupe-Diaz

D0746034

NEW YORK UNIVERSITY PRESS

New York

NEW YORK UNIVERSITY PRESS
New York
www.nyupress.org

References to Internet websites (URLs) were accurate at the time of writing. Neither the author nor New York University Press is responsible for URLs that may have expired or changed since the manuscript was prepared.

ISBN: 978-1-4798-3294-1 (hardback)
ISBN: 978-1-4798-2785-5 (paperback)

For Library of Congress Cataloging-in-Publication data, please contact the Library of Congress.

New York University Press books are printed on acid-free paper, and their binding materials are chosen for strength and durability. We strive to use environmentally responsible suppliers and materials to the greatest extent possible in publishing our books.

Manufactured in the United States of America

10 9 8 7 6 5 4 3 2 1

Also available as an ebook

I dedicate this book to the brave trans voices who opened up to me and shared their stories with the broader world.

I also dedicate this book to my late mother-in-law, Tona Sink, who was an avid supporter of LGBTQ communities and to the victims and survivors of Hurricane Maria in Puerto Rico.

CONTENTS

1

Intimate Partner Violence outside the Binary

For the transgender community, threats of violence, harassment, discrimination, and intimidation are aspects of daily existence. On any given day, violence directed at transgender people ranges from the interpersonal realm to the more broad ramifications of state policy (e.g., North Carolina's House Bill 2) that marginalizes those who transgress the rigid boundaries of the gender binary (male/female).[1] While media and our collective attention are placed primarily on hate-motivated biases and crimes toward transgender individuals, a broader problem remains largely unexplored: trans victimization by intimate partners. I use the term "trans" as shorthand to refer to a broader range of individuals whose gender identity or expression, as Danica Bornstein of the Northwest Network of Bi, Trans, Lesbian, and Gay Survivors of Abuse and colleagues noted, "varies from the cultural norm for their birth sex."[2] This catchall term captures a range of gender identities beyond the biological sex-assigned definitions of cismale and cisfemale. Cisgender people are those whose assigned sex at birth matches their gender identity and expression.[3]

While various definitions of intimate partner violence exist, it is largely understood as a pattern of physical, emotional, psychological, or sexual abuses perpetrated by a current or former romantic partner.[4] Almost all of the available generalizable studies on intimate partner violence focus exclusively on cisgender men and women. These studies typically find that women do experience higher lifetime rates of intimate partner violence when compared to men.[5] Women victims, when compared to men, typically experience more severe injuries that result in hospitalization and more often suffer disproportionate negative outcomes from intimate partner violence such as economic insecurity and psychological trauma.[6] Estimates show that at least a third of women murdered in the United States were killed by a former or current boyfriend or husband;[7] overall, women are murdered by intimate partners at twice the rate of men.[8] In looking at just murder-suicides in the United States, 74 percent involved intimate partners, with 96 percent of these involving women murdered by their current or former intimate partner.[9] While much of the existing evidence shows that intimate partner violence and homicide are gendered phenomena, less is known about the patterns of transgender victimization. This study explores the distinct realities of those who identify as transgender and have survived intimate partner violence by examining phone and online chat interviews and written accounts for the project at the center of this book. Over the course of six months, I spoke with thirteen transgender survivors of intimate partner violence who agreed to allow me to record their experiences and received five additional anonymously written accounts.

Given the dearth of information on transgender survivor accounts of intimate partner violence, the stories in this book served as some of the earliest attempts to describe the dynamics of abuse for the trans community. In sociologist Lori Girshick's compelling *Woman-to-Woman Sexual Violence: Does She Call It Rape?*, the author described this lack of information as a "complete lack of research on interpersonal violence among transgender people," which she characterized as a "serious gap" in the literature.[10] Psychologist Janice Ristock stated that the field of same-gender intimate partner violence research has been dominated by a focus on lesbian victimization and that still "very little work addresses trans experiences."[11] Further, the National Coalition of Anti-Violence Programs (NCAVP), which collects and annually reports data on violent victimization experienced by the lesbian, gay, bisexual, transgender, and queer (LGBTQ) community at large, recently called upon researchers to "focus on increasing the amount of literature on how transgender and gender non-conforming people are affected by intimate partner violence and the unique barriers these communities face in trying to access resources."[12] In answering these and many more calls to action, this book centers on the stories of survival of eighteen trans-identified people.

About halfway through my research, Tom, a twenty-four-year-old black transman from Texas, contacted me to set up a phone interview. Like most of those who responded to the call to participate in the study, Tom e-mailed me with interest and curiosity before we decided on a date and time to speak. Our conversation was briefer than most; the background conversations that typically took around twenty to thirty minutes were shorter and to the point. Tom was raised in the South by a conservative, religious family with whom he sometimes had a contentious relationship but was, at the time we spoke, still in contact. Like the handful of survivors whom I had spoken with before him, Tom volunteered to share with me his experiences with intimate partner violence as a transgender person. He detailed abuse, violence, emotional torment, and public humiliation. This account was still raw. He jumped back and forth between the details of the incidents and how he was dealing with the trauma. Over the course of the interview, I asked Tom how he realized he was in an abusive relationship. He paused at length, giving a short response about how his abuser made him feel: "I knew it was abusive cuz like, she just made me feel ashamed of who I was and all." As I was about to follow-up in the short pause, he added, "Like, every now and then I'll think, just like, how lucky everyone is that they don't have to think about their gender clashing with their bodies and I wish sometimes that I wasn't trans but then I think, no, no, that's what she would've wanted."

It struck me that for Tom processing what made him think about the situation as abusive centered on his trans identity. He described one main aspect of what I would later learn transgender-identified survivors of intimate partner violence routinely faced. As a young transman, he had endured patterned emotional and physical brutalities similar to what many cisgender victims of intimate partner violence report. However, his trans identity made it front and center in the battle toward making sense of his abuse. As with many LGBTQ-identified people, the imagined possibility of being straight or cisgender may provide a temporary mental escape from the hardships of a marginalized existence; however, in Tom's words, this is precisely what his abuser used as part of his abuse—manipulating the external cultural hostility that exists against those who transgress the gender binary in an effort to control Tom's identity.

At the crux of this book's analyses is the goal of detailing abusive intimate partner dynamics among a sample of transgender individuals in order to understand and generate theoretical interpretations about their experiences. How the participants' identities framed the meanings and interpretations of violence and, subsequently, how the process of leaving an abusive relationship was structured for these trans survivors form the center of understanding how intimate partner violence is experienced by transgender people more generally.

Almost by default and continuing today, discussions of violence between intimate partners conjure images of abused ciswomen and abusive cismen: women and men who identify with their assigned sex and gender at birth. Even in a time when our culture has progressed toward the recognition of same-gender couples through either popular culture or the nationwide legalization of marriage equality, the compulsion to try to make sense of the world in rigidly gendered ways is still the convention. Take for example how the public imagines domestic victimization as distinctly feminine all the while conflating violence or aggression with masculine traits. While many efforts have been made to critically reconsider the gendered assumptions behind intimate partner violence, very little has challenged us to think about the experiences of those whose gender identities are more complex than the unquestioned labels we receive at birth.

While much debate exists about the social understandings of gender, it is understood to be more complicated than the decisions rendered at birth. Psychology scholars generally agree that our sense of what makes us feel like a man, a woman, or neither becomes deeply embedded by ages two to four; this is understood as our gender identity.[13] Beyond the internalized sense of what makes human beings identify with a particular gender, externally we express such attributes in ways that are socially understood to signal masculinity, femininity, neither, or both. Humans engage in gender expression daily through the ways in which we carry our bodies and wear our hair, the clothing we select, and much more. Sociologists understand gender as a social construct: a concept that highlights how humans make social categories "real" by attributing meaning to bodies, reifying differences through structure (e.g., gendered bathrooms, sports teams, labor, and wages), and subsequently internalizing such messages. Generally, almost without question, gender has been central to how social scientists and many antiviolence activists have come to understand why intimate partner violence exists, how it manifests, the dynamics involved, and how it is experienced. Despite gender informing much of the understanding that exists around intimate partner violence, mainstream discussions have often taken a rather linear look at gender, mostly limiting the analysis to the two most recognized genders.

Developing the Project

As is the case with many research ideas, my journey toward a trans-centered project on intimate partner violence came about in gradual stages. As a scholar exploring the field, I quickly learned how divisive and contentious the debate over the role of gender in intimate partner violence had been and began questioning some basic assumptions. For instance, do men and women commit equal acts of violence toward one another, or are men the dominate abusers? Meanwhile, I grew more and more interested in the deeper complications of gender—beyond this binary system—to explore how gender informed violence structurally and through interaction.

Today, advocates and scholars alike find that different types of intimate partner violence result in different gendered dynamics. As sociologist Michael P. Johnson generally argued, perhaps the intense coercion that more women experience in intimate partner violence at the hands of men requires the structural power of patriarchy, while more common violence between partners may arise in less patterned and inherently gendered ways.[14] As a queer-identified individual, however, I understood that gender could be experienced more dynamically and in less static ways than commonly conceptualized in the intimate partner violence literature. That is to say that for many individuals, gender identity may conflict with assigned labels or can be understood as more of a journey of evolution and self-discovery. I questioned how a type of violence in which gender informs aggression, communication, identity, and interaction is experienced by those who identify outside of the rigid gender binary, which represents a cultural system of two institutionally legitimized genders. Scholars often refer to that cultural system of two genders as genderism—"a social system of structural inequality with an underlying assumption that there are two, and only two genders."[15] I utilize the term "genderism" here and throughout to describe the structural, institutional, interpersonal, and intrapersonal systems that marginalize, subordinate, and threaten gender variance for individuals who identify as transgender, which includes those who are genderqueer, gender-nonconforming, gender-nonbinary, and/or otherwise gender variant.[16] Further, genderism characterizes a cultural ideology "that reinforces the negative evaluation of gender non-conformity or an incongruence between sex and gender."[17] While transphobia describes fear or disgust against transgender people, genderist ideology more broadly describes how culture regulates the boundaries of appropriate gender expression and identification.[18] In setting up a research endeavor to answer that initial question, I started by first taking stock of what we already knew, in particular, how scholars had come to understand the role of gender and other identities within intimate partner violence.

Tracing Thought in Intimate Partner Violence

Arguably, one of the best ways to begin an exploration of understudied social phenomena is to understand the trajectory of the problem to date. Today, intimate partner violence is viewed as a social problem largely as a result of the efforts of feminist activists and scholars of the 1970s who framed the social problem as violence against women: a phenomenon that exists directly as a result of a patriarchal power structure that fosters a hostile cultural climate against women and enables men to perpetrate violence against them as a means of maintaining control.[19] Within this mode of thinking, the cultural construct of the gender binary is the primary facilitator of the existence of violence against women. In its most rigid application, women are the *only* potential victims while men are the *only* potential perpetrators. The response that emerged from these intellectual exchanges and theorizations about women's place in society provided the foundation for the development of the sociopolitical or sociocultural explanations of the existence of domestic violence. This research generally concluded that violence against women was a "natural consequence of women's powerless position vis-a-vis men in patriarchal societies and the sexist values and attitudes that accompany this inequity."[20]

Though groundbreaking feminist perspectives provided a logical framework to understand a specific type of intimate partner violence, they were limited by an assumption of heterosexuality, or heterosexism, and the "normalization" of heterosexuality, which scholars often refer to as heteronormativity. Early theorization assumed the heterosexuality of victims and perpetrators without question; subsequently, diverse gender identities were also overlooked. By the late 1980s and early 1990s, scholars began challenging these approaches and highlighted their inapplicability to the existence of same-gender intimate partner violence.[21] Since then, a multitude of studies have indicated that intimate partner violence affects the lesbian, gay, and bisexual population at rates similar to those of heterosexual women, although more accurate and recent findings have pointed to higher prevalence among same-gender relationships.[22]

Over decades of research on same-gender intimate partner violence, several key themes have emerged. It is clear that regardless of gender, intimate partner violence exists across relationships and manifests similar dynamics of power and control. Physical, sexual, emotional, financial, and psychological abuses are well documented in patterns that are similar in both opposite-gender and same-gender intimate partner violence. However, important distinctions arise in regard to prevalence rates, dynamics of abuse, myths, and help seeking, among others. Gay and bisexual men typically report higher rates of psychological intimate partner violence when compared to heterosexual men, while gay men also report slightly lower rates of physical violence, rape, and stalking when compared to both bisexual and heterosexual men.[23] Somewhat surprising to some, lesbian and bisexual women report higher lifetime rates of rape and psychological, physical, and stalking intimate partner violence when compared to heterosexual women. Victims of same-gender intimate partner violence also report different patterns of abuses than do their opposite-gender counterparts.

Among the distinctions are the role of homophobia and heterosexism as both tactic and context of abuse. While I elaborate more on this in the following chapter, victims of same-gender intimate partner violence report that abusers use coercive tactics based on sexual identity such as threatening to "out" them to friends, family, or work colleagues and manipulating beliefs in homophobic myths. In *LGBTQ Intimate Partner Violence: Lessons for Policy, Practice, and Research,* the only book to systemically review thirty-five years of existing research on LGBTQ intimate partner violence, sociologist Adam Messinger identified top myths, which in reductive shorthand can be categorized as the beliefs that LGBTQ intimate partner violence is rare and less severe (than heterosexual intimate partner violence), that abusers are masculine, that it is the same as all other intimate partner violence, and that it should not be discussed. The persistence of these myths often makes it more difficult for victims of same-gender intimate partner violence to recognize abuse or to identify as a victim. Additionally, widespread belief in these myths allows abusers to undermine the experiences of violence and entrap victims. For victims of same-gender intimate partner violence who do leave abusive relationships, help-seeking structures are generally best tailored for the needs of cisgender heterosexual women. Survivors of same-gender intimate partner violence often report experiences of misgendering and homophobia by responding police officers and a lack of inclusive shelter space, counseling, and resources. In addition, even informal help avenues such as friends and family may be less available to same-gender abuse survivors due to previous rejection.

Despite the fact that the literature exploring same-gender intimate partner violence and the experiences of gay and lesbian victims has expanded, transgender victims remain largely absent from the research. Decades of research in same-gender intimate partner violence oftentimes lumped trans experiences with those of cisgender gays and lesbians, and little attention has been given to how genderism structures trans victimization and presents barriers to help seeking or to the dynamics of abuse. In one of the earliest trans-specific studies available, transgender intimate partner violence experts Courvant and Cook-Daniels cited preliminary analyses from the Gender, Violence, and Resource Access Survey of trans and intersex individuals that found a 50 percent rate of victimization by an intimate partner.[24] In 2006, the National Resource Center on Domestic Violence reported that of all their reporting agencies, too few had clientele who identified as transgender to garner any statistically relevant information. This difficulty in obtaining transgender samples has often led scholars to exclude trans responses in same-gender intimate partner violence studies or to use just "binary gender identity categories (i.e. only men or women)," which do not accurately represent the diversity of genders within the community.[25]

As a result of the lack of trans-inclusive studies, it is difficult to determine a prevalence rate of intimate partner violence for the trans community as a whole. Within recent NCAVP annual reports, transgender individuals were on average almost two times more likely to experience harassment, threats, and/or intimidation by an intimate partner.[26] In a UCLA Williams Institute report that reviewed existing research on intimate partner and sexual violence within LGBTQ communities, Brown and Herman found lifetime prevalence rates between 31.3 percent and 50 percent.[27]

While feminist intimate partner violence research has critiqued patriarchy, more needs to be done to thoroughly examine patriarchy's reinforcement of the system of two and only two genders and how this contextualizes experiences of abuse. Generally, feminist theorists have held that intimate partner violence is a gender asymmetrical occurrence, viewing men as overwhelmingly the perpetrators of intimate partner violence. Beyond the gendered pattern, feminists have typically described intimate partner violence as a phenomenon that exists directly as a result of a patriarchal power structure that fosters a hostile cultural climate against women and enables men to perpetrate violence against them as a means of controlling women in society.

From this cultural perspective, this violence was not "domestic violence" or "intimate partner violence," but rather was conceptualized as "wife beating," "wife abuse," or "woman abuse." Feminists' efforts were primarily focused on highlighting the evident gendered pattern while shaping a political agenda that would ultimately change our systematic response to the needs of these women victims. In arguably one of the most cited pioneering works, sociologists Dobash and Dobash sought to examine the experiences of abused women in a battered women's shelter through a feminist perspective.[28] Commonalities in the women's experiences led to the conclusion that batterers held rigid patriarchal family ideals. When these victims were perceived to be out of line by their abusers, the abusers would reassert their patriarchal authority in the relationship through violent means. The women expressed that their husbands had certain gender-specific expectations of them as wives and that their violence was a mechanism through which batterers regulated their lives.

While feminist perspectives were readily challenged by the more "gender-neutral" family violence scholars who sought to make oppositional arguments, feminist thoughts based on cultural power dynamics between genders shaped the early direction of inquiry and essentially all of the response systems (e.g., shelters, hotlines, etc.). As the subfield of domestic violence scholarship emerged, it framed the violence as a heterosexually cisgender phenomenon. The broader argument was that men committed the overwhelming amount of intimate partner violence and did so because of the larger patriarchal power structure that constructed women as property in marriage, along with a legal system that supported or tolerated this view and the gender socialization that fostered hostile beliefs against women in our society. While framing intimate partner violence through this perspective highlighted the gendered nature of the violence, it also limited the research to the context of heterosexual relationships with discussions of only ciswomen victims of cismen perpetrators.

Assumptions of intimate partner violence based on theoretical orientation paint the issue with a broad brush that can often prove problematic, particularly when applied to trans victims. The oversimplification of gender resulted in early work that assumed that gender was the primary form of oppression for *all* women, failing to consider the intersecting qualities of race, class, and sexual orientation. This undermined the experiences of women of color, lesbians, economically marginalized groups, and more.

Social theory has grown and developed with the addition of a wider scope of approaches to the scholarship. In particular, black feminist scholars, activists, and critical race theorists revolutionized various subfields by centering black women's voices in social theorization.[29] In particular, feminist legal scholar Kimberlé Crenshaw addressed the intersections of race and gender in how women of color experience violence and is often credited with coining the term "intersectionality."[30] Sociologist and criminologist Hillary Potter described intersectionality as "the concept or conceptualization that each person has an assortment of coalesced socially constructed identities that are ordered into an inequitable social stratum."[31] Within any singular identity-based community, there exist a multitude of various identities (i.e., race, class, gender, sexual orientation) that alter the standpoint and experience of any particular member.

Take, for example, the recent public gender transition of Caitlyn Jenner; her experiences show starkly different realities from those who may not share her unique social position. As a successful athlete and celebrity, Caitlyn has been afforded the ability to access the best health care and transition resources available. Caitlyn advocates for the visibility of trans communities by sharing her story as a transwoman and televising many aspects of her transition via her reality television show. Despite the connection she has established with the broader trans community, Caitlyn has continued to utilize her race and class position to subordinate entire aspects of the trans population. Her personal politics, largely informed by a life of privilege, have often seemed to clash with the broader trans experience.

For example, Caitlyn openly claimed that she "liked" Senator Ted Cruz during the 2016 Republican presidential primary. Despite offering her reservations about him, she lauded his conservative principles as his most important qualities. Primarily motivated by her elite class position, Caitlyn first advanced the notion that economic policy should serve the needs of the rich (e.g., through tax cuts and incentives for the wealthy).[32] Cruz, an openly transphobic candidate, showed no love in return for Caitlyn, buckling down on his stance to deny transgender people equal and safe access to public restrooms.[33] Caitlyn went on to support Donald Trump in the 2016 presidential election and has recently stood by her decision with "no regrets" despite the administration's roll back of Obama-era protections for transgender people, which she simply dismissed as "mistakes."[34] An intersectional perspective illustrates how Caitlyn can afford to support transphobic political candidates at relatively no expense or suffering on her behalf. While she openly identifies as a transwoman, Caitlyn's race and class position allow her the privilege to avoid many unpleasantries and barriers in her life. In a similar way, countless other identities intersect and shape the ways in which social realities are experienced, especially experiences with intimate partner violence.

Building on the broader foundations of intersectionality, Bograd challenged many of the assumptions underlying the dominant feminist domestic violence theories.[35] Applying intersectionality to intimate partner violence demonstrates the effectiveness of a form of theorizing that includes interlocking systems of oppression (i.e., racism, sexism, classism, heterosexism) that shape distinct social localities and ultimately mold interpersonal dynamics, experiences, and understandings of violence and help seeking. While much of the early intimate partner violence work centered gender in the lives of predominately white and exclusively cisgender samples, Bograd conceptualized that intersectionality within the study of intimate partner violence has the ability to "color the meaning and nature of domestic violence, how it is experienced by self and responded to by others, how personal and social consequences are represented, and how or whether escape and safety can be obtained."[36]

Consider, for example, how race complicates earlier conceptualizations of gender. In many ways, womanhood in our society has constructed white femininity as pure and in need of protection, while women of color, particularly black women, have been socially stigmatized for centuries. Cultural narratives of the "Jezebel," out-of-control sexuality, and the construction of "working bodies" have led to distinctly racialized genders experienced by communities of color. The hostile social climates and contexts that surround the violence that occurs for many victims add multiple layers of challenges and obstacles. Individuals are victimized not only in their homes, families, and intimate relationships but also in their own communities, workplaces, and beyond. The daily aggressions of systemic heterosexism, racism, and classism compound the context of the violent experiences between partners. The devaluation of marginalized existences in our culture is often internalized, further complicating the experiences of intimate partner violence. Without appropriate theoretical understandings, research will continue to fall short on adequately capturing the experiences of survivors within historically oppressed communities.

When the inclusion of same-gender intimate partner violence research had recently begun, Bograd argued that the "invisibility of certain populations reflects more their social importance in the eyes of the dominant culture than the absence of domestic violence in their midst."[37] Since then, the field has grown to include gay and lesbian experiences while remaining stagnant in the inclusion of bisexual and transgender populations. The broader invisibility of transgender individuals inevitably led to theorization that exclusively assumed cisgender identity. As a result of that invisibility, the subsequent policy advancements that have changed how our government addresses domestic violence at large have never truly considered the impact of intimate partner violence on transgender lives.

Expanding beyond Early Feminist Explanations

In the early 1990s, psychologists David Island and Patrick Letellier made a provocative break from the dominant feminist paradigm, arguing that intimate partner violence was "not a gender issue at all since both men and women could be batterer or victim."[38] Rather, they argued that the focus should be on the batterer's psychological characteristics, stating that "individual acts of domestic violence are not caused by a victim's provocation, not by a violent, patriarchal society, not by alcohol or by any other excuse." In their explanations of gay male battering, Island and Letellier proposed that violence is learned, that batterers choose to be violent, and therefore utilize it to cause harm and to enforce power and control. While these points were influential in challenging the dominant framework, they did ignore key evidence that intimate partner violence *is* gendered in many aspects of prevalence and dynamics (e.g., injury, outcomes, and self-defense) and that many people without psychological problems batter. As a dominant system in US culture, patriarchy indoctrinates all people (regardless of gender identity) into rigid constructs of gender that promote violence in intimate relationships.

To merge various theoretical explanations together, psychologist Gregory Merrill later proposed an integration of the social and psychological aspects of intimate partner violence.[39] While learning and choosing are primarily psychological or individualistic explanations of battering, he emphasized the *context* of the opportunity to abuse. For batterers, the opportunity to abuse and learn what one can get away with is gendered. Here, men are particularly at risk for perpetration due to the same gender socialization factors to which sociocultural feminist researchers point. Not only are men encouraged to be violent, but they also learn that this violence is often normalized and effective, which, in turn, can further enable abuse.

As an extension to this thinking, it is important to acknowledge that gender is not the only social factor involved; race, class, sexual orientation, and gender identity all contextualize the abuser's opportunity and choice to abuse. The connection of the broader structure to micro-level processes highlights how social context may lead to the perception that one member of the relationship has relatively more or less social power than the other. Power here can be understood as the ability to project one's own desires onto another. With less power, there is a diminished (but not eliminated) capacity to enact negative consequences against a potential perpetrator. This can again be gendered because men in our society are typically ascribed this social power. However, in the power's application, all relationships, regardless of the sexual orientations and gender identities involved, are subject to power dynamics that are informed by patriarchy.

Sociologist Betsy Erbaugh argued that the victim-perpetrator gendered binary in dominant intimate partner violence theorizing is a central factor in the silencing of LGBTQ victims.[40] As a result of this leading framework and limited explanation of violence, the cultural construct of "victim" is gendered—always feminine. This gendered, heterosexist assumption behind perpetrator-victim dynamics assumes that the victim is passive and submissive; it assumes effeminacy. Within the context of same-gender relationships, this pervasive construct of the feminine victim assumes that the victim in the relationship is the "woman" or the passive and submissive member. Conversely, it assumes that the perpetrator is the "man" or the aggressive and dominating member. In same-gender relationships, or really any relationship, the presented gender identity of a victim or perpetrator may not coincide with normative expectations. These normative expectations drive the cultural impulse to make assumptions about individuals on the basis of their presented gender; these impressions are often misguided and do not inform any understanding of the abusive dynamics that are manifesting. Gendered assumptions based on cultural expectations have far-reaching consequences for those responding to or witnessing intimate partner violence. Among the many potential outcomes, gendered assumptions can undermine abuse between feminine partners and/or misidentify abuse between masculine partners.

A Queer Approach—Framing Trans Experiences in Intimate Partner Violence

It is evident that dominant forms of theorization in the field have not adequately captured the nuances of LGBTQ experiences with intimate partner violence. While emphasizing the psychological attributes, situational opportunities, and sociocultural explanations of gender to explain intimate partner violence may provide stronger explanations, turning to a postmodernist framework that emphasizes the power behind language may shed more light on the abusive dynamics experienced by trans victims. Through the critical examination of the power behind language, a more trans-inclusive approach to gender within criminological thought is possible. "Queering" gender in this framework highlights the power that arises through the use of language and discourse that make it a social reality. Gender and sexualities scholars Kath Browne and Catherine Nash explained that queering "can be any form of research positioned within conceptual frameworks that highlight the instability of taken-for-granted meanings and resulting power relations."[41] Through this approach, trans experiences can be examined through the meanings embedded within a genderist power structure that marginalizes their intimate partner violence victimization, shapes their experiences, and limits their help-seeking opportunities. Given that the overwhelming majority of intimate partner violence research and theorization has assumed cisgender gender status, it is hard to think of another concept that has been more taken for granted than the complexities among diverse gender identities.

Most feminist criminological study of intimate partner violence relied on an explanation of gender that was largely either sociocultural or socialized. As noted, these conceptualizations of gender held that the patriarchal power structure enabled intimate partner violence. Outside of intimate partner violence research, sociologists Candace West and Don Zimmerman would later expand the idea of gender as more than an individual attribute or role that was either "naturally" or structurally defined but that gender itself was accomplished or "done."[42] Through this lens, individuals "do" gender according to socially prescribed notions or definitions of what is ideally "masculine" or "feminine" behavior. Thus, gender arises through daily interaction and comes into reality as an outcome of these exchanges. As sociologist Kristin Anderson later added, this interactionist perspective shifted "our thinking from the question of how masculinity causes violence to the question of how violence causes masculinity."[43] This approach effectively framed previous findings in feminist intimate partner violence research that concluded male aggression against women as an action that represented their culturally defined superiority as masculine. Violence thus comes to represent an act of masculinity, one that reinforces or "does" hegemonic masculinity.

More recently, the concept of gender in intimate partner violence has expanded further through a postmodernist framework. Philosopher Michel Foucault explained that power, the ability to get others to do as you please, was rooted in hegemonic discourse.[44] He proposed that the power behind legitimized language was the source of conflict in society that constructed dominant narratives and subordinate or oppositional discourses.[45] For feminist scholars and critical criminologists applying this perspective to intimate partner violence, this meant not that power was simply embedded in preordained structural or social categories, but rather that ways of "knowing" were the root of power. Postmodernism, generally speaking, challenged the notion of concrete categories and proposed that identities were situational, variant, and fluid.[46] Through this framework then, intimate partner violence is still a product of a patriarchal power structure that is also a consequence of structurally informed discourses that marginalize women and create distinct realities across race, class, sexual orientation, and gender identity. Patriarchy, among other systems of oppression, informs the use of violence in relationships regardless of one's own gender identity. Patriarchal norms permeate all relationship types and normalize hierarchal dynamics and the use of violence between intimate partners.

Some postmodern feminists have since departed from the notion that "woman" and "man" are static identities. As gender theorist and philosopher Judith Butler questioned, "what is *meant* by woman?"[47] Butler's proposition was that woman, and therefore biological sex, was just as much a social construct as gender. Utilizing this perspective, gender is not "a singular act, but a representation and a ritual."[48] In this way, Butler located the concept of gender as performance; these acts or ways of being are culturally sustained and represent hegemonic idealization of heterosexual gender.

This approach to gender can be particularly useful for the inclusion of trans experiences in intimate partner violence research. It is by no means the only or best way to work toward a trans-inclusive body of intimate partner violence research, but it starts the process of expanding gender in a field that has overwhelmingly assumed the universality of cisgender experiences. Moving toward trans inclusion is challenging and often controversial when faced with essentialist arguments.

Even feminist scholars have been historically divided on what "transgender" means to the overall concept of gender. Many cisgender lesbian and radical feminists had traditionally opposed the notion of transgender identities as they saw women as oppressed largely as a result of society's marginalization of "female" bodies. From their perspective, to transition from man to woman did not constitute a legitimate "woman," one that had the lived experiences of a "natural female bodied" person.[49] Conversely, those women who transitioned to men were viewed as "giving up" on the cause and shedding their subordinated identities as women to embody the privilege of a man. Because this version of feminism relied on a sisterhood of those born female, those who transitioned in a female representation could never be "real" women.[50]

These arguments have often played out on the public stage, including when Nigerian novelist Chimamanda Ngozi Adichie drew some criticism in early 2017 for what some feminists believed was a transphobic statement she made during an interview. While her literary work has been widely heralded as transformative for feminist thought, when asked on a British news network about trans women, Adichie said, "When people talk about, 'Are trans women, women?' my feeling is trans women are trans women." As a staunch advocate for LGBTQ rights, Adichie later apologized and clarified her statement, but nonetheless the discussion of transphobia and/or genderism within feminism was reignited: are transwomen "women" or are they separate—"transwomen"?

Some feminists have argued that transsexual identities, unlike some transgender identities, support the existing gender binary; they argue that in switching one's physical sex from one to another, only two gendered outcomes are recognized.[51] In many ways, the gender binary is so totalizing and compulsory that even some transgender identities are constructed within the dichotomy of "woman/man," "feminine/masculine." While some have seen flaws in trans inclusion, others have argued that transgender recognition challenged feminism to "move beyond identity politics and into a feminism that based itself on the politics of gender performativity, choice, personal power, and individualism."[52] Despite the fact that many feminists relied on a social constructionist argument for the dismantling of gender inequality, some were resistant to accept biological sex and the body as a similar social construct.

Some scholars argue that the postmodern "feminist accounts of transsexualism and transgenderism have prevailed over radical feminist critiques" and have produced a more trans-inclusive perspective that views gender as an "ongoing process of *becoming* male or female" regardless of trans status.[53] This approach may be particularly critical in incorporating trans experiences in intimate partner violence research. Because transgender individuals do not neatly fit in an essentialist gender binary, broader sociocultural explanations of gender may be limited to explaining only the experiences of cisgender individuals. For this study, moving beyond gender as a dichotomous social construct embedded and regulated in a patriarchal power structure, I viewed gender as a situational power discourse that framed the experiences of abuse for transgender victims.

In this postmodern tradition, discourse or language fosters the domination of individuals through subjective interaction. In its application to criminology, the "language of the court or law expresses and institutionalizes the domination of individuals by social institution."[54] This perspective focuses on how meaning and sense are constructed by victims, criminals, and the larger criminal justice system. As Arrigo and Bernard explained, "Postmodern criminologists maintain that there is a conflict that underscores our understanding of crime, law, order, justice, and victimization. In short, only certain definitions are used to convey society's meanings for these constructs."[55]

Scholars Davis and Glass stated that this form of theorizing, in its direct application to cisgender heterosexual intimate partner violence, "seeks to de-center the dominant homogenizing grand narrative that accounts for *all* violence, for *all* women, in *all* situations."[56] In essence, they sought to deconstruct the binary gender boundary that builds off the victim/perpetrator dynamic as well as the power and control assumed behind it. For example, Arrigo and Bernard stated that when rape victims testify in criminal court, "they must re-present their experiences in a way which is consistent with legally justifiable speech (i.e., acceptable, credible testimonial evidence)." Not adhering to the hegemonic discourse could result in the case's dismal; they further claimed that "the language the victim is required to speak may also be a language that marginalizes and oppresses her."[57] Postmodern criminologists studying intimate partner violence have analyzed the language used by both victims and perpetrators to construct micro contexts of power. Following Foucauldian influence, power is not just structural or held by a group of individuals but rather emerges from the discourse between individuals. For trans victims, the power lies behind the cisgendered discourse that shapes structural responses to intimate partner violence.

Framing for the Study

While there is no singular theoretical framework that solely guided this work, it does operate from and build on existing perspectives. Broadly speaking, the inquiry is situated across queer(ing) criminology, postmodern feminism, and symbolic interactionism. I propose centering trans voices within a budding subfield perspective called queer criminology. Arguably, queer criminology lies at the intersections of critical and postmodern criminologies. The US criminal and legal systems have a long history of criminalizing LGBTQ people, and biases against the community have been documented in the literature across courtroom experiences, police interactions, the carceral system, and more.[58] Similar to the aforementioned ways in which queer approaches challenge assumptions, rules, and power behind gender constructs, queering criminology involves a similar critical lens to highlight the existence of LGBTQ experiences as victims and offenders in the criminal justice system. Today, queer criminologists are pioneering studies and theoretical examinations of the lives of gay gang members, incarcerated transgender offenders, LGBTQ youth, and many others.[59]

While substantial groundwork has been laid for queer criminological inquiry, less work has been done to actively queer victimology. As a subfield of criminology, victimology centers victims of crime as a focal point for analysis. The field has largely been dominated by work that examines the characteristics of victims (i.e., demeanor, social status, neighborhood residency) and their relationships to offenders. Perspectives from queer criminologists provide much of the conceptual language needed to engage with victim-centered research from a queer angle. Gender, sexuality, and other intersecting identities alter the ways in which criminal legal systems view deserving victims and characterize offenders. As a relatively new subfield, queer criminology encompasses the inclusion of static identities (i.e., ensuring that LGBTQ individuals are included in discussions on crime and victimization) but also a deconstructionist approach that critiques the power of criminalization, language, and law.[60] Queer criminologists have criticized the victim focus in LGBTQ research, challenging the ways in which victimization renders subjects powerless and confines analysis to one-directional thinking that does not truly "queer" (i.e., disrupt or break from normative thinking about victim and offender). As such, the research I have done here straddles both of these goals. For one, it is the first such book to include and solely focus on transgender victims of intimate partner violence. By mere inclusion alone, we gain a new insight for queer criminology, possibly for queering victimology. However, trans identity is not static, and therefore the accounts of the survivors often involve discussions of fluid transition, manipulation of identities by situation and context, and trans identity's relation to the broader social structure.

The forthcoming accounts include descriptions of stories of victimization but also illustrate meaning and interpretation; for this, symbolic interactionism offers a perspective that examines the process of defining and constructing realities in social life. Setting out to explore the meanings behind victimization as recounted by survivors, symbolic interactionism informs the research to encompass analysis of the world from the point of view of those being studied.[61] At least in part, the self and identity are characterized as a conversation between the inner, personal drives or desired actions of individuals and the expectations of society. These expectations are regulated by the shared meaning attributed to various actions or the social consequences of action. Meaning is constructed through a social process in which individuals attribute actions not only to others, but also to lived experiences. For survivors of intimate partner violence, reflecting upon their experiences and sharing stories involves a process of interpretation and meaning construction. For example, survivors must describe what dynamics and behaviors they deemed abusive. Further, these conversations may involve how these abusive behaviors were interpreted and what they meant. As such, the present work examines how transgender victims experience and interpret intimate partner violence victimization and how they negotiate the larger cultural contexts that have long ignored these unique realities.

The overall research design of this study was informed by queer and feminist perspectives. Mainly, this meant that I did not intend to locate some form of objective truth, but rather sought to examine accounts of lived experiences and highlight emerging patterns in subjective discourses.[62] This feminist epistemological approach proposes that in order to understand a particular social phenomenon, one needs to first understand it from the viewpoint of those who experience it.[63] Through an examination and analysis of their stories, I sought to illuminate the distinct meanings behind intimate partner violence in trans lives and develop a more refined understanding of these experiences. As such, this study obtained accounts of intimate partner violence victimization as told by transgender survivors through semistructured (and later more open-ended), in-depth interviews as well as through free-write questionnaire responses. These interviews and written accounts represent the sources of the data. One of the overarching goals of this study was to highlight otherwise marginalized voices and account for their realities to further broaden our understanding of intimate partner violence victimization outside of hegemonic, genderist discourses.

While there is significant debate on who should be considered transgender and what it means as far as identity or medicalization, I solicited participants who self-identified as transgender or under the broader trans umbrella. This means all participants were broadly considered transgender (with respect to their more specific gender identities). All respondents self-selected to participate in the study and reported a gender identification other than cisgender male or female. One of the reasons that transgender voices have long been marginalized in intimate partner violence research is the difficulty in securing participants. My recruitment strategies involved marketing the call for participants through LGBTQ organizations around the United States. I utilized my own connections and networks in LGBTQ antiviolence agencies as well as mainstream domestic violence services. E-mails, flyers, and social media advertisements circulated the study call.

In order to maximize my sample, I utilized two different data collection methods to maximize participation from this small and marginalized population. The primary data collection technique involved in-depth interviews; twelve interviews were conducted by phone and one via instant messenger, for a total of thirteen. None of the respondents were local enough for us to meet in person, but in-depth interviews on the phone and instant messenger served as an ideal method of data collection in that they provided me the opportunity to gather extensive detail and ask follow-up questions. On average, the interviews lasted over an hour but generally were under two hours. In-depth phone interviews offered a more comprehensive understanding of experiences with intimate partner violence in a way that survey response items could not accomplish.

While respondents were asked to participate in phone interviews, they were also provided the option to free-write their accounts and answer the interview questions via an online questionnaire format. The online, open-ended interview questionnaire allowed potential participants to describe their experiences with intimate partner violence victimization without having to speak personally with me as an interviewer. Five participants opted to free-write their accounts via the online interview guide. While this format required me to sacrifice the more responsive and in-depth discussions made possible via telephone or instant message, it was important to have this option given the extremely intimate nature of the interview topic and respondents' resulting discomfort in discussing it with researchers. Appendix A elucidates the recruitment and sampling strategies, methodology, and question design in more detail.

The Survivors

A total of eighteen trans-identified respondents who had experienced intimate partner violence participated in this study. As mentioned above, twelve of the participants were interviewed via telephone and one via online chat, and five submitted free-write responses via an online survey link. Although I offered participants whose first language was Spanish the choice to tell their stories in either English or Spanish, all opted for English. Table A.1 in Appendix A provides relevant details of the respondents who chose to use pseudonyms by providing gender identity, race and/or ethnicity, and age; participants described their social backgrounds in their own words.

While a majority of the sample identified as white, there was considerable racial diversity, including three black- and five Latinx-identified participants. The group was also diverse in terms of gender identities, with five identifying as transwomen and three as female-to-male (FTM) transgender, and then a variety of other identifications including transmasculine and transfeminine, genderqueer, transsexual, and transgender stone butch.[64] The average participant was thirty years old. Many survivors were at the early stages of their transition or coming-out process or just a few years into their transition. This may be due in part to the relatively young age of the participants. In Appendix A, I provide more specifics on the analytic and coding strategy used for the stories.

Overview of the Book

The chapters follow the stories of eighteen transgender survivors of intimate partner violence. The second chapter builds upon the first through an emphasis on the contexts of violence as experienced by individuals within transgender communities. The social and cultural contexts of hostility toward transgender individuals provide the backdrop from which the stories are experienced and interpreted. The chapter weaves in introductions to survivor backgrounds and their intimate relationships. The subsequent chapters detail the patterns of abuse experienced by survivors from the beginning to the end of the relationship. Chapter 3 delves into the salient themes of the types of abuses experienced by the survivors. As survivors began to tell their stories, they identified a series of patterned events that were characterized by a combination of physical violence along with emotional and psychological abuses: across their stories, these attacks involved specific aspects of transgender identity, which are then discussed. Chapter 4 explores the process of constructing meaning within the context of abuse and how it affects the process of identity work. The chapter breaks down elements of how abusers controlled victims' gender transition; as the accounts continued, survivors attributed meaning to the events as they tried to explain the motivations of their perpetrator and what the abuse still means to them today. Chapter 5 examines the process in which survivors came to identify their experiences as abuse and the unique challenges transgender victims face when attempting to leave abusive relationships. Finally, chapter 6 offers a comprehensive overview of how these narratives can shape research, policy, and action to improve existing knowledge and services for transgender survivors and move scholarship on intimate partner violence beyond the gender binary. Appendix B offers a reflexive statement that details my personal experiences with collecting and analyzing these data.

2

The Contexts of Abuse for Transgender Survivors

I wanted this to work because, who's going to want me now?
What's my luck of finding another person that wants to love
a trans person?
—Laura

Laura, a thirty-three-year-old black transwoman, found out about my study through one of my online outreach efforts. Asking complete strangers to be publicly open about their trans status while also sharing vivid details about past intimate relationships was a daunting task. Laura was calling in from an area that had been ravaged by a hurricane just three days earlier; I made the hurricane damage the early focal point of our discussion so we could break the ice and get a little acquainted. When I asked her about the storm, she quickly dismissed it: "It's been okay. We didn't really get hit as hard as New Orleans or anything but it, definitely flooded a bit. Pretty bad I guess but now it's cool." Earlier that week, I had seen reports that the area had sustained tens of millions of dollars in damage; no deaths, but several injuries were reported. I quickly got the sense that Laura had developed a tough exterior and sense of self, one that could see a disaster through and come out the other end like it was no big deal. Despite this sense, and like all of the survivors, Laura had endured a history of experiencing violence vicariously early on. I asked her to share a bit about her coming-out story and background. She started off by telling me about her gender transition and struggles with her family:

> Well, it ain't really like a long story and I don't really want to go into all the details but like I already said, I was born in a boy body but I just felt like a girl but sometimes I liked boy things too but mostly just girl. I came from a bad neighborhood you know down here in the South like the projects and shit but like we did okay, like, I wasn't in, you know like a whole lot

of trouble or something. My mom, it was just me and ma cuz my sister was killed, domestic violence actually, so yeah it was just us and we made it like we could. At first ma thought that, well, I guess she thought, like that I was gay boy or something? But it wasn't like that, I was wanting to wear girls outfits. I would wear her stuff if I could get away with it. . . . I didn't know nothing about trans stuff. None of my friends, don't nobody really talk about that and nobody knows about it and I just didn't know.

It was clear that Laura had an early sense of who she was while immersed in an environment that did not reflect it. As we continued to chat, I asked her about her intimate relationships. Almost naturally, given the study call, she focused on her abusive relationship and how they met.

I had met this guy online, on a site where trans people go on to date and stuff and . . . he was nearby and I was into him, he was into me and he just really flattered me online and I was in a rough spot, a tough place in life, it was like eight or nine years ago now so I had just come to terms with being trans and dealing with ma and friends and stuff so yeah, it was nice. It was nice to have someone after me and wanting me.

Like many survivors I spoke with, she emphasized her struggle with feeling desirable in a hostile social and cultural context that defines beauty or attractiveness through a rigidly cisgender perspective. She expressed how often friends would catch on to the abuse and ask her to leave. While I do not know the background of the friend who convinced her, Laura made it clear to me that the friend did not fully grasp her situation as a trans individual. Laura expressed being happy and proud to be in what she considered a stable relationship, despite evident patterns of abuse. She asked me rhetorically, "Who wants to build a life with someone who is figuring out life in another gender and has these issues and my body and all?" Laura's internalization of inferiority, rooted in the fact that she was trans, trapped her in a cyclical spiral that empowered her abuser and left her isolated.

Laura's description of her motivations for maintaining a relationship she knew was toxic stood out to me as distinctly different from those parallel reasons that cisgender survivors of intimate partner violence often report (e.g., feelings of inadequacy) because of the emphasis on how trans people are perceived in the dating world. Laura was not feeling inadequate just because of the abuse but rather displayed a hesitant willingness to tolerate abuse for fear that trans people are not easily loved—not easily found in happy intimate relationships. While this is not true as trans people enjoy healthy and stable relationships, at the time of her abuse Laura felt it was. That specific external force, the social and cultural elements that construct desirability so intimately with gender performance, is part of what enables continued abuses against trans people.

Trans Lives in Context

Each of the accounts has its own individual context, and yet they all shared a broader cultural and social context that threaded through them. A common exercise in early grade school involves practicing the ability to infer the definition of an unknown word by looking at what surrounds it in a sentence. At least in my own educational experience, this process was called finding the "context clues." We were taught to look for ways in which a writer uses an uncommon word while simultaneously paying close attention to the details around it. In a similar way, sociologists and criminologists analyze the surroundings and situations in which human behavior occurs within set patterns and institutions. Context, or those surrounding characteristics of a specific event, holds many clues that describe and explain set actions more holistically. The goal of examining or acknowledging context is ultimately to improve our understanding of what we experience and observe in daily social life.

Turning to context illuminates problematic elements of present-day US culture that facilitate violence in everyday life. This is often a challenging thought process when considering the very personal and individualistic ways in which intimate partner violence is experienced. How does the very structure and organization of society actually foster and motivate intimate violence? For the LGBTQ community, the cultural and social context in which intimate partner violence occurs frames the experiences of violence differently than for heterosexual victims. More specifically, homophobia, heterosexism, transphobia, and genderism structurally disadvantage LGBTQ victims and also foster opportunities for abuse that take advantage of this power structure. The marginalization of LGBTQ individuals works to fuel intimate abuse through the isolation and shaming of victims. In general, many LGBTQ folks endure a wide range of trauma from family rejection to school harassment, all of which fuel high rates of suicide, among other mental health consequences.[1] Several studies have shown the significant role that homophobia and heterosexism play as a tactic of abuse, the internalization of such beliefs, and how it systematically disadvantages same-gender intimate partner violence victims from "traditional" resources such as criminal law, shelters, and services.[2] For one of the few trans-inclusive studies in intimate partner violence, Bornstein and colleagues conducted in-depth interviews with lesbian, bisexual, and transgender victims of intimate partner violence in a study where participants could more freely describe their experiences in detail.[3] In one example describing attacks against victims' queer identities, the authors included one response from a trans participant who was attacked by the abuser as "not trans enough." Attacks by abusers of trans people often stem from external aggression. Laura described how the outside world caused her to navigate spaces cautiously: "I'd make sure someone was with me and stuff but it was weird, you know? Because I felt comfortable in my women's clothes but it's like nobody else . . . would just let me be comfortable."

Overall, trans people live in what can be described as a "trans-antagonistic" culture, an overtly hostile and oppositional social environment that regulates, polices, and maintains recognition of only two genders.[4] As a part of everyday life, these openly hostile climates are normalized and internalized. This pattern of the normalization of trans antagonism contributes to the vulnerability of trans individuals by making it more likely that they will stay in harmful relationships.

While some existing work has opened up the discussion on unique tactics of abuse and structural realities faced by transgender intimate partner violence victims, many do not rely on empirical evidence.[5] For example, Walker emphasized the need for research on trans intimate partner violence while highlighting how trans prejudice and disempowerment structure their vulnerability to abuse.[6] Many of the available empirical studies on trans-specific violence have been limited to incidents of crime in which intimate partner violence was not the focus and have instead examined, for example, hate-motivated violence.[7] As a result, very little empirical inquiry has thoroughly located trans accounts of intimate partner violence in the appropriate critical context.

Transition, Transphobia, and Genderism

At the beginning of each interview, survivors very generally described themselves, telling me briefly about their lives, their family relationships, and their gender journey. For some of the survivors, descriptions of gender identity were sometimes more fluid or perhaps something that developed and changed over time. While many scholars explicitly focus on understanding gender identity development and the trans experience, I mainly used this time to get acquainted with survivor backgrounds without getting too deeply involved in the complexities of transitioning, which could be a separate study entirely. The conversations flowed more naturally as the stories branched out from these foundational parts of their lives. Human beings have told stories for millennia, and each of these stories is given meaning by the surrounding aspects of social life that characterize interpersonal experiences.

In an overview of how heterosexism characterized the lives of lesbian women who had been sexually abused by other women, Girshick identified three levels of analysis: the cultural, institutional, and individual.[8] Following a similar approach, transphobia and genderism can be understood as existing throughout these levels. At the cultural level, we can turn our attention to the norms and values produced through interaction and maintained by institutions. The fundamental order of heteropatriarchal cultures requires the establishment of two and *only* two genders. The norm is first and foremost the masculine or "man." We see this manifest daily in language, for example, when referring to "congressmen" or "mankind"; it seems awkward and inappropriate at times to say "congresswomen" and "womankind."

Beyond language, our culture assumes a linear understanding of sexuality, sex, gender identity, and expression. To be a "man" is also to have a penis, is also to sexually desire cisgender women, is also to be hegemonically masculine and to outwardly express masculine traits. Within these cultural expectations, gender is the dominant precursor from which romantic relationships are formed. John, a twenty-nine-year-old multiracial transman, described the fallout from an early relationship in which he came out as trans to a partner who was presumably a cis-woman lesbian: "I was with my high school girlfriend and I felt like I could just say anything to her but um, I told her that, you know, uh, I'm not just 'butch' but I'm really like, a man, like I want to go by John and I'd like to just pass as more of a man." For a very brief period, John adjusted to his life as a newly "out" transman while staying with his girlfriend. However, things quickly changed, as John related: "We broke up pretty much like that month because I came out as a trans. She was all for it and all but she just said nah, she wanted to be with a woman and that this was over. I mean, I understand, we're still good friends still to this day though but she just wanted to move on. It hurt. It was like my first blow for being trans but I kind of had the feeling, you, that, uh you just know that things are going to change like that."

Rigidly gendered norms often connect with sexual scripts or expectations that often do not consider the well-documented variance in biological sex (e.g., intersex births) and the diversity in gender identity and expression.[9] Survivors like Tom described their gender identity in ways that linked to sexuality—grappling with this cultural emphasis on gender as somehow innately related to sexual orientation. He stated, "I'm a transman. I started transition about three years ago but I was genderqueer or at least always just butch for five years before that when I came out as a lesbian. Um, but, I think I'm more queer now. Like I don't really have a strict preference for women; I've been with other transmen too and even transwomen." Some described that they didn't belong in either masculine or feminine identifications and that they were more fluid. For example, Chris, a twenty-two-year-old white transfeminine survivor, described,

I grew up as a boy so I am biologically a boy but I identify as transfemi-nine or genderqueer but more feminine than anything. I don't want to change my body but I present as female mostly although I don't really care about passing, I just do my thing, that's why I like the genderqueer label. I'm just a free spirit with gender and I don't like to confine my expression. I was always super girly but not in all things, I was actually really into baseball and I played that in high school even. So I don't think the boxes really work for me, I can be both genders at once or neither or just whatever.

Similarly, Todd, a twenty-two-year-old white transmasculine survivor, described, "I am queer because I like the fluidity and the um sort of label without any kind of any commitment to anything that it has to mean. Um, and I just find that it allows me to sort of move fluidly through a lot of different relationships and identities just day to day." Others, like Joe, a white-Latino, eighteen-year-old transman, expressed how they attempted to transition as neatly as possible within the confines of cultural expectations: "For a few years, while I was deeply closeted and in denial about the gender issue, I would go by the genderqueer label because it sounded nicer to say that instead of saying I'm a guy. I'm going to do all this to take care of myself, I just had a problem asserting that to people." At a young age, Joe now firmly identifies as a man who is open about his nonlinear journey toward positive gender affirmation. For Sam, a thirty-eight-year-old white transgender stone butch survivor, a fluid gender identity led to eventual transition: "I spent about 10 years as genderfluid. Then I spent a couple years more on the masculine end of things, visibly gender non-conforming in a way where many people could not tell what gender I was. I transitioned after that."

Producers of culture, most often mere reflections of existing norms, reify the normative cultural binary through a lack of trans representation in broader mainstream media. In a biologically essentialist culture, differences are emphasized as naturally occurring and necessary. This often works to normalize and justify inequality between genders. How the body, reproduction, family life, and sexuality have been culturally constructed and practiced has changed over time and space in a way that demonstrates the artificial quality to gender. While biological and reproductive differences may not be ignored, the cultural stress on legitimizing the differences as innate or natural was openly challenged by the survivors. Rebecca, a thirty-eight-year-old black transwoman, described grappling with cultural boundaries of identity early in her life:

> Growing up, I was always just very effeminate, like, just one of the girls I guess. I had a lot of girlfriends and I identified most with feminine things and that was okay for a while until I started getting a little older. So like, um, my parents started regulating more like when I was in middle school. Before if I wanted like an Easy Bake oven or something I could get it or some other kind of girl toys but when I got to middle school age they

were like, um, just kind of made me or forced me to be more manly and I resisted and went through like this rebellious kind of thing. I got all "Goth" and I could just fit in with those kids because they wore, like, not really "normal" clothes and I could wear more effeminate clothes but just consider myself with them.

In a rigidly gendered culture, trans and cis people alike grapple with identities that often do not neatly fit the socially constructed boxes of "man" and "woman." Survivors described the multitude of ways in which they experienced nonlinear identifications between cultural expectations, self, and the body. Jessica, a forty-nine-year-old white transwoman, described,

> I started, putting highlights in it [her hair], piercing my ears, and being more effeminate and I'm six-foot-three, so I don't really *look* feminine but I have this look and so people knew it was still me it's just that they saw me as more an effeminate type of man . . . then the hormones started so obviously things in my body started changing and now you know . . . living my life as Jessica.

Often, some trans individuals link their identities with biological essentialism, as Anna, a thirty-year-old trans Latina woman, told me: "I wanted to fix my body. I wanted a vagina like a *real* woman." She added, "I was always a girl but I just uh, you know I just didn't fit in my body right." William, a thirty-five-year-old white transman, echoed similar points but further emphasized a desire to be not even *trans* but fully a cismale: "Transition is a huge part of my life and will determine whether or not I can live comfortably. My transsexualism will always be with me and unless there is some way I can magically become a cismale, I imagine it will continue to be the same way." Other survivors described more fluidity and less of the idea of "rejecting" their bodies. For example, Laura told me, "I was born in a male body and like it's not like I completely *rejected* that body but it's like um, I just . . . felt more like, like a girl or a woman rather."

The connection between the body, sexuality, and social practice within the larger social structure contributes to the maintenance of the status quo. The differences exist by utilizing dichotomizing social practices to emphasize innate distinction between the "two" genders. Biology, in this sense, does not determine gender, but gender in a sense can determine the biological. The very same thing that makes social structure artificial is in fact related to the very thing that makes it natural— the social practice. Anna described some of her early social practices in transition: "I started to want to present more like the woman that I was—I am woman. I grew my hair, my nails, I pierced both of my ears and you know, uh, I was always kind of like a smaller, skinny person so I was already kind of—easily effeminate and small so I didn't have to do much to look more like a girl. I have a soft face and I made it softer with makeup." Social practice includes how we "do" our bodies, structure our relationships, and construct our sexualities and relationships. Social practices do not necessarily express natural patterns of biological difference, but they don't ignore natural difference as well. In this perspective, Connell exemplified how people dress the biological body—the construct of power through buff masculine bodies for men or how we dress the breasts of women.[10] She asked, if men and women are so biologically and naturally different, why must we heavily emphasize stark differences in social practice? Connell defined "emphasized femininity" and "hegemonic masculinity" to explain the ways in which people perform and highlight difference while utilizing biological characteristics as well. Social practice in turn then exaggerates these differences that people take as "natural" in an attempt to maintain the socially accepted definitions of gender; biology alone cannot sustain gender categories.

For Casey, the gender journey revealed many more complexities at the intersections of self and identity, the social realm, and the biological:

> It took me a long time to decide to physically transition. I needed to make sure my support system was ready to make that journey with me, and I also felt afraid that I would somehow be turning my back on myself as a strong woman and survivor of violence. Ultimately, an urge for self-preservation won out and I finally started T about 4.5 years ago. I am genderqueer (not male-identified) so I saw it as a compromise, rather than a true solution. I am considering stopping T at some point in the next few years to see how that feels, and also because I want to get pregnant. I am scared that stopping T might be hard on my mental health.[11]

These examples illustrate the diversity of experiences the survivors had with their trans identities. While I did not analyze for consistent themes in the descriptions of their gender identities, I noted that survivors described a wide array of experiences that were all informed through a transgression with dominant cultural gender norms.

Systemic Discrimination

The cultural norms of transphobia and genderism subsequently influence and shape our social institutions. Social institutions take the form of our educational, criminal justice, and health care systems, government, family, and more. Transgender individuals face discrimination across the board in health care, in schools, on college campuses, and in the workplace. The roots of discrimination stem from both invisibility and more blatant marginalization or exclusion.

Both invisibility and exclusion have left the unique health care needs of transgender individuals largely underresearched in medical fields resulting in major gaps in knowledge among practicing health care providers. It's estimated that one in five transgender or gender-nonconforming individuals have been refused health care outright because of their trans status.[12] In the same study, approximately 28 percent of respondents were subjected to harassment in health care settings. In describing his coming-out process, Todd discussed his hesitancy with seeking medical attention for gender dysphoria: "It's in the back of my mind but I am pretty terrified of surgery and other kinds of doctor interactions." Relative to his counterparts in the sample, Todd described a solid economic safety net through his parents, who eventually supported him in his transition: "My parents were supportive of my transition and so they were willing to help me pay for my hormones and doctors' visits." Despite this, he rarely visited a health care provider for fear of bias. In one attempt to seek medical attention after sustaining injuries from abuse, Tom mentioned, "At the hospital I was treated bad but I don't know what for, maybe it's cuz I was trans or maybe because I was black or whatever, I don't know?" These experiences often result in the postponement of care and exacerbated health problems within trans communities. While transgender status has been medicalized (and pathologized) as gender identity disorder, a condition that causes distress that stems from one's internal sense of gender conflicting with assigned sex at birth, insurance coverage for treatments has been more elusive. In particular, states can and have regulated Medicaid programs to exclude transgender beneficiaries from receiving adequate care, including therapy, hormones, and more.[13] For trans people like Laura, the necessary medicalization of trans status became a source of manipulation for her abuser. While getting familiar with me and beginning her story about how she met her abuser and former partner, she described him as supportive, especially of her health care needs. Laura recalled that her abuser would say, "You do what you need to" and "I'll help you pay for the doctors' visits or whatever you need." Vulnerability in health care allows abusers to withhold medical finances as part of the abuse and control.

Overall, trans discrimination in health care is likely to get worse before it gets better. Under the current federal administration, the Department of Health and Human Services is creating the Division of Conscience and Religious Freedom ostensibly to protect health care workers who decide to violate their Hippocratic Oath by denying care on the basis of religious freedom.[14] This includes physicians and nurses who may refuse to treat transgender patients and children of LGBTQ parents or provide abortion care under the guise of religious freedom.

More recently, schools have become a focal point of transgender student discrimination. In our conversation, Anna delved a little bit into her life as a trans student: "I went to school like this [presenting feminine] but eventually I dropped out. I couldn't take being in school anymore after months of torment there. Like even the teachers would say shit and just, uh, like nobody cared and you know, I couldn't tell my parents of course." Similarly, David, a twenty-three-year-old black transman, described, "Where I lived, like it was pretty conservative. You didn't really talk about those types of things [gender, clinical depression] and it was pretty frowned on—where I went to high school there only like ten, not even ten gay kids."[15]

Among the many stories beyond the present survivors, Gavin Grimm, a student at Gloucester High School in Virginia, received the most national attention when his discrimination case was under consideration to be heard by the US Supreme Court.[16] Gavin was assigned female at birth. After transitioning to male, he informed his school that although his birth certificate still stated "female," he was indeed a boy and had his name legally changed. After being openly permitted to use the boys' restroom, word spread in the community, which resulted in several school board meetings with the intent to have Gavin banned from using restrooms designated for boys. The school responded by forbidding Gavin from using the boys' restroom and instead asking that he use a single-stall restroom or the bathroom in the nurse's office. This made him the only student in the school who was required to use a separate bathroom from others. Gavin's story is not an isolated one, as bathroom debates had already been swirling with controversy across several states.[17] Under President Obama's administration, the federal government had interpreted fair and equal use of bathrooms under sex discrimination in Title IX policies. This interpretation was cited by a federal appellate court that decided that Gavin's school was required to allow him to use the restroom that corresponded with his own gender identity. Shortly after, the Supreme Court issued a stay on the enforcement of that decision, allowing the school to continue to discriminate against him. The Supreme Court could still pick up the case, but in the meantime schools can largely ignore the interpreted protection under Title IX. At a time when the National Transgender Discrimination Survey has found that approximately 78 percent of trans students reported harassment and assault, campuses and school districts are slow to respond to the needs of vulnerable trans students. Under current direction from Betsy DeVos, a secretary of education with no previous teaching or public school experience, the Department of Education has stopped investigating and taking civil rights complaints from transgender students barred from using school bathrooms that correspond with their gender identity.[18]

In the workplace, transgender individuals face high levels of bias and discrimination on the basis of their gender identity and expression. Studies generally show that upward of half of the transgender people surveyed have experienced some form of employment discrimination.[19] This includes harassment, being fired, demoted, or passed over for a promotion, and more. Like the more than 26 percent of trans respondents who have reported losing a job due to bias, Rebecca described often feeling like she had very few employment choices in life that anchored her to an unstable intimate relationship: "I didn't have anything so what was I going to do? I had already lost a previous job because of being trans, I didn't want to lose this." Antidiscrimination laws do not comprehensively protect transgender workers from discriminatory decisions made on the basis of their identities. Further worsening protections for transgender employees, in late 2017 Attorney General Jeff Sessions issued a memo to the Department of Justice stating that it would no longer apply Title VII of the Civil Rights Act to protect against discrimination on the basis of gender identity, something that President Obama's administration had begun to implement. Specifically, the memo stated, "Title VII's prohibition on sex discrimination encompasses discrimination between men and women but does not encompass discrimination based on gender identity per se, including transgender status."[20] Significantly, the US Supreme Court ruled in January 2019 to uphold Trump's ban on most transgender people from serving in the US military, effectively limiting even more employment opportunities for transgender Americans.[21]

Among trans people, the struggle for stable employment is well-known. During his transition, John expressed fear regarding his employment security: "I consider myself a lucky one cuz I didn't lose my job, everyone there was cool." Others, like Sam, reported living in fear of being outed at work, often citing previous experiences that led to termination: "If I were outed I could lose my job and I have been turned away before." Among a potential constellation of reasons, employment insecurity among transgender individuals has resulted in staggeringly high poverty rates. The Movement Advancement Project and Center for American Progress has named this "the financial penalty for being transgender in America," citing a rate of poverty among transgender individuals at four times the rate of their cisgender counterparts.[22] While not offering details as to why, Rebecca told me that she "always had trouble with jobs" but that recently she had found "a good, consistent [job] working at a women's clothing store in the mall in the city."

Survivors described a variety of employment ventures but often cited multiple barriers and struggles with poverty. Audrey, a forty-two-year-old white transwoman, was among the older participants in a sample that slanted slightly younger. She was a college graduate with decades of work experience who had lived in several different states. She told me, "I've been slowly transitioning for about the last twenty years and as a result I lost my career. Now I've just been trying to figure out what I'm going to be doing with my life. I wish I could take care of myself a little more and these changes in my life were not just in my sexuality they were in my gender." She added, "The job that I work at now, I'm an esthetician and I only make money when I see clients and it's just been horrible. Sometimes I work forty hours a week at the spa and I make like $150 a week or you know a $180 or $200 so it's been very difficult, even when we had both of our incomes, her [ex-partner's] disability income and mine, to pay the bills, and uh, losing that you know, has put me in jeopardy again of being homeless and not having that." The combined struggles of poverty, job insecurity, and homelessness often leave trans people with few options for income. While often a negative stereotype and an aspect of trans-fetishization, survival sex is a common avenue that trans individuals may turn to for money, housing, protection, and/or safety. For trans people like Anna, "turning tricks" is often the only source of income for extended periods. Anna described a mixture of employment and housing insecurity commonly experienced by not only trans people but queers in general. During a bout of homelessness, Anna said,

> on the street I actually met a lot of gay kids and even some that were trans, like me. A lot of them had been on the street a long time and so they would work odd jobs here and there for money but some of them actually had, like, real jobs but they stayed in these abandoned buildings to live free . . . like one of the gay boys that became my friend he was like mopping floors and fixing stuff at some stores for a few bucks a day and he still lived in the streets so, uh, yeah I thought I could do that, you know?

As she continued to describe meeting other queers, primarily gay men, on the streets or couch surfing, she described how she came to engage in survival sex through a gay man she shared a living space with:

> He shared food with me and you know he was a good friend and helped me but then I learned that he was making more money by trickin' on the streets too like some places around here you can see some people, even boys, trickin' like especially in bad parts and at night so I thought since I already look like a girl and I had my hair long and things, if I could just clean up and you know maybe go as a girl I could get more money too. I didn't like, you know doing it—I was scared like very scared but I needed

the money. I didn't have any skill or even finish school or anything and no money but it was easy to stand around and wait for some dude to hit on me and I just started taking money for what they want to do.

Anna continued to earn a living through sex work until she started receiving more formal employment from a gay bar she sometimes used for cruising and picking up clientele. Anna's life took a more stable turn when she was offered an opportunity to become a drag performer at the bar where she could earn tips; she kept sex work on the side. Having really nothing to wear for performances, Anna was taken care of by a professional drag queen who took her under her wing and offered her a more stable living situation than she had previously had.

> I started to go to gay bars to trick and I came in as a girl all of the time and at one of the smaller bars here I was asked to perform like as a drag queen because they were like "oh my God—fish, fish, fish."[23] Like, they thought I was beautiful and they wanted me and I tried out and I got one night a week at first to do songs and I got to keep my cash tips so I did that and I also trick and then also I met new friends and I started living with other drag queens. One of the drag queens actually I started to live with, she let me sleep on her floor and I gave her like some of my tips to stay there and we shared clothes and stuff and like, uh, yeah she was so helpful to me but I never stopped working the streets.

Anna's housing struggle was not unique across the stories, and housing discrimination continues to be a major obstacle for transgender people in the United States, where research finds that among surveyed trans respondents, one in five have been evicted or denied housing.[24] To date, most states have no protections in housing discrimination laws for gender identity and expression. At the federal level, the US Department of Housing and Urban Development has stated that discrimination against transgender people in housing can be considered sex-based discrimination and is therefore protected. Despite this, a general lack of enforcement and knowledge of rights has continued to leave many transgender people unprotected by the laws.[25]

As survivors continued to describe themselves and their backgrounds, conversations of family and relationships emerged. A prominent commonality across these conversations involved the role of family or support networks during their transition or "coming-out" processes. The family as a social institution serves a multitude of economic and social roles. Among these, families serve as a primary site of socialization, an avenue in which broader cultural norms are both distilled and instilled from caregiver to child. The family has changed throughout time and space as economic structures and cultural norms have evolved. Today, the family continues to follow a broadly patriarchal and isolated function. Deeply embedded in the function of family socialization is the passing down of heteronormative practices of monogamy and intimacy. For many of the survivors, families were not always the most supportive networks during their coming-out or transition processes. John came from what he called a "diverse family background." In a divorced family with four children, all of whom were assigned female at birth, John struggled with his identity:

> It was an all-girl house. My two older siblings were girls and I was of course assumed to be a girl too but I always had this feeling just being different. Being the youngest, I always got the hand-me-down toys and the used clothes so I had to like all of the girl things that my older sisters had and I didn't really question it but I knew I didn't like them, I knew that I wanted boy things but the whole house was deprived of boy stuff obviously. Luckily, I had a friend who was a boy who lived next door to us and I was able to do boy things with him pretty much through all my schooling. I began to express myself more masculine as early as like, maybe, middle school, like, late middle school and then in high school. I was definitely getting rumors spread, people thought I was a lesbian. They'd call me a "dyke" and "butch" and you know, that, kind of thing but never really like to my face I just knew from other people and no one really tried to fight me or anything. . . . I stopped wearing any girl things completely when I could start buying my own clothes entirely in like the tenth grade probably when I was working and going to school.

Unfortunately for John, coming out as transgender resulted in severed ties with his single mom and two sisters. Describing how his mother reacted to his coming out as transgender, he stated, "My mom, she, well, let's say ma was not having it. It would turn into fights like, she would say like 'oh you used to look so pretty' like 'why do you have dress like that, can you please just wear a dress for me just this time' and all and try to like bargain with me and say that she was embarrassed when we'd have to do something formal and I wore like a tie and shirt and uh slacks. So, I had to just, um, I just I needed to leave."

Several other survivors described similar stories of rejection from family members. Audrey recounted that coming out as transgender resulted in the loss of her long-term partner, family, and friends: "Most of my people in my life, my family, had abandoned me at that point." Fatima, a thirty-year-old transwoman who was a Latina immigrant, described her family's rejection but also the additional elements of her community's isolation:

> I just had a long process with that really. It's like, you know, like one of those things that you just kind of know for a long time but there's just no words for it your head or mind or whatever. So if you ask my family I know they will say oh "she was always a very effeminate boy" so it's just been a part of me, I've always thought and felt like I was more female. I do date both men and women though so it made everything weird because as a boy, I wanted to be a girl, but I still liked girls too so I knew I wasn't just gay but I just felt the wrong gender so that I was maybe like closer to a lesbian woman but then again I thought well, I'm a gay boy too? I don't know. I still don't really know, I'd rather just, maybe not care to put a label or anything I am who I am and I'm a woman, I'm a woman who likes other women, men, and trans people. My upbringing was a nice one, no family issues until I came out. Because we were immigrants we were uh, definitely, like, really super reliant on our community and lived with other immigrants, I mean it was the reason we came here, we knew others here. So I grew up with that kind of environment of community. I lost all that. I lost it all. My family was not kind to the gender issues, they didn't understand.

In a similar account, Anna described that she began presenting and dressing as a woman in high school. Her father's reaction eventually led to her homelessness as a teen. She stated, "Dad found out I was dressing like a girl more and he went crazy too, like bad. He was like real bad so he beat me. . . . He said I let the devil inside me and the house and he said I needed to go."

Coming out as trans was often a major disruption in the early lives of many of the respondents. Young people in general are more likely to be very dependent on families for income, housing, health care, and social support. Early disruptions in foundational life stages have the potential to lead to long-lasting consequences, even after some families become accepting. John was raised primarily by his single divorced mother and two older siblings. He detailed his coming-out experience with his mom, his main source of support: "My mom, she, well, let's say ma was not having it. It would turn into fights like, she would say like 'oh you used to look so pretty' like 'why do you have dress like that, can you please just wear a dress for me just this time.' So, I had to just, um, I just I needed to leave. Like, I wasn't thrown out and I know I broke my ma's heart but my last year of high school I just lived with a friend and stayed with my girlfriend too."

While many of the survivors had negative experiences with family and coming out as transgender, a smaller portion of the group either had positive experience or had family that progressed over time on the issue. For a few, family reactions were never a problem. Brittany, a thirty-four-year-old white transwoman, simply stated that "my family supported me, and so did my friends." Similarly, Joe stated, "I have a good support network," and mentioned that he was still living with his mother who was supportive of his transition. In Todd's account, his family eventually came around to support his trans identity: "I basically just tried really hard to work on the relationship and now we've become really close." For Chris, family was among his first supporters:

I first came out as a gay boy when I was in high school. My dad had us moving around . . . quite a bit with his job. He was in fishing and all that up there and mom always found work real easy as a teacher. . . . I didn't have any issues with my family at all. I came out around like sixteen and it was like no big deal. They just said that they had always known and so it really didn't change anything. I was always super girly but not in all things, I was actually really into baseball and I played that in high school even. So I don't think the boxes really work for me, I can be both genders at once or neither or just whatever. . . . I started wearing what I wanted regardless of gender after high school like the summer between high school and college. I went to [university] and just finished last year. So yeah, my family didn't care. I mean I guess they thought it was weird and they would kind of ask about it but I mean it was never a big deal at all.

Within the broader culture and the social institutions that are informed by transphobic and genderist norms, individual interaction and attitudes are shaped. Turning to the individual level illustrates the everyday products of transphobic and genderist culture and institutions. Importantly, anti-LGBTQ messages perpetrated by individuals significantly contribute to the internalization of negative responses. Internalization occurs when negative messages about one's identities become part of how one views oneself in the social world. The negative messages infiltrate self-concept and have lasting effects that increase rates of depression and substance abuse.[26] Psychologists have identified the internalization consequences as sexual minority stress, which encompasses stressors such as "identity concealment and confusion; experienced and anticipated rejection, victimization and discrimination; and internalized homophobia/sexual self-stigma (the internalization of society's negative messages regarding sexual orientation)."[27] Sexual minority stress has been found to be positively associated with increased likelihoods of both intimate partner violence perpetration and victimization.[28] As humans are social beings, daily interactions and interpretations of the world are saturated in a learned context and the specific situational undercurrents that arise. Beyond the LGBTQ community, the constant grind of external hostility wears down many members of marginalized communities. As they contribute to a lowered sense of self-worth among many other consequences, they are an important part of the discussion on intimate partner violence experienced by trans people.

In May 2015, a young trans girl named Mercedes Williamson became national news. Mercedes had previously been dating twenty-nine-year-old Joshua Vallum for about eight and a half months. After a breakup that resulted in the two losing touch, Vallum became suspicious that his friends may have found out about Mercedes's gender identity—the fact that she was trans. He drove to her home in Alabama, where he convinced her to get into his car; the two then drove to his father's home in Mississippi, where he brutally murdered her using a stun gun, a knife, and a hammer. Reports showed that Vallum intentionally murdered Mercedes to cover up his previous relationship, ashamed that he had been intimate with a transgender person and worried that his friends would find out. His subsequent conviction become the first federal hate crime conviction on the basis of gender identity and expression, based on a policy signed into law in 2009 during the early days of the Obama administration.[29] This tragic murder captured national attention, further igniting ongoing discussion on trans murders in the United States, which many activist organizations cite are at increasingly high levels. As might be the case with many transgender cases, the lines between intimate partner violence and hate-motivated homicide or crime are blurred in this case. Motivated by intense transphobia and the fear of external perception, Vallum acted out a murderous rampage against a former intimate partner, someone whom (one could presume through reports) he had previously loved or cared for. So-called "trans panic" defenses have been utilized in US courts to justify the beatings and murders of trans people by those who did not want their sexual encounter with a trans person to become known or who did not realize that the person was trans.

As is the case with all data collection efforts on trans issues, rates of transgender murders are often difficult to determine as surviving families, police, and the media so often engage in misgendering and the erasure of the trans status of victims. The most holistic and centralized estimates show extremely high rates of homicide among transgender populations; this has been described as an "epidemic" of violence against trans people.[30] Consistently, the National Coalition of Anti-Violence Programs (NCAVP) found that the majority of hate-motivated homicides known to the organization are committed against transgender or gender-nonconforming people. Importantly, most of these individuals are people of color. In the most recent estimates, nearly half of the intimate partner violence related homicide victims were transgender, and all were people of color. Across both gender identity and sexual orientation, transgender people are most likely to be murdered by intimate partners. The mounting evidence of increased violence against trans people was marked when in just the first two months of 2017, seven trans people were murdered.[31] This stark variance and distinctive pattern of violence against trans people highlights the significant impact of individual motivations that are direct products of a culture that aggressively polices gender diversity.

Getting an idea of what shapes and influences the public's general attitude toward transgender people is a relatively recent research inquiry. For better or worse, mostly for the better, transgender topics have entered mainstream conversations. Today, Americans have more exposure to transgender people through media and are more likely than before to know someone who is trans. Through popular television shows and movies, transgender celebrities like Laverne Cox, Chaz Bono, and Hari Nef provide a wider range of trans representation than existed in previous generations. This may have an influence on broader individual perceptions of trans issues and trans people simply through humanizing once taboo or unconsidered groups. Interestingly enough, surveys have shown that a majority of the American public thinks it has sufficient information about transgender people.[32]

In an examination of transphobic attitudes among a nationally representative sample of heterosexual adults in the United States, psychologists Aaron Norton and Gregory Herek identified the belief in natural differences between genders as a binary conception of gender as representing one factor associated with negative attitudes toward trans people.[33] Among their findings, men expressed more transphobic views than women, and, significantly, increased individual contact with sexual minorities was associated with more positive attitudes toward trans people. The role of religiosity was explored and found to be significant primarily for women; the more respondents reported receiving guidance from an established religion, the more negative the attitudes they expressed toward trans people. Some survivors noted the role of the church (broadly speaking) in their coming-out processes. Tom, who first came out as a lesbian, stated, "After coming out lesbian, my parents made me go to church counseling all the time, like every week I was in there and they were telling me that I was possessed, asking if I had been abused and all that." Similarly, Rebecca spoke about how her family was first introduced to the idea that she might be "different" by members of the church: "My parents though, it was like they ignored it [being effeminate] for a while but then they, um, someone from church told them: 'you ever think that your boy might be gay?' and it seemed like it was the buzz at church that I was girly and it wasn't right. My parents started praying for me and telling me that they were praying for me to just 'act right,' whatever that meant, they kept saying they just wanted to make me 'right.' I had to talk to the pastor about why I liked buying girls clothes and while they were never like super hostile or anything, they were really clear to me that I was in the wrong." In Anna's account, the church seemed to have little to no influence *before* she came out as a trans to her parents. Her coming out triggered a series of church-related hostilities: "She just thought I was possessed and we didn't even go to the church like all the time, you know, for her to be sayin' that shit but it's what she knew and so she just right away started telling people in the area and sayin' like pray for me." While churches and religious communities may often serve as sites of refugee for many, for the trans people whom I spoke with they were more often sites of aggression.

Intersecting Systems and Identities

The violence experienced by trans people is a direct byproduct of a culture that systematically erases trans communities but also has historically attempted to silence women, people of color, members of the working class, and, more broadly, queers from mainstream existence. The nature of how intimate partner violence is experienced by trans people is firmly situated in this broader context of systemic inequality and structural aggression. Black feminist author and activist Audre Lorde noted that "there is no such thing as a single-issue struggle, because we do not live single-issue lives."[34] While transphobia and genderism were at the center of many of the conversations I had with these survivors, the intersecting problems stemming from economic issues, religion, and race further complicated their narratives. When Tom described (above) receiving bad treatment from a hospital, he talked about not knowing whether it was because he was trans, black, or something else. In mentioning this, I heard Tom centering his trans identity as a way to make sense of potential bias but yet struggling to narrow it down, given the fact that he (and all social beings) encompass a multitude of identities. For people at the intersections of multiple marginalized identities, there is no single unifying experience across one identity. Instead, multiple identities interact to create distinct realities that color life histories and interactions. Across their background stories, survivors described their early lives with their trans status often at the center. This was a product of the study call and my line of questioning, but despite this, interwoven are aforementioned complexities of varying religions, economic backgrounds, races, migration statuses, and more. For example, while all survivors described something related to their family background, the role of family meant something different across varying social locations. For Anna and Fatima, two trans immigrant women, family was an anchor that brought them to a new country. When I asked Anna if she had seen her parents again after she was forced out of the home, she responded, "No, actually. I don't know, the years passed and I would walk by the house sometimes to look in but I never knock or anything—they just, um, they lived without me like nothing and since we immigrated here I don't have any other family really, you know?" Familial isolation took on a different form and meaning, sometimes encompassing a disconnection from their origins.

Looking at violence as a broader social phenomenon benefits from an intersectional awareness through characterizing various systems that foster both structural violence (i.e., poverty, hunger, war, police brutality) and opportunities for interpersonal aggression (i.e., intimate partner violence, homicide). It is no coincidence that *all* of the trans people murdered in the first half 2017 were transwomen and people of color.[35] Trans people today might be living in an increasingly hostile "backlash" culture; based on official measures alone, it has been shown that hate-motivated crimes on the basis of gender identity have been sharply increasing since 2013.[36]

It is clear to see that in many ways the social and political climate of the United States has evolved on some LGBTQ issues (i.e., marriage equality, federal hate crime policies, etc.). However, consider that in November 2016 the US Electoral College system elected a vice president who argued that marriage equality would result in "societal collapse" and that congressional funding for HIV/AIDS support should instead be redirected to "provide assistance to those seeking to change their sexual behavior."[37] Additionally, while governor of Indiana, the vice president issued a retaliatory statement against President Obama's application of Title IX protection for trans students using public restrooms at school saying that he "long believed that education is a state and local function. Policies regarding the security and privacy of students in our schools should be in the hands of Hoosier parents and local schools, not bureaucrats in Washington, DC. The federal government has no business getting involved in issues of this nature. I am confident that parents, teachers and administrators will continue to resolve these matters without federal mandates and in a manner that reflects the common sense and compassion of our state."[38]

Social conservatives often point to "states' rights" in defense of civil rights protections issued by the federal government but paradoxically attempt to use federal legislation to control states' rights to protect LGBTQ rights and women's reproductive freedoms. During the 2016 election cycle, these points made by the vice presidential candidate stood despite clear evidence against conversion therapy and debunked arguments against marriage equality and trans restroom access. Interpersonal violence is intrinsically tied with the structure and organization of society, which has almost inevitably served to maintain and replicate systems of inequality. A multitude of intersecting factors may place transwomen of color at a distinctly higher risk for violence than their white counterparts. Because race is so innately tied with socioeconomic status and physical location, transwomen of color are likely contending with intersecting issues of poverty, racism, everyday street violence, sexism, transphobia, residential segregation, and a lack of support. Violence itself is not merely a product of unequal structures but an innate part of many social systems. Often, the very social institutions that allege to protect communities are culprits of systemic violence against the communities they serve. The police state, schools, and even access to clean water (e.g., in Flint) are highly politicized systems that are disproportionately shaped to disenfranchise poor communities and communities of color. To understand the state of violence against trans communities of color is to grapple with interlocking systems that effectively shut out people of color, trans populations, migrants, religious minorities, and others who have been historically subjugated by white supremacist cis-heteropatriarchy and American capitalism.[39]

Recently, I heard Laverne Cox in an interesting interview with journalist Chris Matthews on trans rights, with a focus on public bathrooms. In the discussion, Cox stated that the issue of trans access was not really just about the use of bathrooms but a fight for the very right to exist in public: "When trans people can't access public bathrooms, we can't go to school effectively, go to work effectively, access health care facilities. . . . It's about us existing in public space. . . . It's really about us not existing— about erasing trans people."[40] She effectively placed the interlocking nature of trans rights with existing systems as being at the forefront of the conversation.

Even the systemic responses to violence against trans people require a deeper intersectional lens. Take, for example, the earlier story of the transphobic murder of Mercedes Williamson. This was the first case in which the federal gender identity hate crime statutes was used to sentence a charged defendant; he ended up receiving a forty-nine-year sentence.[41] Despite the many cases of transphobic violence against gender-nonconforming individuals, it took eight years after the passing of inclusive hate crime legislation, at the federal level, to sentence a defendant convicted of a transphobic hate crime. Interestingly, the presiding attorney general of the United States, Jeff Sessions, who has an extensive history of racist and homophobic bigotry, issued what some might consider a progressive statement: "Today's sentencing reflects the importance of holding individuals accountable when they commit violent acts against transgender individuals."[42] This was an interesting response considering his virulently anti-trans stances such as his aforementioned Department of Justice memo rescinding Title VII protections for transgender employees.

Without proper analytic context, the attorney general's statement might pass as a progressive milestone for an otherwise hostile politician. However, at closer inspection, support for the harsh sentence merely confirms the administration's broader political goal to "bring back" tougher sentencing for all crimes more generally. The statement falls directly in line with the pro-incarceration tone of the current administration of the US Department of Justice, reversing the trend of decarceration that had barely started in the previous administration.[43] Further, the charged defendant in the case was an alleged member of the Latin Kings gang—a group that, despite evidence to the contrary, was among the broader "Hispanic" gangs cited by the Trump campaign as being "out of control" and unmanaged.[44] The forty-nine-year sentence itself was taken as a political victory within the context of the racially punitive administration goals. This was further exemplified by the leading headline for the story featured by the right-wing extremist news blog *Breitbart*, which read, "Latin Kings Member Gets 50 Years for Killing Trans Girlfriend."[45] Unsurprisingly, the focus of the erroneous headline (he received forty-nine years) was on the perpetrator's gang affiliation.

Look no further than the top "liked" comment on the *Breitbart* article, which anonymously stated, "awesome!!! a mentally ill cross-dressing fruitcake, and a foreign gang member are off the streets. America wins this round." Despite the fact that Vallum is actually a US citizen, the message sent and received by extremist conservatives was likely one that had not transgender safety interests in mind but rather an extended expression of white supremacy. While the article title and the comment are anecdotal, they partly exemplify the critique that some scholars have taken toward hate crime rhetoric.

Under neoliberalism, hate crime rhetoric has been couched in framing anti-LGBTQ violence as an individual problem that merges with the interests of mass incarceration and an increasing police state.[46] Meyer points out that hate crime laws gained traction during the conservative "tough on crime" campaigns of the 1980s and 1990s, effectively co-opting movements fighting anti-LGBTQ violence by providing a criminal justice system response.[47] These same punitive movements facilitated continued criminalization of communities of color and gave rise to mass incarceration in the United States. From the neoliberal perspective, hate crimes are the result of bad individuals who should be punished formally through the carceral system. Some scholars argue that a system (i.e., jails and prisons) that is inherently violent toward queer and trans individuals has been problematically framed as the solution to anti-LGBTQ violence.[48] Intersectionality in action and application challenges traditional responses to violence by highlighting the ways in which our punitive answers are rooted in systems with a history of systemic racism, sexism, homophobia, transphobia, and classism. The same lens has been applied to the "domestic violence revolution." From the radical feminist origins of sisterhood and community responses to rape and other forms of violence against women, goals have effectively merged with the neoliberal state. The simultaneous movements to advance the criminalization of violence against women effectively merged with "tough on crime" political rhetoric that started in the late 1970s and truly flourished in the subsequent decades. Often the same system that advocates rely on to take seriously violence against women (now domestic violence, intimate partner violence) as a social problem revictimizes and marginalizes ciswomen, LGBTQ individuals, the poor, and people of color.

The Stories Ahead

The above overview of the social and cultural backdrop contextualizes the forthcoming stories of intimate partner violence as experienced by transgender survivors. The interpersonal and institutional trans antagonism experienced by trans people in the United States is a key site of vulnerability to partner abuse while also being multiplied by many other intersecting realities. The following chapter introduces the former intimate relationships of the survivors. I asked survivors about the relationship(s) that motivated them to answer the study call. My questions started broad and open, asking survivors to tell me about how they met their abusers and about their social backgrounds and to give me an overall sense of what the relationship was like. I identified salient patterns in the types of abuse that was reported and described by the survivors throughout their accounts.

3

"No Man Is Going to See You as a Woman"

Transgender Accounts of Violence and Abuse

He would say like: When are you gonna "chop it off"; you have
enough money yet? You're looking more like a freak now.
—Anna

Throughout her life, Anna had endured abandonment from her family
and migrant community and bouts of unemployment and homelessness,
all while attempting to live as authentically as she could. Anna was the
only survivor I spoke with who openly discussed aspects of past survival
sex and/or sex work. As an employee of a local gay bar, Anna was able
to reduce the amount of time she spent working in more risky environ-
ments (i.e., sex work) and at the time of our chat was finally starting
to feel more comfortable and stable. After frequent rejection, she had
recently started developing close relationships, and this was a source of
strength for her.

While I got to know Anna over the phone, she told me a bit more
about her past and what that meant for her future: "I was alone but
since I made my friends, they were my family now; especially Carmen,
the drag mother."[1] For many trans and queer people alike, friends become the main avenue of social support. In Anna's case, friends ensured
that she had employment, housing, and basic needs met. Beyond basic
needs, Anna's friends were the bedrock of her life—where she found
love and warmth. Anna described difficulty in making intimate relationships work during her years as a sex worker. She met various men, seemingly often for work. I asked her a little bit about her romantic life and
eventually about her experiences with abuse in the context of intimate
relationships. Asking me for further clarity, she distinguished between
being romantically involved with a partner as opposed to men she met
for work: "I experienced a lot of violence from men that I picked up but

that's different, you know, I think they just think they're entitled to do whatever and I was, you know um, not in any place to complain about it because I was the one, you know, on the streets." In her account, Anna described a single case as intimate partner violence, separating violence she experienced from men she "picked up" as something different entirely. In fact, the abuse Anna experienced at the hands of an intimate partner came during one of the steadiest points in her adult life working as a popular drag performer. She told me, "I started dating this guy, he used to come in when I was performing and give me big tips, like, I knew he was loaded cuz there's no way he was giving me like almost a hundred dollars for not doing much, you know, it's not like I'm a dancer or stripping or something; I was just lip syncing, like, to some songs and moving around but he was really into me and I went home with him. And you know it was love."

Anna described her abuser, a business man, as someone who was stable and successful. She described him as "a cisgender male, um, I don't think he saw himself as gay. I mean he went to gay bars . . . he thinks of himself as straight, he just likes transwomen." They continued to date for almost four years before he asked her to move in.

> So he asked me to move in and stuff and it was getting serious but I, I don't know I was like I don't know because I don't think he knew I was still turning tricks every now and then and you know I think he wouldn't like that so but I did move in like and stopped with the tricks because he was taking good care of me and I was able to get more things . . . hormone pills and just even better clothes and makeup and I looked so nice and I felt so good.

The move was something that was not immediately welcomed by her friends. In particular, she described the reaction of the friend she had been living with: "When I moved in, it was nice but I kind of made Matilda sad and kind of angry like she was like you know 'you ditched me for some rando you just met' and like 'after all I did for you taking you in you just walk out' and I kind of maybe ruined that friendship when I left abruptly. I think she was jealous." I got the impression that delving into a serious relationship splintered some of her earlier friendships, something that is not so uncommon for a lot of people. To me, it spoke to some of the underlying volatility in Anna's life, the notion that she often had to choose between people and how those choices would subsequently impact her life.

Anna did not communicate much about the "good times" with her partner (and later, abuser), something that other survivors more readily did, even if briefly. Things began to change once Anna moved in with her abuser: "When I moved in, he started acting differently like he was just not as romantic like, he didn't have to try, like, I was stuck there and my only job was performing." Anna's earlier accounts of fractured friendships gave me the impression that she was becoming more focused on her dating relationship above other aspects of her social life. Feeling increasingly isolated, Anna continued performing and returned to sex work once:

> But you know it [abuse] didn't stop because I stopped tricking but one time I messed up and I just wasn't making enough money and I felt like I was burden at the house because I wasn't paying my share and I wanted to be more independent and I wanted to get my GED and save money for my surgery.[2] I had started saving money for surgery—I didn't have health insurance so I would have to pay for things out of pocket like I wanted breast implants but I needed to save money and also I wanted to fix my body. He found out because I cried and told him and broke down from the guilt and I said we weren't making enough money, I realize too after moving with him that he wasn't really making good money.

While Anna didn't describe how her abuser found out about her continued sex work, she described, "When he found out was the first time he hit me, he hit me, like, slapped me and said I was a dirty bitch and a whore and that I was worthless . . . he said a whole lot of shit and that I was nasty and filthy and that I gave transwomen a bad name—that I was a stereotype." In a commonly reported pattern among abusers, Anna described that the following day, her abuser was "soooo apologetic." She detailed him saying, "I'm sorry, baby. I'm so sorry. You know I didn't mean that and here I got you this makeup and I got you a new dress and heels."

For Anna, increased isolation fostered the opportunity for an escalation in violence. Her voice grew slightly shakier as she described the worsening situation. She took a short breath as I recalled her earlier descriptions of being routinely cut off by friends and family well before the violence from her partner had begun. In an attempt to stay afloat financially and make progress in her medical transition, Anna continued to engage in sex work, fearing that perhaps she was trapped living with a man she loved but who had also turned abusive. His mounting jealousy culminated in the most severe violence that Anna described to me. I was not prepared to hear the intense details and gruesome brutality that she had experienced, much less imagining her lived reality.

Anna's ex-partner began to take on the role of an abusive "pimp" as she tried to become more independent from him. She described to me what she recalls him saying: "'Fine! You want to get money then fine you gonna let others have you anytime then I can to and I'm gonna follow any other man you get with. . . . I wanna fuck you after they do' and he started to come on to me and I didn't know what to do because I wasn't really in the mood and, you know, like I didn't understand what . . . he wasn't making any sense." She thought, "What are you doing right now?"

Anna took another short breath:

> And he pushed me down and he held me hard, like, down on the floor and I kind of struggled but I was so shocked like, what do I do? I have to let him just do what he wants or he's gonna hurt me and plus I was the one that messed up so I deserve this? And he forced himself on me and he hurt me, like, he normally used to make me comfortable but he hurt me on purpose and I screamed and he kept going and I was crying and crying and he didn't stop and he put his hand on my face, like, and said stop crying, baby, stop and put his hands on my face and after he was done he said um, "See I don't need to pay you cuz you live here feel free to get out any time if you don't like it."

As Anna made attempts to regain some semblance of financial independence away from her abuser, he co-opted her strategies and began to exploit her sexually. The romance and intimacy she had described was gone, and now Anna described living in total, paralyzing fear: "it was scary." The escalating sexual abuse turned into outright torturous humiliation—sometimes in public:

When we went out, he would like, see if someone at the bar wanted to fuck me like he would get drunk and even if we were at like a straight bar he would say like "you wanna fuck her—the 'shehe' is with me she's a freak and cheap" and people would like just be like "get away from me" but he liked to humiliate me in public and then actually what was so bad was that one time we were out and somebody told him that he would pay him to "have me" to like get with me and like he wanted my ex and him to like gang me and he would make the deal and I'm just not even part of the conversation he would just come home with this dude or even multiple guys sometimes just like nasty dudes they aren't even friends like I don't know where the hell he was um, getting them but it was too often but I would say like twice a month and he would say here you want trick money do it with me, we'll make the money together and I can watch and join. "This will work out, baby," he would say like that this is perfect we get to stay together and I can still make the money for my surgeries but he had to make the calls and he made me do these things with the men.

Anna continued to detail the escalating intensity of repeat sexual violence, manipulation, and exploitation that all seemed facilitated by repeat attacks on her trans identity, her transition, and her overall self-worth. As Anna spoke more about what appeared to be the peak of regular sexual violence to which she was subjected, I asked her how she was surviving, reacting to all of this. She quickly responded, "Well I didn't know what to do really." Anna described to me how she wanted all of this to stop while continuously being psychologically assaulted and eroded by her abuser. Anna regularly pushed back, vocalizing her trauma:

I did say, you know like, "NO, I don't want to do this"[3] and he would say, like, "You'll never get the money you want then, how about you find someone else to support you then huh? Get the fuck out—leave whenever you want see if anyone is going to give you what I did to some whore tranny slut like you. You're lucky I'm even here for you—you know men think you're gross and that you're just a man in a dress. You have a dick and you can't hide that shit, no man like me will want you. No man is going to see you as a woman and even if you get one, they just wanna sleep with you they don't want to love a circus act like you."

These attacks occurred with such frequency that Anna eventually felt like "he made a good point." She added, "It's hard that I'm just not able to pass all the way and that I want to live as woman but I may not be attracting the men I like or find what I want in a man without passing more and without the transition so I let myself just shut down when he brought men over, I just shut down. I just didn't think about it and I just had to just like . . . pretend I wasn't there." When Anna did push back, often mentioning that she regularly stopped or tried to stop the abuses, her abuser's responses relied on transphobic and genderist brutality, policing, and dehumanization.

At this point in my study, Anna was the fourth trans-identified survivor of intimate partner violence whom I had spoken to. It started to become evident to me early on that the emotional and psychological manipulations experienced by trans survivors were deeply saturated in the devaluing of non-gender-conforming expressions, identities, and ways of existing. Some of these discussions had already existed in the broader assumptions made by those examining dynamics of abuse in trans intimate partner violence. In existing studies, researchers had discussed how transphobia and genderism are utilized by abusers to structurally disadvantage trans victims.[4] What results is the ability of a perpetrator to utilize existing trans antagonism to further coerce victims. As a result of a victim's gender-variant status and the transphobic culture that permeates all aspects of social life, perpetrators may tear down victims by attacking their trans-status. As Brown stated, "Non-trans perpetrators are acutely aware of the individual and institutional vulnerabilities faced by trans people and these vulnerabilities feature explicitly in the abuse tactics and harm done."[5] In another example, abusers may undermine trans identities by intentionally using the wrong pronouns, ridiculing bodies, or destroying tools used to communicate gender (i.e., breast binders or breast enhancers). Brown added that abusers may regulate victims' perceptions of their own ability to pass as the gender they wish to present; this often includes tormenting victims into thinking that they are not "believable" men/women, that they do not look like "real" men/women, and taking advantage of the lack of structural support for gender identity and expression protections against victims with threats of "outing." Despite a lack of generalizable data, a few scholars and activists have identified potential tactics illustrating that these abusers may deteriorate trans victims' sense of self by isolating them and making them feel less than human or undeserving of love. Others have gone further and argued that transgender individuals are especially at risk for partner victimization due to shame, isolation, or loneliness.[6]

For trans people of color like Anna, the threat of violence ranging from strangers to family members is distinctly heightened. Beyond interpersonal threats, systemic and institutional violence against trans people of color is disproportionately documented in the limited available reports on violence in the LGBTQ community.[7] Queer and trans activists have long expressed the epidemic of violence experienced by trans people in general, more recently calling attention to the complex intersections of race and gender identity. With a specific focus on homicides, antiviolence advocates and activists alike have noted that the vast majority of trans victims of homicide are people of color, more narrowly, women of color.[8]

As I noted earlier, when I asked Anna about her experiences with intimate partner violence, she made a reference to *all* of the types of violence she had experienced and took a brief moment to clarify what I meant by the narrow focus, setting aside what she called "a lot of violence from men." Beyond the interpersonal and physical aspects of violence, Anna spoke of being separated from her immigrant community and family, never having stable employment opportunities, and constantly needing stable and safe shelter. It is impossible to retell the stories of trans intimate partner violence without noting how interpersonal and systemic forces both facilitate abuse and fuel ongoing patterns of oppression that are reinforced by our very institutions, often the ones that may have been created with the intention of mitigating abuse.

In this chapter, I examine two major themes in the accounts of violence and abuse as detailed by the trans survivors of intimate partner violence. As survivors opened up about their victimizations, patterns emerged in the dynamics of abuse across the stories. More specifically, this chapter highlights how anti-trans cultural and social climates foster opportunities for violence, embolden abusers of trans partners, and emotionally erode victims, often entrapping them while abusers rely on external transphobia and genderism. The patterns in abuse illustrate the centrality of a trans-antagonistic culture in the techniques of manipulation and degradation used against trans victims.

For this study, with the goal of collecting data on intimate partner violence in the trans community, I analyzed the eighteen stories utilizing an approach that allowed me to remain open to emerging themes within the data themselves while openly acknowledging the existing queer, identity work, and feminist orientations that loosely guided my thoughts as I interpreted the data. This means that as I heard these stories and subsequently analyzed them, I was open to the search for themes that emerged directly from the accounts while also acknowledging an interest in the manifestation of gendered dynamics and identity within the stories. These interests often shaped my follow-up questions in the moment and led toward the refinement of my conclusions. I offer more details in the Appendix A.

The latter sections are organized by two major themes of abuse that emerged in the accounts: genderist and transphobic attacks. I argue that transphobia and genderism exist as two distinct and prevalent mechanisms in the abuse experienced by the survivors. While transphobia can be understood as the broader fear, discomfort, and prejudice against transgender individuals, genderism characterizes a culture in which two and only two genders are acknowledged, legitimized, and institutionalized. Beyond the two and only two system, genderist norms subordinate femininity in contrast to dominant heteromasculinity. In the data I have collected, transphobic attacks by abusers expressed disgust toward trans identities and people. Abusers who engaged in transphobic attacks weaponized the known trans-discriminatory elements of society to marginalize the victim's identity. Distinctly, genderist attacks reinforced the gender dichotomy by policing "appropriate" expressions of gender. Additionally, genderist attacks relied on hegemonic constructs of masculinity and femininity to regulate the boundaries of a victim's gender expression. For example, transphobic attacks directly targeted transgender identity as "freakish" or "disgusting," while genderist attacks told victims what "real" men/ women did, behaved, or looked like. Survivors spoke about these two prominent attacks the most across the accounts.

Over the course of recent years, as I have shared some of these accounts in professional meetings and dialogues with scholars and activists, a common question arose regularly: "Did the abusers know the victim was transgender *before* the start of the relationship?" While I cannot be certain about the origins of these curiosities, I believe the line of questioning is rooted in a couple of assumptions. It may be an attempt to rationalize the abuses experienced by the victims. For example, in one presentation, a fellow scholar asked this very question but then quickly followed it with "because I would understand a lot more of these hostilities if perhaps the abuser did not know the partner was trans." These assumptions are so prevalent that even two survivors here prefaced their stories of abuse by disarming the questioning, stating that, from the start, they always come out as trans to all potential dating partners. Regardless of the intent, this line of questioning surrounding the "out" status of trans people in the dating world often attempts to justify cisgender violence against trans people and largely stems from a trans-antagonistic culture.

In chapter 2, I briefly mentioned legal defenses like "trans panic" and other similar justifications for violence perpetrated against trans individuals. There have been cases in the United States and the United Kingdom in which transgender people have been charged with sex offenses for not disclosing their trans statuses prior to a sexual encounter (e.g., Justine McNally's case in 2013).[9] Legal scholars have since argued that the law has too often denied the full existence of the trans individual.[10] Law professor Dean Spade pointed to *Littleton v. Prange*, in which a judge ruled that a transwoman defendant was "created and born a male. . . . There are some things we cannot will into being. They just are."[11] Such assumptions propel the myth that one's sex assigned at birth is the only gender identity and expression that can be recognized.

The data in this study and others have made clear that these assumptions that transphobic or genderist attacks occur because the victim does not identify their trans status are fallacious, as in many cases the abusers were also trans identified. Second, this line of questioning assumes that people who *choose* to date trans-identified individuals cannot possibly be transphobic or utilize genderist attacks. I argue that in fact everyone, regardless of their own identities, is saturated in a culture that is hostile to trans people, and therefore anyone can utilize transphobic and genderist elements of our society to control and manipulate trans partners. It is important to note that *who* these abusers were is crucial for some context, but it was not central to the study. Instead, I asked about some basic demographics (race, gender identity) of the abusers while focusing primarily on the story of the relationship and subsequent abuse.

When I first got the all clear to begin recruiting survivors for this study, I was anxious with a flurry of questions and doubts swirling around in my head. Would I be able to reach enough people? What is "enough"? How would I be able to comfortably get total strangers to open up to me about extremely sensitive, personal, and often traumatizing events? Like any qualitative researcher, I knew I had to warm up and have topics prepared to discuss early on that did not relate directly to the topic and then eventually get to the experiences that would provide the data for this study. Within days of the initial call, I got my first e-mail response to the study call. After the first three interviews, I developed a smoother rhythm and relied less on prepared follow-up questions, letting the conversation evolve more organically.

The Relationships

During the interviews, I typically began with a brief intro and talked about something current. Topics ranged from major weather events to regional stories relating to the survivors' localities, sharing a bit about our personal experiences in those places and more. I asked all survivors to describe their background a bit: basics about demographics and family background, their transition processes or coming-out stories, and so on. Once we were engaged in conversation, I broadly asked survivors to share with me the experience or experiences that led them to respond to this study call. For all but one of the interviewees and one of the open-ended questionnaire respondents, the relationship they spoke of was the only one of their prior relationships that had been abusive. Brittany was one of two interview respondents who had been in more than one abusive relationship. Brittany was a working college graduate who had close ties with her local polyamorous community and a "pretty busy social life." She stated, "I've had trouble with abuse in a couple relationships. One lasted two and a half years, and the abuse started after about a year, verbal, emotional. She ended up breaking up with me partially because she felt bad about how she treated me. The second one was worse verbal, emotional abuse lasted for about six months, and she lived with me." Brittany spent essentially all of our time telling me about the story of the second abusive relationship, which she deemed "worse," though it was shorter than the first.

Sam was one of the five who submitted written stories and reported experiencing three abusive relationships. Sam wrote that they were typically in polyamorous relationships and had transitioned to their current gender identity about ten years prior: "I have been in 3 abusive relationships. I was in [one] abusive relationship for about 9 months 11 years ago. Second, I was in a relationship that began 9 years ago that was abusive as well. That relationship lasted for 3 years. Third, I was in a relationship 4 years ago that lasted for 5 months that included psychological abuse, sexual abuse, and spiritual abuse. . . . This was a long distance relationship." In total, eighteen survivors discussed experiences with twenty-one abusers. Despite the fact that only two participants had experienced more than one abusive relationship, the increased frequency of violence experienced in the context of romantic relationships for trans people is a well-documented problem.[12]

During each interview conversation and for all written stories, I asked survivors basic follow-ups about who their abusers were, demographically speaking. The majority of the abusers, fourteen, were identified as cisgender, while seven were described as fitting under the broader trans umbrella. Six of the relationships were interracial, while the remaining fifteen were described as relationships in which their eventual abuser was of the same race.

In the following sections, I provided an overview of the relationships as described by survivors. These descriptions cover a broad range across survivors; some talked at greater length about their relationship(s) prior to the abuse; others remained briefer in detail, focusing instead on experiences with violence. The patterns in storytelling reveal a cultural product and were influenced by the design of the study. As a cultural product, stories about domestic violence might take on the form of beginning with the good, developing the beginning of early abuse, detailing cycles of abuse, and then (at least for these folks) eventually surviving or escaping.[13] The characteristics of my inquiries naturally followed this structure, starting with the details on how survivors met their abusers, how things escalated or turned, and then eventually how they all left. Both my line of questioning and the cultural pattern of storytelling shaped the direction of the accounts, as described above.

"I Saw the Good in Her"

The dating lives of transgender people can be complex and are relatively understudied. In the broader dating world, intimate desires are contextualized by a culture that assumes the "naturalness" between genital anatomy and sexuality. In the social world, where people are all clothed, gendered social signifiers (i.e., makeup, clothing, hair) and markers are taken for granted as an assumption of biological sex (i.e., penis/vagina). Attractions occur first with bodies fully clothed and with a direct assumption between the gender presented and biological bodies. Transgender people present a potential disruption to these assumptions because these assumptions revolve around a heteronormative construct of sexuality that necessitates penis-vagina penetration. As heterosexuality continues to dominate structures and patterns of dating, transgender people may find themselves potential targets for hostility and isolation. Schilt and Westbrook argue that heterosexuality relies on the gender binary system (man/woman) and its assumed natural link to biology.[14] As a result, even when heterosexual and cisgender individuals react to trans people as their socially designated gender (their authentic self in public), sexualized interactions remain regulated by heteronormative assumptions about sexuality and genitalia (i.e., man = penis = heterosexual; woman = vagina = heterosexual). Studies have found that the prevalence of heteronormativity at the intersections of gender and sexuality affects how trans people adapt in the dating world.[15] For example, the "buy-in" to heteronormative dating practices with their reinforcing gender roles may seem to make trans people more socially acceptable and appealing, but efforts to conform to these norms might have psychological consequences. Some studies note that those trans people with less rigid acceptance of the gender binary report lower levels of damaging internalized transphobia.[16] While the dating context paints a hostile picture for transgender people involving gender policing, violent reactions, and rejection, overall transgender people continue to lead satisfying lives with healthy relationships.

While I asked all survivors to share with me their stories of intimate partner violence, they all first detailed how everything started. The types or characteristics of relationships varied, and not all respondents voluntarily spoke about aspects of their romantic life outside of their stories of abuse. Most of the survivors, as Todd exemplifies, had been dating their abusers for years. Todd had spent four years with his abuser during their college years: "We started dating when we were both eighteen and stopped when we were both twenty-two and between those years there were lots of things that happened." Survivors met their former partners and would-be abusers in a variety of ways. Brittany met her abuser while they were looking for work in the area: "She lived about a couple hours away from me and was looking for work, so I let her move in with me while she looked for work in Madison. This was at the beginning of the relationship." After they met through mutual friends, Brittany began dating and living with her abuser at a quicker pace. John also met his abuser through mutual friends:

> We met through mutual friends so I was finishing up school and she was there too but studying real estate and someone had told me that she was interested, like that she'd see me around and ask about me and so I didn't believe it until we kind of had like uh, a blind date set up so um, it just started like that. At first honestly though we weren't jiving like, I was going and passing as a man but she knew I was trans and she was fine with that, she was like bisexual or something so she didn't care really she just thought I was attractive so we saw each other for a bit but it uh, it really just grew on us like we just loved each other's company and I was happy and well, uh really happy that someone like her was interested in me. I fell for her real fast. It was pretty, uh, it was like pretty nice for a while. We moved in together just under a year being together, it was all good I mean like that first year, you know everything was like fine.

Conversely to others who moved a bit quicker with relationships that started through mutual friends, Fatima had dated her abuser for some time before they decided to move in together. She met her abuser through an online dating site: "Yeah, we dated for over a year and then he had to move for work. . . . He got the place, I quit my job, and then I found work up there." Another survivor, Laura, also met her abuser online. She talked a bit about how she met him and how she felt at the time:

> I had met this guy online, on a site where trans people go on to date and stuff and he was in Little Rock and he was nearby and I was into him, he

was into me and he just really flattered me online and I was in a rough spot, a tough place in life, it was like eight or nine years ago now so I had just come to terms with bein' trans and dealing with ma and friends and stuff so yeah, it was nice. It was nice to have someone after me and wanting me. . . . We started seeing each other regularly after some weeks of chatting. First it was just like the regular things, normal things like, like dinners or movies or whatever but then we started seeing each other every day. He started saying things like that I make a beautiful woman in the bedroom, that I'm sexy, and all this and I don't know it all just, it just, happened fast and I left my roommate to move in with him across town in probably, just like, maybe eight months but definitely less than a year so it was quick but I was just so happy.

Not surprisingly, the trans folks who responded to the study call met their former partners in many of the same ways anyone today would enter a dating relationship. A few met online, others eventually married their former partners, and some were even what might be considered "high school sweethearts." Tom shared a few details with me about meeting his former abuser in school:

I was with this person since like senior year of high school. We went to the same high school, she was a lesbian, and she's a woman. And at first it was a lesbian relationship and um, yeah we were fine then and everything was good. It was nice to have someone at the school you, just not, not just being a friend but she was my partner and I think we were visible and proud and it was good. We went to neighboring colleges; she was about just twenty minutes away from mine so we saw each other every day as normal, stayed at each other's dorms when we wanted and all that. I was always butch she was more like femme but not like extremely but I was real, real butch and she liked that.

Similarly, David met his former partner in high school: "We went past high school. . . . I went to college for a semester but then I got really depressed there too and she started living with me there." Other survivors had school-based stories of when they first met their former partners, including those starting off in college. Chris told me, "We met at a queer group on campus and zie was really awesome person all around. We liked the same things, we bonded over games and movies and I never really got the hint that zie was going to be a total psycho."[17]

Many of the relationships in the study spanned several years. For Jessica, the relationship crossed decades; she was the only survivor who reported being legally married to their former abuser for a number of years as the abuse intensified. Distinctly, while all other survivors were seemingly at varying stages of transitioning or openly questioning their gender identity, Jessica was the only survivor who was not openly considering their trans status at all during the early years of the relationship. Jessica described a more complicated journey with gender in a cis-heterosexual marriage. While she was not initially out to her abuser as transgender, she stated, "She [the former spouse, eventual abuser] knew two years prior [to getting married] when we were dating . . . we dated five years and married twenty-three. So she knew for twenty-five years." Jessica's abuser entered their marriage knowing Jessica's trans identity and was, in Jessica's words, "very supportive. She didn't quite understand but the following day she came home with a bra and panties and a skirt for me. She went shopping and she bought me some clothes."

As Jessica opened up more and more to her former spouse, the responses seemed relatively positive at the surface level. She often cited throughout her account the ways in which her former spouse was supportive of her journey, primarily through the provision of material items—women's clothing, makeup, and more. For Joe, the youngest participant, his abusive relationship started off as more of just a causal dating process; he had no intentions of pursuing the abuser. Joe met his abuser while working on a theatrical production:

> I didn't have any interest in this guy even as a friend he was just this guy, "scoping" around the cast who had been there for ages, he was about nine years older than me give or take. He was overly affectionate with me. I would just sort of brush him off from time to time and I would be just like, whatever its some dude in the background and it just sort of progressed from there and he'd get all up on my case, he'd spend time with me if I was doing work in the theater, he'd put his arm around my waist and if I tried to get away he'd get all sad and just be weird, I got a weird vibe from him from the start but I just sort of rolled with it.

Joe was the only survivor who reported getting "weird vibes" or other potential warning signs of abusive behavior from their former partners. Despite these signs, Joe talked about what drew him into the relationship: "This [choosing to date his former partner] is where I went wrong. I was like, okay I've never been in a real relationship, I'll just have a little fun and break it off and just do whatever I need to do and enter a relationship with this guy and it was okay at first. He just wanted to, like hold hands and be cute and that wasn't my thing but I went with it because I was curious about what other people were doing and I guess about a month after the relationship started or so, he started to get really weird."

Similarly, Owen, a nineteen-year-old Latino transman, described entering his abusive relationship with the pretense that it would be more of a fling that later turned more serious: "I was early in my medical transition and was open to casual sex and 'dating' (dating being more so a casual affair, nothing serious). I met a man who was about nine or ten years older than me who happened to be interested. I was looking for fun and casual sex, not a serious relationship. As I began to spend more time with him, however, it became apparent that he wanted a 'forever' sort of relationship. True love and all that, you know?"

Some survivors talked about the struggles with dating while trans. Rebecca opened up about these early challenges and how they contextualized how she met her abuser:

> I met my ex online on OkCupid and since I pretty much pass, I have had surgeries and all and I'm all woman, I'm not necessarily out as trans, I just pass as a woman but I think my trans identity is a big part of me and that I'm pretty open about it but I just don't put it out there but I do tell men that I'm planning on dating; I tell them right away.[18] Usually they stop talking to me and we never meet in person but this time was different. This time he was interested in meeting with me which happens but it almost always just ended in like an eventual hook-up and then that's all it would be about and nothing else. So fast-forward, we hit it off right away; it was all great at first. He didn't really mind that I was born or assigned male when I was born but he did ask a lot of questions about it. Some of the questions were kind of offensive but I mean it was typical and it all seemed pretty cool.

In describing relationships that began online, Fatima echoed some of the same struggles that Rebecca did. In particular, I found it interesting that both Fatima and Rebecca immediately prefaced their stories of online dating with a statement clearly defining that they were out to their abusers as trans before anything began. Fatima told me,

> I met him online. It was on PlentyOfFish, I was out as trans there, I was not hiding anything, I was like twenty-five so it was five years ago when we started to talk.[19] I usually met anyone I dated online because, it was just so much easier than like having to talk about myself in person. I had bad experiences with both men and women who didn't know I was trans at first and then I had to say something later and it just ended there so I thought this way it's like up front and just there. And you know we just did the typical thing, we met in person, we kept talking in person and it just, like uh went on from there. We fell in love, yadda yadda you know, the same story, it was no like big deal, he seemed like perfect, I felt like oh my god here it is, this is what I needed this is what I have been looking for. He was stable, he was good looking, he was just everything and he loved me for who I was and that's just, that's something that I knew not to take for granted.

Audrey was one of three survivors who described dating within polyamorous relationships. Polyamorous relationships typically involve multiple and simultaneous open relationships with all parties involved fully consenting to and agreeing to the practice. She described what it was like to meet her former abuser within the context of the polyamorous relationships.

> A friend of mine invited me out to this bar he goes too and he also invited a whole lot of people because it was also his birthday thing. So he was doing the birthday on St. Patty's Day and invited a whole lot of friends and there were only actually two people that showed up: myself and her [the abuser] and um, it had been two and half months since I left my partner so we kind of hit it off at the bar and then went home and we fooled around but then after that we got serious about each other, but I had another girlfriend too that I was seeing, you know I don't really practice monogamy at all so I was seeing another girl and her [the abuser] but you

know that [the relationship with the abuser] kind of developed into an emotionally monogamous relationship where I was seeing her exclusively and then shortly after I went through periods of homelessness and she [the abuser] left the person she was with and then we ended up moving in together . . . about ten months after we had first started dating.

Brittany told me in less detail that some of her relationships were poly. As I asked follow-up questions on her past relationships, she stated, "It was a poly relationship from the beginning." However, the story of abuse she chose to focus on was not one that involved others in the same way her poly relationships had in the past.

As these examples illustrate, the types of relationships varied throughout the stories and included dating relationships, cohabiting partners, and a married couple. The origins of the relationships are diverse and encompass the wide array of contemporary dating rituals. In the following section, I introduce the types of violence and abuse experienced by the survivors.

"Every Day, Wherever She Was, I Lived in Terror"

Most survivors, as noted above, spoke only briefly about what their relationships were like before the abuse began. This pattern is likely explained by the interviewees' knowledge that the focus of my study was on their experiences with violence in a past intimate relationship, and my line of questioning on background information was briefer than my more specific inquires on experiences with partner violence. After conversing in brief detail about their abusers and their relationship(s), I asked all survivors to very broadly share with me their story of abuse. At this point in our conversation, I took the time to restate the purpose and goals of the study more colloquially in order to gain a better understanding of trans experiences with violence in intimate relationships.

My decision to examine these accounts of violence and abuse with descriptive intent before conducting more in-depth analyses was determined by the lack of research data on trans intimate partner violence victimization. In early rounds of analyses, I began identifying commonalities and trends in the stories described by survivors. With data lacking in this area, descriptive accounts of the violence may have identified different types or dynamics of abuse and violence that had not been previously been discussed in the available cisgender literature.

Generally, I found that survivors' stories spanned various types of abuses, including physical, sexual, emotional, financial, and psychological violence; these are typical aspects of abuse that are well documented across sexual orientation and gender identity. While all survivors experienced some aspect of physical violence, most focused primarily on the emotional and psychological aspects of the abuse. While there is no set standard definition for emotional abuse within the context of intimate relationships, it can be understood as the "use of verbal and nonverbal communication with the intent to harm another person mentally or emotionally, and/or to exert control over another person."[20] These abusive actions can span a wide range of behaviors including threats, coercive control, verbal aggression, and exploitation. Some scholars argue that emotional abuse is more common than physical and sexual violence in intimate relationships and is often reported as the worst experience of intimate partner violence.[21] The most recent NCAVP report on LGBTQ intimate partner violence showed that in their samples abuses such as verbal harassment (18 percent) and threats and/or intimidation (13 percent) together made up more of the common experiences than physical violence (20 percent) alone.[22] Varying by situation and context, emotional abuse can be interpreted differently based on the power dynamics inherent in any given relationship. For partners with a stronger sense of power and control, emotional abuse tactics may be trivialized; in contrast, those with less power may be disproportionately more affected. Scholars understand this as a reflection of a broader cultural problem that tends to marginalize the real impact of verbal and nonverbal styles of psychological aggression.[23] Significantly, research consistently finds that emotional abuse is often a precursor to physical violence.[24]

As most intimate partner violence studies that are inclusive of emotional abuses find, every survivor in the study described a combination of physical and emotional abuses that occurred regularly or periods of psychological manipulation punctuated with more physical violence. Todd experienced various types of violence:

> We had, I guess, a really long relationship that um . . . spanned many cities and many kinds of forms. We had a long distance relationship and

then open relationships and then we sort of kind of did this thing and that this thing; it was always morphing into another form and I guess. I mean we started dating when we were both eighteen and stopped when we were both twenty-two and between those years there were lots of things that happened. . . . We had different forms of violence that happened throughout the relationship. . . . Um, that weren't that apparent to me in the beginning but I guess as the relationship progressed, they became more prevalent.

Like other survivors, Todd described the complexities in identifying and putting a name on the actions of his abuser. David echoed, "I didn't know she was being abusive because she basically cut me off from like everything. All my friends, I didn't have friends anymore, she would cut me away from family and try to get me as mad at my family as much as possible." David described the difficulty in even retelling the story:

To tell you the truth, I don't really remember the beginning. I don't remember really, cuz there was some like, there was too much for me to just remember all of it. It's hard to separate it out. There were other things happening around it, outside the relationship. She wasn't like, she wasn't physically abusive until later on. She was maybe like, sexually abusive but like she would lure me into it. I don't know, she never like forced herself on me but she would like, I don't know like, try to start doing whatever she wanted to do. There were times where I was like no, I wasn't really in the mood but she was like, she would just go anyway.

Jim, a twenty-one-year-old white transmasculine survivor, echoed these complexities in naming abuse:

It is difficult to describe because it was a pattern of behavior, but some examples are: she pressured/guilted me into sex ("if you loved me, you would do it"); she would continue touching my chest after I told her not it made me uncomfortable; she would get mad at me for being depressed (I have clinical depression) and make me feel like everything was my fault, and my feelings were not valid, and imply that she must know better because she was older. She also made me afraid to leave the relationship by using emotional manipulations such as threatening suicide if I left.

William wrote that his most common experiences were "in the form of controlling and manipulative behavior, verbal abuse and anger, black-mail, and suicidal threats." These nonphysical descriptions of abuse were common, and some survivors detailed a bit more than others. In her account, Audrey told me about early signs of emotional manipula-tion that she attributed to the kind of person her abuser was. Audrey openly criticized her abuser, disparaging her for engaging in sex work and attributing those characteristics to how the violence began:

> She was very good at manipulating as you would suspect from somebody who's lived on the street and made her living off of uh, sex. She would try to find things that I would be sensitive on and she would attack me on, so whether it was my appearance, whether it was my intelligence whether it was um, my inability to make a good living right now. Whatever she thought would be my weak point she would you know, try to make me feel bad. She then would make it seem like me loving her or being with her would fix all of these problems I had, it was always about putting me down and then try to be the one that could save me.

These aspects of emotional and psychological manipulation or control echo decades of findings on partner abuse and parallel the experiences of heterosexual women as well as gay and lesbian survivors.[25] Jim's written account started off with a description of his very first intimate relation-ship, which was emotionally abusive: "I experienced emotional abuse in the past, from the first romantic partner I had. It was all emotional and verbal but I sometimes became afraid she would physically hurt me when she got very angry (she sometimes would punch things, but never hit me)." A common thread across most stories was the intense severity of the emotional abuse and its subsequent impacts. Casey wrote:

> It was an emotionally traumatizing relationship. I think she had very se-rious mental health issues that she wasn't willing/able to get adequate support on, but the way it played out was that she was very emotionally abusive toward me. Much of the abuse involved threats of suicide or self-harm, particularly if I saw certain friends or family members of mine or wasn't present enough for her. There were a number of very dramatic "suicide attempts" in which she didn't cause any self-harm, but scared

the living shit out me and our mutual friends. We had to call the cops several times despite our values, and I spent a lot of time visiting her in mental hospitals as a part of forced hospitalizations that were also against my values. I remember smiling through our visits then sobbing as soon as I got into the elevator to leave. Every day, wherever she was, I lived in terror that she would die. It was so gut wrenching and terrible that I really started to lose my shit. I just couldn't cope. I made her the center of my world and restricted my activities and dreams in the hope that doing so would keep her from hurting herself. I lost many friends and hurt people I loved with my neglect. She was constantly leaving me scary, cryptic notes or messages and then disappearing for a day or two, so I didn't know if she was dead or just being weird or getting back at me for something I might have done. I worried about everything I said to her and everything I didn't say to her. Our relationship went through the standard tension building-incident-honeymoon cycle and eventually the cycles got tighter and tighter.

Some survivors, like Laura, described the origins of emotional abuse as rooted in regular fights: "He continued to be abusive for months after [her abuser began sexually assaulting her], the physical aspects were either just as bad or more brief but still it just got more frequent." The escalating nature of violence described by most participants also echoes similar patterns experienced by heterosexual, cisgender individuals. Adding to his early descriptions, Todd told me about what he described as a situation that was getting worse and worse. Like many others in this study, Todd was not a passive bystander in his abuse, but instead he regularly attempted to resist the violence and create distance:

It definitely got a lot worse—at the beginning I just thought it was Steve's personality and that I wasn't dealing with it the right way cuz we had broken up briefly last summer and I was realizing that I was kind of stuck in this relationship and situation that I didn't know how to handle or really how to interpret and uh, we ended up—I don't know. . . . It's kind of hard to say we ended up getting back together. I felt a little coerced about it from different angles and I told him that you know, if we got back together I wanted to take things slow and then we ended up moving in together which I told him I didn't want to do but he made it very clear to me in multiple ways that if I wanted to be with him we had to live to-gether or that if I cared about him at all we had to live together. So I took on all of these roles, like that I didn't want like being a roommate and then he became financially dependent on me which became a huge issue but I do remember thinking last summer that we had a relationship that wasn't really going in the direction that I wanted it to be going and that I was somewhat fearful of him in different ways but I wasn't really able to articulate that to myself until I would say it got really bad um, the last six months. The last six months was pretty much the worse.

Similarly, Audrey described "putting up" with the evolving situation in hopes of seeing a change. She added, "I kind of put up with it and worked through it and I told her from the very beginning to never hit me. I won't tolerate violence in this or any relationship, but there were definitely other forms of abuse."

For survivors like Anna, the abuse didn't necessarily worsen but in-stead increased in frequency over time. She told me,

Well it didn't really, like, get "worse" but it got more frequent—he was just less patient with me and stuff but I mean it was already bad—getting raped regularly and then the verbal abuse was so bad. I guess I stayed for like about, wow like a long time really. I tried to leave a couple of times but I just didn't have a way like to stay gone, you know? I stayed like over four years that way. Toward the end, because it was happening more, like he was having more outbursts especially if he had a stressful day he would be easily pissed at me for anything at home and he would just go off and yell and scream at me.

Several survivors, most notably transwomen, experienced frequent repeat physical and sexual violence. This is somewhat echoed in some of the existing research that shows higher rates of sexual violence and stalk-ing related violence among feminine trans and gender-nonconforming individuals when compared to their cisgender counterparts.[26] I started this chapter with Anna's story with an abuser who was a former client during her time as a sex worker. She engaged in sex work as a means to earn extra money and because she had difficulty obtaining a job. Anna's abuser regularly raped her and in a scene that she described earlier in the chapter, his motivations were rooted in jealous rage. Similarly, Laura described routine sexual violence: "He would force himself on me yes, he would just need to have it when he wanted and that was that, no questioning it. I was too afraid to even say no and so I just did what he wanted even if I didn't want to."

While transwomen described acts of sexual violence as routine or central to their accounts, other survivors also described more physical and sexual abuses, including transmen. Owen wrote, "Despite my disgust with vaginal/anal sex, he would force me into it and make loving comments about how we were 'truly' together." Sam also wrote about frequent sexual violence throughout all three of their abusive relationships. In the first relationship, they described, "the abuse mostly consisted of sexual abuse (including nonconsensual BDSM, and nonconsensual sexual labor), threats/menacing and psychological/verbal abuse and coercive control, but also included isolation, threats, and financial abuse. In addition, medical neglect played a significant part in the abusive dynamic." Others described frequent physical attacks at the center of their experiences. Rebecca told me, "He would have no shame in shoving me, he's punched me, and he's slapped me. One time I fell and he even kicked me in the sides."

While all survivors experienced different types of abuses that could be classified as physical, sexual, emotional, or psychological violence, a major focus of many of the stories included mostly psychological, verbal, and emotional abuses. For example, Sam wrote about one abusive relationship: "It was all emotional and verbal but I sometimes became afraid she would physically hurt me when she got very angry. She sometimes would punch things, but never hit me." Symbolic violence such as punching objects or hitting walls is a common tactic of abuse across all types of partner violence. The intimidation or threat of violence carried by symbolic acts serves to reinforce emotional and psychological attacks. For many survivors of intimate partner violence, the violence that unfolds over time may be varied in frequency and type. For example, Todd described struggling with many types of abuses as they are generally difficult to recognize or label as intimate partner violence given the focus on physical violence: "When it comes to violence that's always a hard word for me to define because I understand physical violence of course . . . that sort of tangible thing. But other forms of violence, uh, for me are a lot harder to understand and spot and I think those were the most often occurring circumstances and manipulations." Laura echoed a similar story when reflecting upon her experiences. While her experience involved severe violence, she reflected on how she felt during the early stages of her abusive relationship when much of it involved verbal and psychological torment: "I didn't think it was abusive, I mean, I know it is now but, it, it like hurt my feelings so bad. He crushed me." These accounts confirm findings across the intimate partner violence literature that describe abuses that leave no physical mark are not only difficult to label but also very often among the most damaging to survivors.

In the following sections, I separate out two major and salient themes of abuses against transgender victims: genderist and transphobic attacks. In earlier sections, I argued that genderism and transphobia are distinctly separate aspects of the emotional and psychological abuses experienced by survivors. Both genderism and transphobia rely on rigidly patriarchal cultural norms and structure. However, they are distinct in how they manifest within the accounts of abuse. At a cultural level, genderism characterizes a system of two and only two recognized genders while maintaining rigidly defined heteromasculinity as the norm and subordinating femininity. Interpersonally, genderism manifests in how we police and regulate the "natural" order of two genders with masculinity as a privileged expression. I argue that transphobia operates differently—more of a direct, prejudicial bias against those who self-identify as existing outside of the gender binary (cismale/cisfemale). These types of abuses emerged as prominent aspects of my conversations with the survivors. As their stories illustrate, while many of these types of violence and abuse involved psychological and emotional torment, they also manifested through or in tandem with physical and sexual violence. Notably, not every survivor's story centralized trans identity in the context of the abuse, but these were the most common ways in which they described their experiences.

Genderist Attacks

The utilization of genderist attacks was prominent throughout the accounts of violence and abuse. These attacks were characterized by the way in which participants described the origins and tactics of the violence. While these were recounted as primarily verbal, emotional, and psychological attacks, they were often experienced in tandem with physical or sexual violence. A genderist culture such as our own motivates and facilitates policing of two appropriately recognized expressions of gender. Genderist attacks are innately buffered by a reliance or emphasis on biological sex and secondary sex characteristics. The illusion of the "naturalness" of sex propels the social regulation of gendered boundaries. In this way, abusers rely on rigid understandings of two socially recognized and legitimized genders with one (masculinity) constructed as superior to the other (femininity).

Brittany was one of two survivors who characterized their relationship with the abuser as open.[27] Brittany was in an open relationship with an abusive partner who would police her gender performance by attempting to regulate her behaviors. Brittany stated, "She would say my promiscuity was more like a man than a woman." Despite having mutually agreed to an open relationship structure, Brittany's abuser regularly policed her sexuality by reinforcing traditional aspects of femininity. Brittany added that her abuser would micromanage a variety of daily behaviors as misgendered performances: "Sometimes she would say I didn't do something like a girl, like how I wash my hair." For Brittany, basic everyday behaviors were policed by her abuser through a lens of what was an appropriate gendered action. If Brittany acted in ways that were not traditionally feminine, her abuser would reinforce the notion that she was not being the most proper woman that she could be.

Beyond genderist attacks that were intended to regulate daily behaviors through the constant critique of gendered performances, many of these abuses were directed against a victim's personality or character. As gender is embodied through performance, it is also a characteristic of one's personality and was the site of many reported attacks. As I got to know more about Todd's previously abusive relationship, he described how his abuser would get in his head by mentioning aspects about his personality that were not traditionally masculine. This worked to erode Todd's sense of masculine self during a time when he was actively coming to terms with this aspect of his identity. He described, "At a certain point he held um, I guess traditionally masculine characteristics over me like 'if you were more of a man—you would do x, y and z' or um, if you had more honor and integrity you wouldn't be acting like this or why can't you just talk to me face to face like a man that were specifically gendered that were supposed to be used as threats against my character or my transition."

Todd described something most other survivors identified: emotional and psychological assaults that policed gender expression. Through these attacks, abusers manifested their power to police gender appropriateness and control intimate and personal aspects of these survivors' gender expression and identities. Genderist attacks can be an attempt to disempower victims. Audrey described the effect genderist attacks had on her overall sense of self and which she described earlier as manipulative: "When I talk about her attacks on my appearance, I mean her attacks on my passability as a woman. Just general comments about, you know, my appearance and not being passable."

Throughout the accounts, I found that not all aspects of genderist attacks were negative; some manifested as ways to "positively" reinforce traditionally accepted ways of expressing one's self-identified gender. I use the word "positively" here to indicate that attacks can also be complimentary—a show of positive reaction to illustrate acceptance of one behavior of gendered action. Just as negative genderist attacks may regulate the boundaries of appropriateness as defined by a genderist culture and the abuser, a positive attack rewards a limited conception of the victim's gender expression. Laura described this to me as she was telling the early parts of her story, how her abuser liked certain things she did (e.g., wear dresses, makeup, etc. at home): "He started saying things like that I make a beautiful woman in the bedroom, that I'm sexy. . . . He really liked when I dressed as a woman at home though, like that was his thing, it would be a treat for me to be a woman at home. Like dressed as one and stuff."

In addition to regulating and policing gender expectations, abusers often reinforced the superiority of masculinity against those victims who were femininely identified. As a component of genderism, abusers attacked femininity and directed severe violence against these survivors. Notably, Sam wrote about their second abusive relationship with another trans-identified abuser, "I was particularly targeted by his misogyny in very intense ways as part of the abuse particularly directed to my femme gender presentations." In Laura's account, like those of several other respondents, she described being early into transition and progressing through what was that current relationship with a partner who was seemingly supportive. In an instance in which a fight over what Laura was wearing and how she was presenting herself escalated into physical violence, she recounted, "He stopped me. He pinned me against the wall and he slapped me and said, 'You wanna be a bitch? You wanna be a bitch that bad? This is how bitches get treated.'" Laura's abuser regularly policed her feminine expressions through verbal and psychological degradation that marginalized and subordinated femininity. In this example, the perpetrator physically abused Laura and made the direct connection between the violence and her femininity. Essentially, her abuser regarded her femininity with contempt and deserving of violence and cruelty.

Returning to Anna's story shows how she experienced similar abuses that reinforced the subordination of femininity. Anna was engaged in sex work throughout the relationship and the abuser had been a former client. Earlier, Anna expressed that engaging in sex work allowed her to earn extra money with which she could meet her transitional goals, which included several surgeries and hormone therapy. Like a few of the other participants, Anna had difficulty getting and maintaining employment due to her trans status. She had not quit her sex work while they were dating, and the subsequent physical and sexual abuse was one of her many experiences with this partner lashing out violently: "When he found out . . . he hit me, he hit me like, slapped me and said I was a dirty bitch and a whore and that I was worthless and . . . [that] he should've known better with a slut." In addition to the physically violent attack, Anna's abuser utilized these gendered verbal attacks that degraded womanhood and her femininity. To him, she had violated the boundaries of her appropriate feminine expression, and the genderist attacks were a reminder of what kind of woman she was—a woman deserving of violence. Genderist attacks involved the policing of gender performance and the reinforcement of traditional or hegemonic notions of gender. By utilizing genderist narratives that exist in our culture, abusers were able to manipulate and control victims' emotions and psychological well-being. By disempowering victims, abusers gained control and established a power dynamic that subordinated the other.

Transphobic Attacks

Distinct from the genderist attacks described by survivors, most experienced patterns of transphobic attacks. These attacks were directed specifically against their trans status and further served to keep victims disempowered and isolated. Similar to the experiences of many gay and lesbian survivors of intimate partner violence in which homophobia and heterosexism were used to abuse, perpetrators in these accounts utilized the existing transphobic culture to attack their victims. As Jim described the early days of dating his abuser, "She said that it was very difficult to date a trans person and made me feel like I was a burden . . . this behavior affected my self-image negatively and impacts me to this day." He added, "I transitioned during the relationship. I am not sure if the abuse started before or after but I believe it got worse over time. I definitely recall the way she treated me changing after I came out [as trans]. I don't know if my trans status played a role in the abuse or not. She did try to shame me. . . . I think she was a little mad about me transitioning. Since she was a lesbian, she didn't want me to change my body. But she also didn't want to just break up with me, so she became resentful and lashed out at me, instead."

Abusers disparaged victims' trans status and identities by belittling bodies, making victims feel that the abuser was doing *them* a favor in staying, stereotyping and misunderstanding their transition processes, or threatening to "out" them. In Anna's story, her abuser went so far as ridiculing her in public spaces. This was particularly devastating to Anna as she prided herself on her ability to pass as a ciswoman and described herself by stating, "I was always kind of like a smaller, skinny person so I was already kind of, easily effeminate and small so I didn't have to do much to look more like a girl. I have a soft face and I made it softer with makeup." In one instance of a public display of humiliation, Anna and her abuser were out at a bar when the abuser began to tell others loudly that she was a transwoman. During the night of this part of her experience, Anna's abuser not only outed her in public but also made attempts to sell access to her body. As previously described earlier in the chapter, Anna's abuser frequently pimped her out without consent. As she recounted, "He would like, see if someone at the bar wanted . . . me. Like he would get drunk and even if we were at like a straight bar he would say like 'you wanna fuck her? The "shehe" is with me! She's a freak and cheap' and people would like just be like get away from me but he liked to humiliate me in public." While she detailed only this one experience, she noted that her abuser picked hostile locations (e.g., a straight bar) to out her trans status and ridicule and objectify her.

As with Anna's experience, abusers commonly relied on transphobic tactics that instilled fear of not passing or fear of being outed as trans to others. Rebecca described how her abuser constantly harped on her insecurities by frequently telling her that any of the men passing by who looked her way would never love or want to be with her if they knew who she "really" was: "He would ask about other men that worked at the mall, like this one in particular he said, 'I seen the way he looks at you' blah blah and then follow it by 'you better be careful cuz he find out you were really a man he's gonna flip out on you.'"

In many of the accounts, the notion that trans people were not "real men" or "real women" was cited as a tactic of abuse. Laura described that her abuser would refer to her as a liar for passing as a woman. In one argument that severely escalated, Laura stated that her abuser was angered by her new position as a secretary and that he took issue with her working with the public: "He just said, 'You really think you're something, you're just gonna be like this ebony princess answering phones and batting eyes at strangers and shit, sitting around like you this fine woman lying to everyone is what you're doing.'"

Abusers commonly relied on the notion that because these survivors were trans, others would not "understand" them or would view them negatively. Jessica described that her abuser weaponized her trans status, threatening to shame her among her friends, family, and community: "She was manipulating me but because no one else knew [about Jessica's trans status] other than our children, I was afraid that if I made things into a big deal that, uh she would then up end up not only leaving me and then leaving me bankrupt because I couldn't afford the child support but also then go around and telling everybody how much of a freak I am and so this eventually did happen." As with the genderist attacks, these tactics left victims feeling that beyond the context of this abusive relationship, the world is also unfriendly to transgender individuals. As Anna described what her abuser would say regarding the outside world, "No man is going to see you as a woman and even if you get one they just wanna sleep with you they don't want to love a circus act like you."

Similarly, Laura described how her abuser simply hated her trans identity the more she became public with her authentic gender presentation. She noted that as she became more open with her gender expression, her abuser started to became more hostile: "He just got real distant at first like quiet and all but like we was still good but then he just got mean and meaner and then violent." During a time when Laura started presenting publicly as the woman she was, she noted that it was "the first time I had ever seen him this angry and the first time he violently attacked me in this way, he had attacked me before but it was arguments like about wearing, dressing up as girl to the wrong place but he didn't even let me explain." Abusers like Laura's routinely emphasized that the general public would be hostile to people who were trans in an effort to instill fear in them by weaponizing external societal transphobia. To Laura's abuser, the general public was "the wrong place" to be visibly trans. Laura added, "He just hated me or at least trans-me, my trans-identity. I just don't understand. I still don't understand. He didn't mind being seen as gay. What was I doing that was so wrong? I just wanted to be me but it's like he didn't like me, he wanted some other me. He wanted some cross dresser in bed and then that's it. He would never address the problem. The trans problem."

Fatima met her abuser online and, like the majority of the survivors, entered a relationship as an openly trans person. She described that her trans status was never an issue in the relationship but that her abuser avoided being "seen" with her. After over a year of this isolation and feelings of insecurity largely instilled by her abuser, Fatima confronted him and told him that she felt as if they were purposefully not seen together very frequently in public. Fatima described her abuser's response:

He got upset, he got really upset and was like well um "Well I mean Fatima, I see a lot of people around, that place is small-minded there and with work you know, who knows if they would see me and then talk about me and that could really hurt me" and I said "See you what? See you with me?" and he said "Well no, no hun, I'm just saying people are small-minded and they'll judge" and like all this other shit he started saying like basically that I was right, he was not wanting to be "seen with me" or whatever. I couldn't believe that. It just hit me like a ton of bricks, like I mean, I do fine with passing and I try not to be consumed by it but this um, now with him saying that I just got like so um, like I don't know like hypervigilant about it, about what I looked like.

In her account, Fatima's abuser tells her that he in fact has been isolating her and that it's about others' transphobia and not his. In externalizing blame, her abuser is shifting the focus away from his own behavior but also amplifying the role of public others who may be judging her trans status. As she described, these experiences fueled preoccupations with self-image, centralizing others' potential transphobia in how she evaluates herself. John also explained that his abuser's transphobic attacks were some kind of reflection on her own problems: "She would just say I was worthless . . . that I wasn't like the man I wanted to be. She'd ridicule me. It was just such a power play for her you just can tell now looking back that she has issues. She was putting me down because of her other problems but that probably gave her satisfaction."

In Anna's experience, her abuser often ridiculed her transition processes, utilizing transphobia. As Anna described, her abuser would say, "You're looking more like a freak now with looking like a full woman but then have that shit between your legs." Similarly, Owen wrote that his abuser "would make fun of my transition." The frequent degradation of trans statuses not only became a tactic of abuse but also characterized what the violence meant to the survivors. In the following chapter, I delve a bit deeper into how survivors characterized the meanings of violence, that is, how they described the perceived motivations of the abusers.

Power and the Social Context of Genderism and Transphobia

In thinking through the power behind these attacks, the emphasis on how social and cultural contexts shape the opportunity for abuses to occur within intimate relationships becomes critical. Chapter 1 featured Tom's first quote, which exemplifies the impact and significance of understanding how genderism and transphobia manifest in abuses experienced by trans people. Despite having left his abusive relationship, Tom described his internal battle with wishing he was not trans. As a survivor of intimate partner violence, he described not only genderism and transphobia as central to the attacks he experienced but also how they continue to make him think about what his abuser "would've wanted." While traditional feminist models argued that the patriarchal power structure fostered the opportunity for men's violence against women, the stories in the present study illuminate the microcontexts of power within relationships that are largely informed by the larger social structure. Through this perspective, while social and cultural contexts can grant one member of the relationship more power than the other, ultimately the power is constructed between two partners. For example, the patriarchal power structure informs a social system that recognizes two and only two genders while simultaneously defining one superior gender and subordinating any and all gender variance.[28] While this characterizes the social context, power is made real through interaction and in its application to the present study; it is constructed through language and discourse. The power is not necessarily conferred on any one partner according to their category in the social structure but rather is constructed in the context of the intimate relationship.

Transphobia, which embodies the negative attitudes toward those who are gender variant, stems from a genderist system that recognizes only two genders and accords one of them dominance. As noted, the use of transphobic verbal and psychological attacks was a particularly salient theme across nearly all of the participants' accounts of violence and abuse. Munson and Cook-Daniels proposed that transgender victims of intimate partner violence are highly susceptible to transphobic attacks by partners as a result of the larger social and cultural environment that facilitates violence toward those who are gender variant.[29] This finding is evident throughout the accounts showing that this is indeed a prominent dynamic of the verbal and psychological abuses perpetrated against transgender victims. This pattern of abuse was prominent even in cases where the perpetrator was also transgender (seven of the abusers were identified by respondents as non-cisgender). Audrey described her abuser as genderqueer and stated that the abuser "retained her female name and her female pronoun. She just feels like she lives her life right down the middle so she didn't really feel the need to change anything like that." In another example, Chris described his abuser as "biologically male but genderqueer identified, also feminine mostly." Todd attributed some of the violence to the fact that his transgender abuser was not getting help for his transition: "For me, my partner was also trans-identified so the fact that I was able to start hormones and he wasn't, he used to manipulate me in multiple ways." These accounts illustrate that while abusers utilized genderist and transphobic attacks, the abusers were not necessarily cisgender themselves or in the category of gendered privilege. While the social and cultural contexts facilitate and make possible these attacks against gender variance, the power used to control and manipulate victims is constructed through the use of existing language regardless of the abuser's characteristics.

Through the policing and regulation of gendered expectations and marginalization of trans identities, abusers subordinated their victims. These tactics served to cripple victims' self-concepts and established an abusive power dynamic that relied on a trans-antagonistic culture. Whether the abusers were cisgender or not, the existing genderist and transphobic social and cultural contexts fostered the opportunity for these abuses to occur.

These accounts of genderist and transphobic attacks that emerged as the most salient themes in the patterns of violence provide evidence and support of existing claims made by scholars and activists that trans identities can be a central component to intimate partner violence. While other scholars have echoed many of the same tactics of abuse, including undermining trans identities, ridicule, manipulation, and other genderist or transphobic attacks, few have provided empirical evidence of these potential susceptibilities to abuse.[30]

For trans survivors of intimate partner violence, these attacks served as a constant reminder that they were inferior and deserving of abuse or violence. Through the recurring devaluation of their trans identities, many of the participants became more isolated and further ensnared in abusive patterns. Genderist and transphobic culture permeates these relationships and encouraged or at least partially motivated the abuses.

Given that the majority of the survivors were early into transition during these abusive relationships, it is possible that these tactics against trans identities were not only more common but potentially more damaging. As our conversations progressed, survivors moved from talking about escalating patterns of abuse and citing examples throughout to discussing what the experiences meant for them at the time. While each conversation varied, my questions probed how the survivors made sense of their experiences and what meanings they ascribed to them. Survivors would often discuss the motivations of their abusers, how they perceived their transgressions, and ultimately what they thought the abuse was about. As they recounted what had happened to them, they constructed stories about abuser motivations and why they felt these abuses occurred. In other words, sharing these stories of victimization at the hands of a partner they once loved, survivors began to construct what the abuse signified, why the abuse was directed toward them. What did abusers seek to accomplish?

A majority of the survivors described their abusers' motivations as controlling their gender transition and trans identity. Specifically, abusers controlled aspects of bodily changes and how/when participants expressed their gender identities. In the following chapter, I refer broadly to this as "controlling transition," and then more narrowly I specify ways in which abusers actively discredited the identity work of the respondents. While everyone engages in identity work, which is the active construction of our identities through social interaction and feedback, this is an area of heightened vulnerability for trans people. Given the evident marginalization of trans identities, the ways in which abusers undermine the identity work of trans victims are important to note. The following chapter analyzes a critical yet underexplored aspect of abusive intimate relationships—how abuse can be understood as interactional control through which abusers direct or manipulate a victim's identity work and presentation of self. The chapter first brings together social-psychological and intimate partner violence backgrounds to better understand dynamics of abuse in intimate relationships and ultimately offers some insight into "why victims stay" in abusive relationships, in relation to the manipulation of self-concepts.

4

Meanings of Violence

Controlling Transition through Discrediting Identity Work

Moving beyond the descriptive accounts of abuse, survivors delved deeper into how the abuses affected them and how they made sense of the experiences both then and presently. Laura's formerly abusive relationship was introduced earlier, one that began online and flourished into what she considered one of the most promising. At one point, her and I got focused on the day she went to submit her legal gender confirmation. This was a significant day for her, but she recalled it being stressful; she told me her abuser "tried to stop my appointment to change my [legal] gender." She added, "He would say like, 'Oh but I had something planned for us that day' and he would make something up. And he just did that like twice and finally I was like, I don't care I'm going to file this paperwork. That turned into his screaming the same things he used to, it's like it was no different again, he would just get me so upset I wouldn't leave." I asked Laura, "How did it go?" curious to hear if she had made it in on time to submit her gender confirmation request. That specific day, thanks to a friend who had agreed to go with her, she ended up making it to the appointment to file the necessary paperwork. Laura continued to tell me how she now understood her abuser's actions as disruptions to her transition goals. I inquired a bit further on how she left that day to get a sense of what she was feeling and how she now interprets why she had stayed home from appointments in the past. She added, "I wanted this to work because, who's going to want me now? What's my luck of finding another person that wants to love a trans person? Who wants to build a life with someone who is figuring out life in another gender and has these issues and my body and all?" Laura expressed a specific vulnerability that many survivors echoed, a fear of romantic rejection based solely on their gender identity. Taken as whole, the accounts reflect how survivors saw much of what their abuse meant as tactics to control their transition processes. Analytically, it's crucial to dissect the ways in which gender transitions were controlled by abusers, specifically as related to active identity work.

Controlling Transition

For many transgender people, transitioning from an assigned gender to one that more accurately represents their internal sense of self is a lifelong and active process. Like the survivors in the current study, trans people may be at varying stages of transition, including but not limited to the social and psychological realms of identity development and medical interventions (e.g., hormone therapy, gender confirmation surgery). Given the true diversity in gender identification and expression, many trans people may not desire or even benefit from medical transitions. Much debate exists around whether gender is "reassigned" or "affirmed," whether transition is lifelong or a finite process.[1] Trans scholars often critique the public fixation on the transgender performance of "putting on" gender (e.g., putting on lipstick) as if it were a costume or a temporary act instead of seeing simply who the person is innately.[2] Regardless of the path, gender transition is a complex psychological, social, and public process for many.[3]

While there were varying aspects to how abusers attempted or followed through with their desires to control the transition process, the broader theme of controlling transition was salient throughout the meanings constructed behind abuse. To most survivors, the abuse was perpetrated to gain control over their development and served to further disempower victims. When reflecting and making sense of their reality, survivors saw many of their experiences with abuse as attempts by abusers to control transition and define them on the abusers' own terms. In maintaining power and control over victims, abusers often took charge over victims' lives and controlled a central (and often vulnerable) aspect of identity—gender transition. Given that the majority of the sample was relatively young and early into the transition processes, abusers found ways in which to manipulate, regulate, and control victims' gendered expressions and identities.

A closer analysis of the stories revealed an active pattern of control that directly targeted the identity of these survivors. While controlling transitions was a broad pattern evident in the ways survivors reflected on what their abusers' motivations were, the accounts illustrated more specific mechanisms for how identity was marginalized.

Identity and Intimate Partner Violence

Utilizing an identity work perspective was essential in understanding the theoretical underpinnings of survivor experiences. Of central concern to researchers studying identity is how people present themselves to others interactionally. For instance, sociologist Erving Goffman argued that people will use tact because of mutual desires to maintain their own face.[4] Throughout daily interaction, identities are presented, reflected, and reinterpreted by both the actors and the audience. Schwalbe and Mason-Schrock defined identity work as the process of signifying one's identity to others in such a way that it will arouse desired responses from audiences, while Snow and Anderson considered tactics by which stigmatized groups' constructions of personal identities uphold their self-worth.[5] This line of research acknowledges that others play a role in self-identity construction, including the need for joint action for successful signification.[6] The current chapter, however, examines the place of others from a different perspective within the context of an abusive relationship. It examines how people can be understood as actively working to direct others' desired identity work and presentation of self in an undesired fashion, or discrediting identity work.

While identity work includes activities contributing to the presentation of identities, in research with a fellow scholar and coauthor we put forth the term "discrediting identity work" to account for an individual's engagement in activities that direct another's identity construction away from desired identity signification.[7] Although research has examined the construction of a "victim identity" or a victim's identity work,[8] the present chapter expands from sociologists Weinstein and Deutschberger's call to focus on the implications of an individual's behavior on the definition of the situation and narrowing lines of action, in order to examine identity-related issues in the context of intimate partner violence.[9] From a Goffmanian perspective, focusing on potential discrediting is particularly critical because transgender identities may differ from those of so-called normals, so that (1) their "attempts to avoid devaluation and discrimination generate problematic social and economic circumstances that . . . in turn may further undermine self-worth" and (2) whether or not they accept the label, they must "deal with the interpersonal difficulties created by a discrediting public identity conferred by other people."[10]

Two primary strategies of discrediting identity work were evident in the accounts: altercasting and targeting sign vehicles, including controlling through props. Rather than claim generalization to the larger trans community, the analyses instead offer generic strategies of discrediting identity work directed toward transgender individuals who are actively negotiating identities from transitional, marginalized positions.

Control through Interactions

Connecting back to previous points, much of the early work on intimate partner violence framed the use of violence as one part of men's attempts to control women's current and future behaviors within the context of intimate relationships. Individuals' sense of who they are in intimate relationships is largely constructed through their partners' perceived reactions.[11] Control has been understood and defined as the purposeful or tactful exertion of power over a romantic partner through the use of fear, threats, and/or physical or emotional violence intended to manipulate the victim in some form.[12]

The concept of control within the existing intimate partner violence literature evolved from identifying desires to manipulate or restrict decision making to conceptualizations of coercive control. As Stark explains, the coercive control model originated from literature applying theoretical learning approaches to examining those being controlled in nonfamilial settings, such as war prisoners or institutionalized individuals.[13] As the coercive control model developed in intimate partner violence studies, scholars emphasized severe dependency as motivating abusers, drawing parallels to terrorists holding victims hostage in an attempt to extort their desires. Stark's coercive control model expands upon these propositions by emphasizing the power behind the cultural context facilitating men's ability to entrap women within intimate relationships. Existing research has generally lacked an explicit focus on identity construction that is necessary to better understand mechanisms of socially controlling others' identities within the context of abusive relationships.

Understanding Identity Work

Employing an identity work perspective helps to address this. In line with Snow and Anderson, I understand identity construction as encompassing elements of identity work processes.[14] Identity work entails the "range of activities individuals engage in to create, present, and sustain" identities that are socially acceptable and confirming of self-concepts. The self-concept comprises how individuals think and feel about themselves as an "object of reflection."[15] That is to say that individuals negotiate their self-concepts according to their meanings and definitions of self (self-identities), their perceptions of others' reactions to themselves, and the internationalization of these perceived meanings.[16] Therefore, drawing on processes of identity work further reveals the importance of interactional negotiations regarding how others (like potential abusers) can influence the identity work of transgender partners.

An identity work perspective is useful as it brings attention to the activities people perform—and the work this entails—to signify a particular identity to others. These identity negotiations involve sign vehicles, or signifiers, which include any tool that helps convey a "particular kind of self," such as clothing, gestures, facial expressions, popular culture consumption, and political choices. These signifiers also include what Goffman defined as props; such material objects can be seemingly limitless because "contact with all and any material objects in the world gives a human a chance to put his or her self into play."[17] Cultural messages attach meaning to certain ways of acting, posturing, and moving—even the act of walking can signify femininity or masculinity, so that through embodiment individuals can utilize their bodies to signify particular meanings.[18]

However, reactions within interactions carry meanings that can confirm or deny presented self-concepts.[19] For example, individuals may more or less consciously make "demands" of others, as we bring expectations of others based on their social "category and attributes" into interactions.[20] Individuals bring into an interaction their expectations for others to both support and realize a norm associated with particular categories; if the other's actual social identity fails to uphold this virtual social identity, interactional tensions, discrimination, or potential discrediting actions can occur. At the same time, Goffman notes that individuals who "fail to live up to what we effectively demand" of them may still be "relatively untouched by this failure."[21] Accordingly, the actor's interpretations of others' interactional feedback is a critical component in their corresponding identity work. Therefore, the present focus is on how the survivors I spoke with and read from constructed the abusers' actions, and I apply the theory of altercasting to examine their perceptions of abuse. In other words, I seek to make sense of abuse from the victim's perspective. This helps to better understand how victims can perceive their abusers' actions as discrediting identity work, affecting their own identity work.

In relation to such influences, prior research suggests that control can enter into relationships if individuals perceive their own identities as being questioned.[22] Sociologists Burke and Stets defined the process in which one projects one's identities and then perceives feedback aligning with what one thinks of oneself as identity verification; however, when individuals do not have their identities verified positively in relationships, they may act more aggressively or controlling in an attempt to counter.[23] Additionally, while Goffman predominately focused on "cooperation in face-work" by arguing others will help in restoring someone's face if they lose face, he did explain situations in which aggression can enter interactions.[24] Aggressive face-work involves a person using proven tactics for saving face in a planned manner to gain rewards, such as increased status.[25] This turns the interaction into a "contest" instead of a performance, with the intent to one-up the other individual; based on this, Goffman stated an audience is "almost a necessity" to support this contest. However, his focus was on everyday examples (e.g., "comebacks," "squelches"), so that the interactions relate contextually to losing face, but he did not extend his research to the greater consequences associated with victimhood and abuse.

Drawing from Goffman, Weinstein and Deutschberger claim a critical component to interactional negotiations is the definition of the situation.[26] The definition of the situation involves accounting for "symbolic cues" to infer the behaviors one can take in order to elicit desired responses. Due to this, individuals can control or direct another's presentation of self by limiting options for signification through manipulating the definition of the situation. When successful, this "altercasting" can "cast" another into a particular identity—an identity of another individual's choosing.[27] Weinstein and Deutschberger therefore offer insight into how forms of control can enter into relationships by drawing attention to how individuals can work on others' self-presentation, versus only their own presentations of self.

Weinstein and Deutschberger argue that in one dimension of altercasting manipulation can occur through an actor constructing an identity for the targeted individual who feels they require the actor's support, help, or comforting. A second defined dimension includes when the targeted individual feels interdependence with the actor and perceives their fates or interests as intertwined. Last, in relation to the dimension of "degree of freedom allowed" by the targeted individual, the actor can limit the range of behavior of the targeted individual by decreasing the number of responses allowed, in turn increasing the likelihood of the targeted individual adopting the roles and behaviors desired by the actor. By connecting symbols valued by the targeted individual with a constructed identity, the targeted individual effectively would need to reject their ideal identity to reject the constructed identity.[28] In these ways, the actor's actions are targeting the ways in which another constructs their identity and, to a certain extent, define the possibilities for another's identity. Even with such innate connections to interpersonal control, research is lacking directly connecting altercasting with intimate partner violence.

Critical to examining the social recognition of transgender intimate partner violence, previous work has helped to shed light on connections between identity work and the construction of intimate partner violence as a social problem. Sociologist Loseke examined the divide between formal definitions of wife abuse and definitions deriving from the lived experience of abuse.[29] In culturally recognized, public definitions of wife abuse, abuse is recognized as "extreme" and physical—and therefore often linked to visibly present marks of abuse.[30] Related to this, Leisenring found that women, in their identity work, at times both claimed and distanced themselves from the public definition of victim. Most relevant to discrediting identity work, Leisenring examined how "mandatory arrest policies shape women's identity work during their encounters with police officers," specifically focusing on "unsuccessful" or "failed" identity work when police officers denied their self-presentation strategies.[31] Leisenring argued women believed their inability to "proactively define the situation in their favor" led to failed identity work.[32] Arguably, one way women explained this was according to men's knowledge of the criminal justice system through prior intimate partner violence experiences, which they believed gave men the "upper hand" in defining the situation to the police in such a way that framed their partners as the abusers. While focused on individuals' interpretations of their own identity work, such research still shed light on situations in which others could direct victims' identity work.

As one's identity work is susceptible to influences from others' direct mediation through these interactions, one aspect of such interactional negotiations needing further clarification is the ways in which an individual's actions can negatively influence another's identity construction. Based in this prior research, interpersonal control and forms of manipulation appear critical to processes of discrediting identity work, especially as it relates to transgender intimate partner violence victimization. It is evident that more is needed to understand manipulations of others' identity work within abusive intimate relationships, particularly in considering perceived control and manipulation of self-concepts versus a more narrow focus on a "victim identity." Therefore, rather than examining the construction of victim identities or processes of overcoming stigmatization to create desired identities, this chapter examines the identity construction process from an underexamined perspective of discrediting identity work. For transgender victims, experiences of learning and practicing how to perform gender offer striking instances of identity (re)formation, which can bring to the surface processes of others' discrediting identity work.

Importantly, survivors' stories can be considered a form of identity work in and of themselves. Therefore, I draw from these stories to examine processes of others preventing positive identity construction, as narratively understood by transgender people who have experienced the abuse. The narrative format thus includes sense making within the context of a research setting.

Comparing the patterns in the data to existing literature helped develop focused codes identifying major ways in which survivors defined how their abusers manipulated desired identity construction. Their stories thus helped account for their vulnerability while revealing how abusers discredited their identity construction and presentation of self through altercasting and using sign vehicles against the victims, particularly in relation to manipulations of emotional insecurities, and controlling props and the usage of props.

Discrediting Identity Work

The stories reflectively revealed ways in which victims made sense of their experiences of intimate partner violence. First, the chapter reviews how victims' accounts helped to define the stage, from a dramaturgical perspective, on which abusers could act out the manipulation of victims' identities. This examines the victims' accounts for why they were vulnerable and how their own perceived needs created the stage for abusers' discrediting identity work. Next, while survivor accounts helped make sense of their experiences, they additionally described a more subtle yet powerful construct of abuse—the controlling and directing of one's identity construction. This control occurs through two generic strategies of discrediting identity work: (1) redefining the situation to focus on participant-defined insecurities, a form of altercasting; and (2) targeting sign vehicles, including regulating gender transition treatments and controlling through props. As noted, gender transition treatments may include medical interventions necessary to alter physical sexual characteristics (e.g., hormone therapy). Such tactics also suggest insight into one reason why victims stay in abusive relationships, as abusers are actively—whether more or less intentionally—manipulating victims' identity construction; these identities are not necessarily confined to a "victim identity," but include victims' self-concepts during the time of their relationship.

Altercasting: Manipulating through Insecurities

Stories of interpersonal control revealed survivors' constructions of abusers' exploitation of their self-defined insecurities, including aspects of their transitions interpreted as increasing their vulnerability to such exploitation. Accordingly, the process was defined as one component of discrediting identity work through altercasting, based on abusers drawing from insecurities to place victims into identities self-described as insecure and former identities. The survivors' stories highlighted their self-identities, offering insight into how manipulative abuse affects the looking-glass self, as they described adjusting their own views of self beyond responsive behaviors, suggesting this process over the course of time can lead to the internationalization of these casted identity traits.[33]

Altercasting involves defining the situation, so that situations can be directed in ways toward conversational topics that limit the roles others can adopt, leading to either greater or lesser comfort for the others interacting.[34] In other words, this process consists of "casting" the "alter" (other) into a particular role and is thus closely related to the dramaturgical presentation of self. Stories that went into greater depth built on the desire for stability to explain how partners drew from former or insecure identities in order to make victims feel compelled to stay in the relationship, even after abuse increased. Such stories, therefore, shed light on "why victims stay," due to a form of altercasting that directs victims into an insecure or undesired identity.

In making sense of self-concepts, individuals can use stories to reflexively reconcile what was expected to happen and lived experiences. Earlier, I noted that much of the narrative quality in the stories follows cultural patterns. Being asked to reflect on past experiences sets the stage for individuals to draw from master story patterns, which can be understood as resources for individuals to understand and coherently construct their identities. As Mason-Schrock explained in relation to transsexuals constructing stories of a true self, respondent accounts are based in part on a "master account" of falling in love that circulates in Western culture, as romantic narratives can be used to justify decisions and new self-concepts. As noted in earlier chapters, survivors drew from similar story patterns surrounding the significance of intimate relationships.[35] Additionally, for transgender individuals, desires for relationship stability may keep them involved in abusive and harmful dynamics.[36] The stories upheld such findings, as they accounted for a strong desire for stability through the maintenance of a long-term relationship; this in turn can be understood as setting the stage for how abusers' manipulated the definition of the situation.

For instance, Rebecca described her abuser as one that exploited through desired support through stable relationships. Halfway through our conversation, I asked Rebecca about what she was feeling during the peak of her abuse; what kept things going even when they got so bad? She replied, "It's easy for that person to just look from the outside and say 'just leave,' but when I've literally lost so much over the years; it's hard to 'just leave.' I wanted so badly to have stability that I just made myself put up with him. I thought it was a small price to pay for the stable home."

According to altercasting, abusers' manipulation of identities and victims' self-presentation can merge when victims sense they need the abusers' help, comfort, or support. These traits can be seen through survivors' accounting for abusers being able to maintain relational control through victims' desired support for stability from the abusers. As with Rebecca's explanation of how she changed herself in reaction to her abuser ("made myself put up with him"), John made sense of the ways he adjusted his perspective in response to the labels he felt were conferred to him by others, in accordance with his abuser's actions: "I didn't really think it would ever get like this and also, I was in love and I had it good so I just thought, I don't know. I had been single for two years because my long-term girlfriend left me after coming out trans. So maybe I thought this was like a rare thing that I should try to fix. I had other trans friends and they all didn't have relationships or couldn't keep one so maybe I was trying to be like the one that had a success."

John's description offered insight into how these desires for stability can relate back to a positive sense of self; in describing wanting to be the one with "success," he defined the relationship as not only offering stability, but also demarcating a path toward desired identity construction, based on associations of a normalized path ("success") with the maintenance of a long-term relationship. Victimization can thus occur when abusers take advantage of these desires to direct the victims toward former, undesired identities. The stories suggested this direction was possible through accounting for their vulnerability, based on their willingness to sacrifice for stability through long-term relationships—and the need of their partner to accomplish this. Chris emphasized how much hir perceived vulnerability, rooted in their trans identity and queer sexuality, made hir justify the abuses zie was experiencing:

> I didn't want to engage in penetrative sex. Zie would say things like that I wasn't really meant to be in a relationship. Like that all relationships

had to be about sex and that I wouldn't really attract anyone unless I was willing to do things that people expected of me, sexually that is. I just ended up accepting that as fact; that out there, we just lived in this world of relationships where a certain type of sex is expected. I think of myself as queer sexually because I don't need to engage in penetrative sex to be having sex but that was just not an option. For some odd or just weird reason I thought, well he already knows this about me and zie was still willing to stay with me and I'm happy to be with another genderqueer-identified person so maybe I should just count my blessings and not be picky about everything. It's hard to think now, that rejecting sexual abuse, essentially, rape, was something I thought was being "picky"—it's scary that I hit that low, that I felt I wasn't worthy of a healthy relationship because my sexuality was weird or that my gender was weird and people won't understand me so no one will want me—so maybe I thought, well at least I have hir.

Survivors' descriptions of "changing their minds" additionally revealed perceptions of abusers controlling their decisions by taking advantage of fears based in transitions; through the lens of dramaturgy and narrowing lines of action, such vulnerabilities created the stage by which abusers could direct their identity work toward positions in which they continued needing support. For example, Joe, a survivor who I noted was early in his transition process, stated,

I do feel like it [being trans and transitioning] made me more vulnerable. I was in a really sensitive and kind of unstable place and I was trying to find my footing and I just, it's not a good; it's an ideal time for an abuser to strike. They take advantage of your fears or your uncertainty. . . . I remember like, I was actually changing my name legally and I changed it on my own and he wanted to know my birth name um, and I refused to tell him . . . [explaining] "That's not your business; that's not what I go by," and he got really angry and that was the first time he got really angry at me . . . from the start, he wanted to control the entire process in some form.

Here, Joe offers explanations of how he was controlling his identity work in the way he desired, yet his abuser targeted relevant identity-related changes to control and redirect Joe's focus back to points of instability. For transgender individuals, the selection of a name encompasses the active construction of a new identity. By seemingly forcing Joe to refocus on his birth name, for instance, his abuser prevented Joe from moving forward into his desired identity. Related to this, Tom discussed his abuser's control over his actions and his own redefinition of identity based on the abuser's use of guilt to direct Tom away from certain actions and back to issues of (in)stability and loneliness.

> I didn't want to break up with her and when I tried to leave she would just guilt me back in, or if she didn't, I would just change my mind—I'd feel lonely or something. When you're going through changes it's best to have a steady and consistent home and intimate life, you know, and I thought I was doing the right thing with just keeping this the way it was. . . . She just made me feel ashamed of who I was and all. Like every now and then I'll think, just like, how lucky everyone is that they don't have to think about their gender clashing with their bodies and I wish sometimes that I wasn't trans, but then I think, "No, no—that's what she would've wanted."

Making sense of his actions in relation to stability, Tom explained how his abuser perpetuated his current instability through creating an environment of guilt, which is in opposition to providing support for desired identity construction. Tom's story offers insight into his negotiations of his abuser's actions by interpreting his own guilt and shame regarding "who he is" as a desired result of his abuser's discrediting identity work. Such interpretations reveal how victims perceived discrediting identity work as affecting a sense of a core identity. The stories consistently highlighted how abusers took advantage of their desire for or felt need of support through creating a "void," creating a situation where abusers' work kept victims unstable in their sense of self. Rebecca discussed how abusers took advantage of insecurities:

> I always had a good sense of self, like since I transitioned years ago before him, I really came to be myself—who I was—but he just had this way of pulling out old insecurities, ones that I had put behind me, like he just knew where I was vulnerable and he knew what to attack. I got really down on myself and preoccupied with my looks since he went after that

a lot. . . . After a while, I felt just defeated, I was now just basically back to what I had been feeling like years ago, I was self-conscious, timid, I started isolating myself from everyone.

Rebecca constructed how abusers directed their roles back to the difficulty of transitions and "who I was." These interactional tactics directed conversations toward topics found to be destabilizing (e.g., looks), shifting the interaction to one with a power dynamic. Participants' descriptions of the following incidences explained how abusers' verbal manipulations particularly controlled the role the victim took and, beyond this, the way they viewed and defined themselves. Audrey's story encompassed this manipulation of self-concept by describing how her partner attacked points of insecurity, including successful presentation of her desired gendered self. Similarly to how Rebecca described her partner pulling out "old insecurities," Audrey explained how her abuser would "pull" the positive things away. These actions can be seen as creating a void the abuser could take advantage of through discrediting identity work to redirect the victim's identity work:

> Her attacks on my passability as a woman . . . it was an attempt to manipulate me. To take away something that I was feeling good about and you know, how I was able to present myself as female, and learning how to look beautiful, and look pretty, and the way I dressed, and the way I see myself, and trying to turn that into a negative for me. It was taking away those things that I found self-fulfilling and trying to pull those away so that there would be a void there, that she could come in and fill it.

Through a perspective of altercasting, this "proactive stance" increased probabilities that the situation would place the victim into a former, undesired gender identity by creating a focus back on looks—a point of insecurity.[37] Audrey's long list of the items her abuser attacked revolved around the way she saw herself, limiting the choices for her desired identity construction and "self-fulfillment."

Throughout our conversations, survivors discussed how they perceived their partners taking advantage of stated vulnerabilities surrounding their gendered identity transitions. In relation to the dimension of "degree of freedom allowed" abusers limited the range of behavior of the victim by creating an ideal role of what it means to be a "man," limiting the desired identity traits that the individuals could fit in to fulfill their ideal identity.[38] Rather than redirecting the situation to focus on old identities, abusers redefined the desired identities to increase the difficulty of the victims being able to fulfill those roles. Todd made this point to me when he described his partner holding "traditionally masculine characteristics over me like, 'If you were more of a man, you would do x, y and z,' or 'If you had more honor and integrity you wouldn't be acting like this,' or 'Why can't you just talk to me face-to-face like a man?' that were specifically gendered—that were supposed to be used as threats against my character or my transition."

Todd's account showed the interconnectedness of threats to his gendered identity—stated by Todd as his "character"—transition, and discrediting identity work. This echoed my conversation with John, who also defined a "power play" through which his partner was understood as reverting John to a place of insecurity, emphasizing the power of verbal manipulations:

> I was so proud of myself and everything that I had accomplished and I had done it all on my own, and I been out as trans, I got the things that I needed to do it, I went through it and had to deal with so much loss [i.e., jobs, family] but then, on top of all of that shit, all that I had to deal with before, she came in and had to do that [abuse] to me. It was just such a power play for her. . . . I didn't think of myself as like, a soft, like you know—I'm a tough man, I really am, but I would've never thought that words could just bring someone down like she did. All those insecurities and all that, she got into it.

This story explained the "ideal" identity of John—being a "tough man"—and how the abuser was able to, through social proximity to the victim, have increased opportunities to reconstruct the interactions with the victim by knowing the insecurities and redefining the situation around those insecurities. Similar to Audrey's description of the abuser creating a "void," the void can arguably be seen as the "role" the abuser is directing the victim toward, defining the situation in a negative rather than more supportive consensus. Survivor stories constructed the tactics by which another person caused them to change their internal perceptions of self, *beyond* their expressed emotions or presentations of self. Such versions of "power plays" revealed forms of altercasting in which abusers limited the range of behavior, accordingly reducing the options by which the victim could act. When in the positions defined by the participants as vulnerable, these verbal power plays can lead to an increased need by survivors to following through with the suggested roles. The stories therefore revealed a combination of societal narratives, including the social desirability of monogamous relationships and love, with self-defined vulnerabilities that participants perceived as taken advantage of by abusers; this was accordingly accomplished through discrediting identity work.

Targeting Sign Vehicles

Stories also suggested abusers directed signification of desired identities by positioning themselves as gatekeepers of sign vehicles. More specifically, the survivors' stories suggested a turning point in their transition process at which time the abusers more explicitly targeted props or gender transition treatments, and whether the props were internal or external, constructed the props themselves as the seeming target of violence. This can contribute to keeping or placing victims in a liminal state because, to a greater or lesser extent, abusers controlled when, where, and how victims could present desired identities. While props are integral to individuals' presentations of self, for individuals transitioning, the centrality of props for successful self-presentation can be even more significant in expressing desired gender identities. Identity work can therefore be discredited through the targeting of physical changes and props that participants classify as especially important to their personally defined achievement of desired identities and the acknowledgment by others of those desired identities. Again here I revisit how participants made sense of their vulnerability, basing their vulnerability to abuse in their reliance on props and revealing transition points that appeared to trigger particularly violent discrediting identity work. Beyond this, the examination of survivors' perceptions of how abusers targeted props shows how these tactics contributed to the undermining of their desired presentations of self.

While in stories of altercasting survivors defined stability through relationships as the primary point increasing their vulnerability, in the case of sign vehicles participants also first explained points of vulnerability, but specifically explained how their gender transition treatments and increased reliance on props for desired identity signification made them more vulnerable to abusers. The stories suggested that once survivors reached a place in which they felt they were gaining ground and closer to achieving desired identities, the abuser worked toward discrediting this identity achievement through targeting gender sign vehicles. Particularly as certain survivors felt they had completed their transition and achieved a desired identity, this felt as though they were going back and forth in time between desired and undesired (former) identities. Such stories therefore revealed concrete examples of how abusers controlled the signification of identities in abusive intimate relationships.

Commonly in my conversations, respondents described how they were attempting to act out their identities (e.g., sexually queer) and how their abusers prevented them from doing so. For instance, Laura's account situated the targeting of hormones—a gender transition treatment—during a point in her transition when she had begun to feel confident enough to wear a dress for a dinner date. The conversation focused on this particular night after I first asked Laura about her abuser's reaction to her becoming and feeling more like her authentic self. She had already told me she was out as a transwoman from the start of the relationship, but I followed up with an interest in learning more about his support for her advancing her transition. I simply asked Laura, "Was he supportive?" Laura, with hesitation, replied,

> Well, it seemed like yeah, well, yeah at first he didn't really seem to mind you know he was like "yeah baby, yeah babe you do you," "you do what you need to . . . I'll [the abuser] help you pay for the doctors' visits or whatever you need." And I mean, after that, after we had been together for over a year, is when we had this talk and it seemed fine and all. But then when I changed my wardrobe he really started to take it serious. Like, I had started hormones and T blockers and the meds I think it was a lot for him. He just got real distant at first, like, quiet and all but like, we was still good but then he just got mean and meaner and then violent.

I asked Laura to describe what she meant by his reactions to her advancing transition. It was then that she turned toward the night his responses began to escalate in severity.

Well, I guess it started with the first time I just wanted to go out during the day time with him to eat lunch and he was like "yeah, it's cool let's go baby." We were getting ready and all and I started putting on all my [women's] clothes and hair and did my makeup and everything. By then, you know, I had been on T blocker and hormones for a while so I was softening and I was working my voice better and I just felt like more comfortable being able to do this. When I was almost done he came in the room and was like "whoa whoa—baby what are you doing, what are you doing?" "I thought we was going out for lunch, what are you doing?" and I was like well, I want to go like this, I want to go as me—this is what I want. He said, "nah nah—you ain't ready, you look like a drag queen you look ridiculous," and I said [to her abuser], "But I thought you said the hormones were working and I feel like my voice is better," and I had gotten this new bra that had the breasts in it and I looked real good. He said, "Please don't do this to me right now, I can't." . . . He just was like "No, this is gonna be a problem baby . . . you're gonna be miserable and you know I think you look good but that's for home, baby—please, you look like a freak."

Although her partner had appeared supportive of her transition, his disparagement of Laura as a "freak" can be seen as attempting to regulate her public presentation of self through props. Such discrediting identity work occurred through classifying her desired presentation of self as a "problem." Laura described her abuser's violence in one physical attack as directed toward her newly performed top surgery for breast enhancement, highlighting additional forms of vulnerability during transitions: "He slapped me and pushed on my chest and pushed on my surgical scars and made them bleed. . . . He said he wasn't going to date a confused person, he couldn't be with a mentally ill person, he said 'I know you're crazy, I know you got problems in the head.'"

In some stories, abusers undermined victims' transition processes, again when a change was first occurring. Tom described his abuser's attacks upon beginning testosterone hormone therapy (T): "She started getting really suspicious of me like, because I was on T, she thought I was going to get out of control sexually and she started just regulating everything. She was always checking my phone and asking me questions. If I didn't answer to her, she would scream; she even broke my phone at one point." Similarly, Sam wrote that the main way their transition was attacked by their abusers "was in the jealousy of my relationships with other masculinely gendered people that contributed to the isolation and psychological abuse. This was attributed to the idea that transguys turn gay after they start T." The assumption made by abusers that T made individuals more likely to cheat was also referenced in David's account as he described to me that after his transition "the longer we were together the more it just became about sex, and especially after I started T, then it was really about sex, even if we were emotionally together. . . . I don't know how to put it into terms there was just no connection no romance. I think it was about [her] control, it was just about [her saying] 'I'm going to make you do what I want.' It [T] made her turn on me more, like I was on T and more sexually interested so that could play some kind of role." While he emphasized that he did not think transitioning was a cause of the escalating abuse, he cited her mischaracterization of transition medications as a potential reason for sexual jealousy or intensity. Overall, the abusers' attacks constructed and perpetuated stereotyped and suspicious assumptions about the transition process, targeting a physical prop that could enable desired identity work, yet could also be controlled during the transition process in order to manipulate the victim's presentation of self. The assumptions about hormone therapy also gave the abuser a sense of justification to control Tom's interactions with anyone outside of the relationship. Similarly, Owen wrote, "He would blackmail me, emotionally abuse me, threaten suicide, and do everything in his power to make me stay in a 'relationship' with him. . . . [He] threatened to make me pregnant among other things. He prevented me from getting on testosterone until the relationship ended with numerous threats of suicide and other things." Such accounts for how abusers attempted to restrict victims' transition actions echo closely well-documented findings on intimate partner violence and the restriction of women's movements to within the home.[39]

In the process of controlling props, abusers additionally objectified the victims, affecting their ability to embody and live out their desired identities by regulating the victims' signification through gender identifiers. Such objectification could, in the extreme, turn the victims into "props" themselves that could be manipulated through abusers' directives. When I asked Joe if he felt that his trans status or transitioning progress was somehow threatening to his abuser, he quickly replied, "Oh he told me outright what [transitioning] meant to him." In relation to physical alterations and treating the body as an object, Joe explained, "He would say 'I can handle you physically modifying the upper half of your body but if you change the lower half of your body it's wrong' that you have to keep what you have, you have to use it, you have to get over it and make a baby with me. It was just a threat to him . . . for me to be, like . . . I hate to use this because I know there are so many types of relationships but I am a dominant person, and he didn't like that, he didn't like that I would take charge of this [transitioning], he didn't want me to." Joe never did agree to pregnancy with his abuser, but his account explained his abuser's attempts to control his physical transition, an important component to his construction of his desired identity; not only this, the body was objectified following genderist expectations of reproduction. Joe added,

> He would use [transitioning] as a constant scare tactic. When I had finally gotten the means to pay for top surgery for example, he would talk about how he and I would go to the surgeon place and take care of me but that wasn't in my plan at all. I had someone else in mind and when I told him that, he would do the dramatics like "why am I not good enough for you?" or regarding the hormones it would be like "why do you have to do this?" "we could go in together and talk to the therapist together." It was what I felt personal, my personal thing to do, he would turn it about him or both of us together and he would just sort of use it. He would try to keep something that was personal and for me to deal with, he would turn it into like, an issue to talk about with me, he would just use it as a guilt trip thing regularly.

The control of the body as an object can also be seen through Sam's story: "I was genderfluid at the time [while dating]. I was told I could not transition before him, and was often not allowed to present in masculine ways. I was ordered to embody particular genders by him and the people he traded me to for goods/services."

Such interactions related to assumptions about how others would look at the victims and how the victims would act outside of the home. While hormones and biological changes overlap with props in enabling signification a gendered identity, gender transition treatments additionally cross into issues of sex, such as abilities to have children, and sexuality, as related to concerns for becoming sexually "out of control." Arguably, many of these accounts suggest the real need to expand researchers' definitions of physical abuse beyond specific violent acts to include the ability of another person to control one's physical makeup. For instance, Fatima's case revealed the interconnectedness of props and gender transition treatments, as bras, silicone, and surgery ("did more on my face") to targeting sign vehicles for abuse through discrediting identity work. Fatima described,

> I started doing [wearing] some of the things he got, like, the better bras and silicone; I even did more on my face, like the lips and cheeks [referring to surgeries], that were just easy one day things. He would praise me for that and then do stuff for me, like things that I had been asking to do; like just more public things. I started to just lose myself; I was just now this thing. This, like experiment or something, of his to use and "doll up." It only made me more depressed, which made him more angry, and then that's when he got colder, more distant, more angry, and kind of like violent.

Fatima's explanations suggested a process of objectification, offering concrete examples of discrediting identity work with repercussions leading to increased abuse. Within the context of these abuses, the manipulations of constructed gender ideals become apparent even when more or less consciously drawn upon by abusers; in Fatima's account, she expressed how an emphasized femininity was expected and regulated by her abuser. The connection between the body, sexuality, and social practice was drawn from by the abuser in ways that regulated the embodiment of gender through the reinforcement of heteronormative ideals. These tactics of control not only affected survivors' ability to use props to support their presentations of self, but arguably made them into objects or props themselves. Jessica's story also helped explain this aspect of targeting sign vehicles: "She could often do anything she wanted you know? She simply just had to pick up lip stick or you know, a pair of nylons for me and throw me a bone like 'here I got you something' that was supposed to forgive anything she chose to do and I really felt like she was manipulating me." Abusers' actions can be interpreted as using gifting in a seemingly compensatory fashion to "make up" for their past manipulation of self-signification. As opposed to destroying props, partners' actions that appeared to be an attempt to compensate for their actions through the purchase of props exemplified an additional point of control. Beyond this, such gifting in turn can also direct future presentations of self, adding another layer of direction through controlling props. These stories thus echo Stark's research supporting gifting as a way to make up for abuse by revealing how gifting can perpetuate control by further objectifying the victim, so that within the context of an abusive relationship in which the victim is transgender, gifting takes on a unique dimension.

Just as such objectification of abusers turned sign vehicles, or props, against the victims, stories additionally shed light on the critical connections between the props (e.g., a dress) and expression of her desired gender identity (e.g., being "a woman"). For example, Laura explained, "He started to rip up my clothes. It was a nice outfit, I loved that dress; I went out just grocery shopping in it but I loved it and I always got compliments on it. He ripped it up; he took a knife off the table and ripped it close to my skin and he cut me. He cut me while ripping it up and yelling things and he said, 'You wanna be a woman so bad.' And he kept ripping up my dress and turned me around." Although Laura's description explained how she was also physically injured, her story clarified the dress as the abuser's target. Related to this, Tom explained how "sometimes she would hide my chest binder just to ruin my day, knowing I couldn't go outside without it." Survivors therefore constructed the importance of these props to signification of a desired gendered identity, and thus to the abusers' ability to use these sign vehicles against victims. Rebecca also told a story in which the abuser not only physically targeted a prop, but verbally targeted her transition and presentation as a "real woman":

He shattered my favorite perfume. . . . We weren't even fighting over perfume but he quickly tried to justify it like, he said, "You only wear that perfume for everyone else you don't wear that for me, you just trying to get other men." Blah blah and he said, "If you ain't gonna look like a real woman you might as well smell like one right?" He would just say mean things like that to attack me. He'd start trying to put me down all the time and making feel bad.

While not broadly acknowledged within victim research, gender identities and expression of such identities critically rely on outward appearances. Thus, accounts helped to explain the importance of external props for upholding gender identities, which in turn directed their presentation of self through their transition.

Instead of enabling embodiment of their partners' desired identities and their ability to act accordingly to gain recognition of these identities, abusers directed through discrediting identity work not only how victims presented themselves, but how they technically could embody their desired identities. Therefore, discrediting identity work through targeting sign vehicles had similar results to altercasting, as the abusers' statements accompanying their actions could bring attention to an ideal gender identity that abusers were making more difficult for their victims to achieve. This included physically blocking forms of self-presentation, whether through the abusers' own actions or through their degradation of their partners' presentation of self.

In the process of targeting sign vehicles through controlling gender transition treatments and props, discrediting identity work can direct victims' future presentations of self and guide their identity work. In very similar ways, the stories of these survivors upheld similar findings in intimate partner violence research indicating that the extension of self through the use of material objects may be a site of potential attack by abusive partners.[40] This is an underexplored area in intimate partner violence that has the potential to shed light on trans-specific experiences with abuse. While all individuals utilize props in the presentation of self, for transgender individuals these props serve a unique role in aiding their construction of new gender identities (or rather, the construction of their actual, authentic gender identities). Discrediting identity work can occur through the victim being treated as an object, so that the abuser regulates the victim's signification through gender identifiers. Victims' stories exemplified how these transitions and identity signification are extremely embodied, so that the control of one's body can be considered one of the most personal aspects of identity work. This was demonstrated through their stories explaining vulnerabilities particularly focused on how abusers regulated the hormonal and surgical changes, which contributed to signifying desired identities. Therefore, to undermine people's ability to control their own body is an extreme form of controlling presentation of self.

As pointed to in social-psychological identity research, signifying identities requires the support of others, as people must understand and accept others' presentation of self. However, this chapter adopted a different perspective to understand another aspect of this acceptance, in that people must also support—or minimally not prevent—the ability *to* signify. Although identity research can be guided by the assumption that people will coordinate their actions to support smooth interactions, the analysis of these stories here is intended to bring additional attention to the instances in which someone does not do so. Examining these stories through these perspectives contributes to the understanding of identity construction and the direction of individuals' signification of self, particularly in the realm of abusive intimate relationships.

Survivors' stories surrounding their experiences of abuse accounted for their understandings of how others manipulated or directed their identity construction. Throughout the bulk of my conversations, survivors first explained how their transitions made them particularly vulnerable to manipulations, with abusers manipulating their self-identities by exploiting insecurities through altercasting. Second, participants described how abusers directed participants away from signifying their desired identity by controlling their props and regulating physical treatments and thus their presentations of self. Manipulating their definitions of self, significations of self, and bodily experiences additively affected their self-realization and contributed to the objectification of the victims.

As these stories revealed how the survivors felt they were more vulnerable to abuse because of their transition, it is possible that others who are more actively and consciously performing work to establish a new identity may be more vulnerable to discrediting identity work. Beyond providing a potential theoretical insight into how transgender people experience intimate partner violence, this perspective may also apply to others seeking stability. For instance, Ebaugh examines an extensive number of individuals exiting past identities.[41] Those going through exiting processes may be more vulnerable to abuse, although future research should also examine whether the exit's voluntary or involuntary nature affects individuals' perceived vulnerability.

The findings in these stories uphold that an abusive relationship is a matter of control and manipulation. While control has been explored mainly as it manifests for heterosexual cisgender women who are victimized by male intimates, the stories of transgender survivors of intimate partner violence emphasized how the undermining of identity disempowers victims across gender identities. The stories revealed the importance of maintaining a form of control through resistance to empathizing with their partners' perspectives.

The inclusion of transgender voices in the examination of how intimate partner violence victimization plays out in the lives of many provides new insights into these realities. Specifically, the stories illuminate the significance of how controlling transition contextualized the ways in which trans victims understand and express their experiences, while also exploring why and how they felt targeted by their abusers. Further, the stories expand our understanding of how discrediting identity work manifests in abusive relationships in which the victim is transgender. Throughout the stories, an emphasis on the importance of trans-specific vulnerabilities in stages of transition, the significance of props and physical markers, as well as the reinforcement of heteronormative expectations are central. Beyond how this framework aids in examining transgender victimization, the findings might also suggest the need for additional inquiry into intimate partner violence, deriving from altercasting, in relation to couple identities. As the abuser's identity is tied to the couple identity, changes in the partner's identity—particularly salient in the case of gender transitions—can in turn affect the abuser's identity. As Miller and Caughlin explain, "Although this situation is similar to classic altercasting, it is different in the sense that it refers not just to the individuals' identities in encounters, but also to who the couple is (and who the partners are to each other) as a unit. They are not only coming to an interactional working consensus, or an agreement between others' behavior and one's own definition of self that must be achieved during interaction; they are instead negotiating what kind of couple they are."[42] Such perspectives can offer insight into why the newly performed surgeries, for instance, can be trigger points for abuse, as these physical and visual changes affect the abuser's identity as the victim's partner.

Regardless of the gender identity of the abusive partner, power dynamics may involve the control of and degradation of gender variance as illustrated in discrediting identity work. For those in direct service to intimate partner violence victims, these stories illustrate dynamics that are understudied. Further, the narratives of emotional exploitation of insecurities illustrate how these unique dynamics may contribute to a common problem addressed in the field of intimate partner violence—why do victims stay? As told throughout the stories, transgender victims may be more susceptible to marginalization and isolation within the context of abusive relationships. Few scholars have noted this distinct aspect of isolation as a major contributor to trans intimate partner violence. Walker noted that "at a recent conference on transgender domestic abuse, it was suggested that some trans people may stay with an abuser because 'being with someone is better than being with no one at all' especially when their social circles are minimalistic" (speaking about the LGBT Domestic Abuse Forum).[43]

As my conversations with these survivors dwindled down to an end, I began asking about the eventual exit from the relationship. Since I only spoke to survivors who had left their abusive relationships and were not currently experiencing intimate partner violence, this offered an opportunity to understand not only how transgender survivors left their abusers but their hindsight perspective looking back from the other side. While the literature on the help-seeking behaviors of intimate partner violence survivors is plentiful, it has lacked a trans-inclusive perspective. In the following chapter, I present how these survivors struggled to identify their abuse and subsequently leave.

5

Processing Victim Identity

Walking the Gender Tightrope

As Tom began to tell me more about his abusive relationship early in our conversation, his initial responses began with him grappling why and how the abuse began. Recall that Tom met his abuser in college while the two attended neighboring institutions and during a time that he was experiencing family isolation. While chatting with him about his background and transition, his responses jumped into a process of sense making for the abuse he experienced by his former partner. He told me, "I don't know if it was school stress or what, but she just started getting really short with me. It's like anything would piss her off and I was just waiting for her to blow up any time." He described a volatile person who had once been supportive, stable, and loving. Tom added that despite his slight changes in gender presentation and ongoing transition, his partner "was supportive. . . . It was not like a make or break kind of thing, we stayed together so it wasn't that crucial." I followed up more about what he meant that his former abuser had begun to get short with him. He told me, "Her verbal attacks and breaking things and all . . . it just got worse. Like, she would hit me. If she got into a jealous fit she would slap me or punch me and I just didn't do anything, I wasn't going to hit her back. She just always wanted to be in control it was like an obsession with her that she just know everything and run the show."

Tom described scenes of escalating tensions that were turning more and more physical: "It went from controlling things and yelling frequently over nothing to just more physical things and breaking things and the physicalness got more violent like harder. She would be more severe with it. One time she threw a router at my head, like right at the back of my head." In slight shock, I replied, "A router? What do you mean? Like, a wireless router like for internet?" He answered, "Yeah, yeah she was real cray. She just grabbed anything around her sometimes and she threw at me while I was turned around and I fell out cold and I hit the front of my head too on the way down so I just went out cold." At this point, my assumption was that he probably needed medical attention. Maybe his abuser would call for help? I clumsily asked: "How did you wake up?" To my surprise, Tom told me that his abuser called 911:

> She called the ambulance. They came and she told them that I tripped on the router cable and fell and hit my head. The story was stupid and it just didn't even seem right and you know, they didn't even question her at all. They just took her word for it like, what?! That made no sense and I woke up in the hospital and I'm sitting there thinking, oh she's gonna get in trouble and nobody had even accused her of doing anything!? They just bought that story hook line. And since nobody asked me what happened, I just didn't even want to start anything. I remember the hospital, they put my [old] name on my bracelet and they called me "ma'am" all night and even when I said, I go by "Tom" they just didn't even bother to remember, it was like they didn't care. So to me, it just seemed like clearly I wasn't a priority, I wasn't a victim, I was just some butch woman who fell out and thankfully this girl was there to call the ambulance. I knew then that people just, just weren't going to get me or get that situation or anything. They're just going to think I just, I should just deal with it.

Getting Out

Tom echoed what many survivors also experienced—an unwillingness among formal help service providers to recognize their situation and properly identify abuse. In chapter 2, I briefly mentioned Tom's experiences with hospitals after needing attention from intimate partner violence injuries. He openly questioned the treatment he received: "At the hospital I was treated bad but I don't know what for, maybe it's cuz I was trans or maybe because I was black or whatever, I don't know?" The complexities of his encounters with medical services highlight what research has consistently shown—patterned racism in American health systems has created and maintained disparities in care across racial groups, with African Americans often receiving the lowest quality attention.[1] Taking into consideration the well-documented biases against transgender patients with a case of intimate partner violence, it is clear that Tom's experiences didn't occur in isolation but represent a common pattern for transgender survivors of abuse.[2]

Across the stories of survival and eventual exit, engrained inequalities often structured the ways in which trans victims both responded to abuse and were responded to by help providers. While there is no singular or proper way to leave an abusive relationship, for survivors access to helpful others and pathways out often facilitate the exit. These paths are all contextualized by the disparate social recognition of the abuse experienced and the real need for access to resources.

"If I Think This Isn't Really What I Want, Why Can't I Just Get Out?"—Todd

Toward the end of each of my conversations, survivors discussed how their abusive relationships came to end. For some, this part of our talk came organically; they spoke at length about their abusive experiences and then subsequently how it all ended. For others, I asked a bit more directly, "How did you get out?" All of the survivors in the study had left their abusers and thus described and constructed their process of identifying the abuse and seeking help if needed or desired. The process of identifying abuse (and subsequently identifying as a victim of intimate partner violence) is one that is both personal and socially informed. The idea of being victimized or being a victim is one that carries with it cultural significance. In terms of its application to intimate partner violence, the broader heteronormative and genderist culture assumes a certain dynamic between perpetrator and abuser. Specifically, it assumes cismale perpetration and cisfemale victimization. Grappling between actual lived experience of intimate partner violence victimization and this broader cultural narrative about what it means to be a victim, participants constructed the process of how they came to see themselves as victims of intimate partner violence. This process of identifying as a victim and recognizing their experiences as abuse signaled the stages of exiting the relationship.

Some debate exists across the fields of interpersonal violence regarding "survivor" versus "victim" terminology. This debate is characterized by an emphasis of meaning behind language, societal interpretation, and individual healing.[3] Some argue that the word "victim" elicits the notion that someone was helpless and/or taken advantage of.[4] Similarly, others argue that the word "victim" captures only part of the eventual "survival" process. Oppositely, the word "survival" represents a holistic turnaround from the abuse experienced; it signals endurance and perseverance. Throughout the chapters, I have emphasized the importance of language in understanding the construction of meaning behind experiences of violence. Additionally, I have framed my conversations with survivors as aspects of storytelling guided by cultural patterns of narrative. Arguably, the ways in which the respondents spoke about how they left their relationships illustrate the process of moving from victim to survivor. The stories can be seen as part of active identity construction (see chapter 4), repeating the experiences to others as a mechanism of moving beyond and healing. Tehrani notes that "today, story-telling is being used to assist in the healing process for people facing a wide range of personal and psychological problems."[5] I asked respondents about not only how they left but how they came to see themselves as victims or at least how they identified the behaviors as abusive. Across the chapters, I have often toggled between the words "victim" and "survivor." I have used these somewhat interchangeably but often within a time-relevant context; if I was speaking about the experiences they had during the abusive relationship, I would refer to them as victims. If I spoke about them after the fact or in a sense to signal the post-abuse analysis, I switched to survivor. Even this became tricky; as the forthcoming sections will indicate, not everyone thought of themselves as a victim in the "traditional" sense. Some may have identified their experiences as victimization but perhaps shed the idea of identifying as a victim—notably for Tom, it was the fact that others did not see him as a victim that informed how he identified with the abuse. Queering taken-for-granted victimological concepts like "victim" and "offender" creates room for the interrogation of these categories. The categories often rely on criminal-justice-oriented definitions that sometimes may not accurately reflect the role of agency even in these abusive contexts. The experience of violent victimization can be nonlinear; that is, some survivors resist, fight back, and sometimes even choose to avoid systemic help for fear of escalating violence or revictimization. Often, victimological approaches to intimate partner violence frame victims as staying in abuse only because they have been so worn down or defeated. For many of the survivors I spoke to, this might actually be the case; but for some, it wasn't. Instead, the field and the systemic response could benefit tremendously from acknowledging the fact that often victims know best. They're closest to the situation and may also have the best sense of perceived danger.

In the following sections, I explore two of the most salient and consistent patterns that emerged as respondents described leaving their abusive relationships: "walking the gender tightrope" and the challenges of "navigating genderist resources." First, by "walking the gender tightrope," survivors utilized gendered language when discussing their victim identities. Specifically, they constructed the notion of "victim" as hyperfeminine and passive. Even for those whose gender identities were more feminine, there was an evident rejection of the idea that they were that kind of victim—a feminine and passive victim. A major component of this process involved others outside of the relationship acknowledging and confirming their victimization. Survivors invoked the idea either that others would not take their victimization seriously because of their gender or that they would simply not be believed.

Second, most of the survivors sought some form of help from either formal or informal resources. Examples of utilizing formal resources included calling the police, pursuing legal action, or going to shelters, while informal resources involved reaching out to family, coworkers, or friends. In describing these experiences, survivors described what I termed "navigating genderist help resources." Several of the survivors experienced and encountered structural barriers to formal help on the basis of their trans status (further complicated by intersecting identities). Specifically, many help-seeking resources are structured from a genderist perspective: assuming two and only two genders while also assuming the needs of victims to be the same as those of cisgender individuals. These experiences ranged from genderist or transphobic discrimination in the courtroom and at the hands of law enforcement as well as hospital and shelter staff. Notably, most survivors described that informal resources (friends and family) were most helpful.

"As I Tried to Get Out of the Relationship, the Real Abuse Began"—Owen

Broadly speaking, help-seeking can be understood as the process by which victims of intimate partner violence first identify their situation as problematic, which may be followed by a need for external assistance that can involve navigating formal or informal avenues in an attempt to remedy the situation or leave an abuser.[6] Part of my guiding inquiry at the final stage of my conversations was to understand how transgender survivors of intimate partner violence described their help-seeking processes.

Help-Seeking Barriers for LGBTQ Survivors

While much of the existing knowledge on help seeking for same-gender intimate partner violence has often lumped trans experiences with those of gays and lesbians, there are some significant similarities worth noting. Homophobia and heterosexism are often the central concepts discussed in the help-seeking literature, while less attention has been given to how transphobia and genderism structure the eventual exit from abusive relationships and present barriers to help seeking. In general, survivors of intimate partner violence typically face a number of challenges to help seeking, including poor response from law enforcement and service providers, financial inability to leave abusive partners, and a lack of access to shelters.[7] However, for LGBTQ survivors of intimate partner violence, both formal and informal help-seeking avenues may be much more limited than those for heterosexual ciswomen. Early studies examining gay and lesbian survivors of intimate partner violence and their help-seeking behaviors indicated several challenges to the accessibility of formal resources by introducing homophobia and heterosexism into the overall discussion as barriers to help seeking for gay and lesbian survivors.[8]

First, homophobia may play a role in whether or not victims of same-gender intimate partner violence even come forward and seek help. Because same-gender relationships are already marginalized and characterized as inferior, the literature illustrates evidence for a reluctance of both the community and survivors to report victimization.[9] For many in the community, the perception exists that disclosing same-gender intimate partner violence victimization sheds negative light on an already oppressed population. As McLaughlin and Rozee argue, this "maintains the silence about same-gender intimate partner violence and reflects an acute awareness of societal homophobia."[10]

Beyond individual struggles with reporting same-gender intimate partner violence, systemic responses to abuse in intimate relationships have been historically limited to the needs of heterosexual ciswomen. Studies have shown that for lesbian women, domestic violence shelters and resources are not perceived as viable options for help in their distinct situations.[11] For gay male survivors, these shelters and resources may be even further out of reach, as many of these programs have traditionally been centered on ciswomen.[12] Beyond shelters and other domestic violence resources, law enforcement has shown to be a problematic resource for victims of same-gender intimate partner violence. Renzetti's pioneering study showed that lesbian victims were reluctant to call the police as they perceived officers to be homophobic or indifferent to their victimization.[13] Of the few respondents who had police interventions, all reported their ineffectiveness. One respondent reported being called a "queer devil" by the police, while another described that the police "basically took the attitude, 'so two dykes are trying to kill each other; big deal.'"[14] Other scholars have also found that LGBTQ victims of intimate partner violence consistently had negative experiences with the police or negative perceptions of the police, and these experiences influenced their reporting.[15] These factors all play a role in the fear of revictimization by police.

In reports by the National Coalition of Anti-Violence Programs (NCAVP), almost a fourth of their sample experienced a "misarrest" by the police in which either the victim or both the victim and the perpetrator were arrested, and 29.7 percent called the police and received no arrest.[16] Further, 7 percent reported homophobic abuse at the hands of police. A multitude of other studies have gone on to show that legal and law enforcement remedies are often the least sought forms of help and the least helpful among LGBTQ victims of same-gender intimate partner violence.[17]

Much less is known about how transgender survivors navigate or experience the help-seeking process. The overwhelming majority of domestic violence resources are designed for women and work from a cisgendered assumption. Moreover, domestic violence shelters are known to be both inaccessible and dangerous places for transgender victims. Arguably, how social systems define "woman" typically dictates who is labeled a deserving victim. As Brown stated, this gender-based admission process often puts both female-to-male (FTM) and male-to-female (MTF) trans-gender victims in unique situations that force them to either "pass" as female (for MTF) or reject their identity and accept help at a women's shelter.[18] Erbaugh explains, "The gender identities of the participants in a given relationship may counter normative gender stereotypes, and first impressions based on gender-normative assumptions will not reliably reveal which partner has the upper hand in an abusive dynamic."[19] This cultural construct has consequences for reactions from the police, who may approach lesbian battering as a "cat fight" or gay battering as a fight between roommates. Because gender is a strong social "precursor" to the social understanding of intimate partner violence, it's important to note how trans survivors are responded to in avenues of help.

Unique Challenges in Help Seeking

In recounting their experiences, survivors discussed how these abusive relationships came to end. The process of identifying as a victim is one that is both personal and socially informed and is a crucial step in the help-seeking process. The notion of being victimized or being a victim is one that carries with it cultural significance. In these accounts, par-ticipants' most salient and consistent pattern involved what we termed the "walking of the gender tightrope"; that is, throughout their accounts, participants regularly utilized gendered language when discussing their victim identities in the help-seeking process. Specifically, they con-structed the notion of "victim" as hyperfeminine and passive. Even for those whose gender identities were more feminine, there was an evi-dent rejection of the idea that they were that kind of victim—feminine and passive. A major component of this process involved others outside of the relationship acknowledging and confirming their victimization. Survivors invoked the idea either that others would not take their vic-timization seriously because of their gender or that they would simply not be believed.

Walking the Gender Tightrope

As survivors discussed and reflected upon their victimization and how they came to view the abuse as problematic and themselves as victims, a gendered discourse emerged that constructed "victim" as totally submissive and in many ways traditionally "feminine." Several of the survivors discussed feeling conflicted with this regardless of their own gender identification. Anna described her thought processes and grappling with the notion of being a victim of intimate partner violence. As our conversation came to a gradual end, I asked Anna if she identified as a victim of intimate partner violence. She first responded, "Well, bad things happened to me, right, and I am at a point now where I realize that technically I was being victimized but I just don't really identify as a victim because, I don't know?" I followed-up with, "Well, what does being a victim of intimate partner violence mean to you?" She and others invoked the heteronormative and genderist cultural narrative behind intimate partner violence victimization and stated,

> Well, like, I wasn't just some helpless housewife or something like getting punched in the face and then apologizing for her husband or some shit like that I mean, I guess it's hard because I still feel sometimes that I put myself in that situation but also because I just think victim means that you lost, like that you lost: something happened to you that was bad. But for me, I don't want to think of myself as "I lost." I didn't lose—bad things happened to me and I was able to get up and pick up the pieces and move forward and learn. That's not like "victim" to me.

Anna described grappling between what she knows it means to be a victim of intimate partner violence, which is largely informed by the larger heteronormative and genderist culture, and her actual lived experience. By specifically identifying the idea of "helplessness" with a battered housewife, Anna was comparing her experience to what she assumes most people expect from victims. She added that while she never fought back, "I would yell back and sometimes I kept a weapon nearby like, maybe a knife or something just in case something got really crazy but I never did." She added that she vocalized her desires to leave on various occasions: "Sometimes I would tell him like, 'I'm not taking any more of this. I'm leaving.' And he would just be like 'Where are you going to go? No one is going to feel sorry for a tranny hooker' and so there wasn't like, a specific event that happened but it was more like, I tried again to talk to a coworker and she kind of made me realize that I was being abused and that I deserved better and she wasn't a friend of my ex so she wasn't involved and she said come to my place and get out." Anna's abuser degraded her trans status not only as a tactic of abuse but also as one that limited her help seeking. By manipulating the idea of what a proper victim is, Anna's abuser essentially told her she was not one—at least not a respectable one whom people would "feel sorry for."

Other survivors shared similar struggles in their process of identifying as a victim that invoked the idea that a victim was submissive, traditionally feminine, and one who did not fight back. In another example, Rebecca described, "I wasn't gonna be just any victim, I had to just butch up and survive." She told me more about how she felt in the moment when contemplating leaving:

> I didn't have anywhere to go you know, I had no church network like I did growing up, they were long gone from my life, my family was gone, my coworkers only really just tolerated me, and I had a few trans friends I met early in transitioning but that was years ago we rarely stay in touch, just Facebook if even, and then I just accepted that this was my fate. . . . I didn't have enough money to just leave either so it was just a bad situation all around. I shouldn't have left myself so open to him especially now looking back like, there were just a lot of things that he could latch on to to bring me down.

Given the situation she described, Rebecca felt like she needed to "butch up" and deal with it.

Part of the gendered narrative behind victimization was the belief that victims "lose" and "don't fight back." After Laura described to me a violent scene (see chapters 3 and 4) in which her abuser physically brutalized her shortly after a surgical procedure, she described her reaction: "I was screaming, I was screaming and I punched and scratched him back but I couldn't get away. . . . I tried, I tried it's not like I wasn't like these other people who just freeze up, no I tried but my whole upper body was just sore and he was beating on me I was on the ground and he kicked me." Like many others, she essentially distanced herself from a typical expectation of a victim because she fought back.

Survivors discussed their concern that they would not be believed by others during the process of seeking help. While this isn't a uniquely trans experience, respondents invoked a trans-specific quality to their perception of how others viewed their victimization. This involved a process in which survivors grappled with what they thought others expected of an intimate partner violence victim and their actual lived experience. For example, in Tom's opening story, he described the significance of others not viewing him as a victim and did so in a way that invoked the gendered discourse behind "victimhood." To him, others would see him as "butch" and able to handle it himself and that his abuser was just a "girl."

In a similar fashion, Rebecca echoed an account that included how others would perceive her victimization since she was "male bodied" and larger, unlike her abuser. I asked her, as I had others, if she viewed herself as victim. She simply replied, "Well yes, what happened to me and what was happening was just uncalled for and I didn't deserve that treatment. I didn't do anything to him to be put through that." More to the broader point of identifying abuse in the moment, I asked her, "Did you feel you were being victimized while it was going on?" After an elongated pause and pensive "hmm," she told me,

> Hmm, well . . . that's different cuz, I feel that way now but to think then, I mean I knew it was wrong for sure. But because I was putting up with it I felt like I had no one else to blame but me. Plus, I just couldn't talk about it. When you can't express what's going on you can really go through it. Just live day by day if you can't really take time to take in what's going on and put it out in words. I knew that I felt like I didn't want to talk about it because it was wrong and my life was going to look a mess and on top of it I didn't have anyone to tell it to anyway but I mean, what if people didn't understand how serious it was. I mean, even the friend that finally took me in said, "Why didn't you just beat him up? You're bigger than him." I think others would just see that I have a big build, I mean I was born biological male so that means I can just beat him up too and just deal with it that way. So I thought, well, I mean, I'll deal with what I can. Like I said, I never just didn't do anything, I protected myself too.

Reexamining how she felt in the moment, Rebecca looked back and recalled how her own body made her less sympathetic to others. Even a helpful friend characterized Rebecca's body as one that should have been more resistant, channeling genderist interpretations of her body as masculine. This is something one might expect to be told to a cismale survivor of intimate partner violence; for some transwomen like Rebecca, the genderist reading of bodies minimizes the abuse experienced.

Similar to Rebecca, others described accounts in which they were expected to "handle things" on their own or otherwise would not be validated by others. As John described while our conversation began to wind down, "I didn't think of myself as like, a soft, like you know, I'm a tough man, I really am, but I would've never thought that words could just bring someone down like she did. All those insecurities and all that, she got into it. . . . I wanted no one to know, I just wanted to handle it myself and see if I could just make it stop. I didn't really think to do anything about it but, um, I don't know." For John, contending with the notion of being victimized and his masculinity meant that he should help himself and not reach out. This was evident not just in those who were masculine identified; similar patterns were reported by most survivors as they struggled with processing their victimization. It was clear to me that regardless of gender identification, the notion of being victimized embodied a disempowered status these survivors sought to distance themselves from. While Audrey's story mainly focused on emotional and psychological manipulations, there were bouts of physical violence that prompted me to ask her whether the mainly nonphysical elements of the abuse still made her afraid. She responded,

No. No, I was always very confident in myself and my ability to take care of myself. That's why I put up with all of her stuff. I felt safe and capable of handling the situation and I thought I could help her, you know? After the violent incident, I began to feel a little bit afraid for my safety because I really didn't think she would get to that point. It was very surprising that she would get to that point so I did fear a little bit for my safety but you know, she was big enough that she could hurt me, I'm only about fifteen pounds heavier than she is though I have a much higher height difference. She could have definitely hurt me, so it became, you know, I can deal with the mental and the verbal and emotional because I ended up detaching for a very long time and you know after all that I've been through in my life I'm very good at emotionally detaching from things but with the violence, you know I wasn't willing to put up with that.

Audrey confidently told me that she was never all that afraid; she started to have more fearful concerns, but for the most part she described her desire to, again, "deal with it." As she spoke about dealing with it, like Tom and Rebecca, she referenced bodies, comparing her body to her abuser's and whether she could defend herself or not. By referencing height and weight, Audrey was focusing on key gendered characteristics of bodies or at the very least signifiers of a body that can take on abuse (i.e., more masculine bodies).

Navigating Genderist Help Resources

In the majority of the accounts, survivors left abusive relationships with the help of friends and family. However, for most this was neither the first nor the only help resources they sought. When discussing more formal avenues of help, many of the survivors either had experiences with or held strong perceptions about law enforcement and the criminal justice system; few contemplated shelter resources. This is not unique to trans populations, as victims of intimate partner violence report negative experiences or perceptions of police, judges, attorneys, shelter workers, social workers, and more. However, unique to the trans experience is the reality that most formal avenues were constructed with heterosexual, ciswomen victims in mind. When describing their experiences with seeking help or reflecting on their available options, survivors recounted stories of exclusion, isolation, and how genderism structured or limited many of their available options.

For many, especially those who had experienced severe physical violence, the option of involving police was contemplated, called on by others, or called on their own accord. While there was no universal experience, most respondents had strong negative perceptions or interactions with the police. Depending on the context of the story, I asked the survivors if they called the police. For example, Todd endured four years of abuse that ranged from physical to emotional but also financial. His abuser had become financially dependent on Todd, often syphoning off funds that didn't belong to him. At this point, I was curious to know what Todd's exit strategy was looking like. I asked him, "During the four years, did you go anywhere for help? Any sort of assistance—friends or family? Or even something more formal like counselor or police?" He answered,

Well, I had become at that point pretty isolated from my friends because Martin didn't like certain relationships in my life or he thought others were making me think badly about him or whatever and so I talked to maybe one friend . . . two friends. My roommate and then another friend about how I didn't think the relationship was really what I wanted but I felt really . . . I felt really dumb. I felt defeated. I don't know—very powerless. I couldn't make changes in my life that I wanted. I didn't start talking to a counselor about it until . . . I don't know, more recently. And we sort of had to go back between is it a failure of communication . . . trying to figure out what was wrong but I didn't really, ever seek help in the way that I know I need help and I know I need to get out of this relationship until very recently. I was doing it to myself. I put myself in the situation to get hurt and knew I would get hurt so when I got hurt it was my fault. At first it was because I cared very deeply about Michael and thought there was a way we could work it out and that it was that we weren't communicating right or missing the conversation somehow but then it just escalated into me feeling like and I was also like trapped financially. I couldn't afford to move but he couldn't go anywhere either. He had no money or anywhere to go and I felt responsible for that and by moving in with him I told him I'd support him in certain ways so I felt like I was . . . . Um. Just not . . . that I had made a commitment that I had to follow through with. Basically.

At this point I replied to Todd: "Right, that makes sense. Because, I mean, you were not free to make a decision when you have others that depend on you as a well . . . or the other way around sometimes." I asked again, somewhat differently, "Did you ever have to get the police involved or legal assistance?" Todd replied,

Umm . . . we had a conversation that went very badly. He made all of these threatening body movements and made all these threatening movements saying he was showing a lot of restraint and "you're lucky your roommate isn't hurt" and I thought those were physical threats of violence and that was like to me sort of like the okay that's tangible I can take that to the police—I can take that where ever. I went to my counselor with it and he gave me the number to some detective somewhere and I tried to do everything before I called the police. Um I guess the day I was going to call the police, it was the day he eventually left. So the police never got involved. I left the house and told him he had to move out. And it was about two weeks or maybe seventeen days before he moved and I had to go to the landlord and tell them that Martin had not paid rent in the full year we had lived there and I wanted to take him off the lease. And I had them send an eviction notice to ask him to leave the house.

While Todd had been given a contact number for what I assumed was a detective well versed in domestic violence cases, he refused to use it. I followed up on his hesitation to call the police, and he described what several other participants did, a fear of how police would respond to his case:

> I didn't want to call the police for lots and lots of reasons. One because I don't feel comfortable around the police and the situation was so much worse than I thought it could be I guess I couldn't imagine, I couldn't emotionally take a step back to what really needed to be done. But the police, there was a high likelihood that there would be some kind of discrimination based on our gender identity. . . . They wouldn't understand the names or the pronouns or some kind of discrimination. Or they wouldn't take it seriously or something like that. I also just didn't want to have. I didn't want to have that on my record, I didn't want to put it on Martin's record that there had been domestic violence issues or whatever. And I just . . . it wasn't a type of situation that I was surely ready to deal with . . . and I was going to call the police because the threats were continuing and he began threatening himself like threatening to commit suicide and his mom was threating me and basically I couldn't keep staying at friends' houses I needed to get back to my house and life.

While it is no revelation that across the board, victims of intimate partner violence show some reluctance to involve police, trans people face the distinct realities of harassment, disrespect, marginalization, and brutality by law enforcement. Many of the participants felt reluctant to involve police because of this fear of discrimination. This perception led to the majority of respondents not seeking any legal assistance at all. For survivors like Joe, who endured aggressive disruptions to his medical transition process, getting formal help was just not an option. Curious to know how Joe successfully managed to leave an intensely controlling situation, I asked him, "Were you the one who cut it off, could you describe the process of getting to that point, calling it off?" He responded,

> It was difficult um, I had a hard time being rational. I was very angry all of the time. All I could really comprehend was that, something had to happen, something had to change, I didn't know what. And then, just after so many times of him taking from me and just playing it off like it was normal for people to take from each other and be like what he was to me, I wanted him out of my life. I didn't want to deal with him anymore, he was a leech he took my energy my time. He was just, he took a lot from me and I was tired of it and someone said wouldn't it be wise to just cut him out, if he gives me more stress just go to the police, and I never did go to the police. I don't trust them because of my situation. . . . I had just heard a lot of bad things, um it's a different situation. Someone who is um, trans, being abused by someone. I was torn by the whole the "men can't get raped mentality" that people had taught me growing up, the whole "you are a freak" police will see you as the attacker instead of the victim it would just be a whole mess and I didn't want to draw it out further I was afraid of the police, I was afraid of what other people would do if they found out.

Joe's concerns are not without basis. The 2015 National Transgender Discrimination Survey found that 58 percent of respondents reported harassment by police officers related to being transgender.[20] More broadly, in the latest report by the NCAVP, researchers found that of the few LGBTQ survivors who have interacted with the police for help, 19 percent found the response to be indifferent or even hostile.[21] Beyond a perception of transphobia in the police, Joe expressed a major concern that police would misunderstand the situation.

For some survivors, negative accounts of the police were not just perceptions but actual experiences and interactions. When John had neighbors call the police more than once and after one of many violent incidents escalated, he found himself injured and locked away in the bathroom as they arrived through the front door. I asked John what his strategy was, what he ended up doing. He detailed his process while also describing his abuser's final plea:

I tried to work extra hours cuz it kept me away from home and it also net-ted me more money to leave. So I finally just got at least like enough for a security deposit and one month's rent and I told her to her face, in the middle of a fight, I'm leaving. And she did her usual like turn around, she just got on the floor like all "I'm so sorry please baby don't leave, you're all that I have" and it used to work but I had already paid for the other place, it was all ready to go, I needed to go. So she saw I was leaving and then it was like no more apologies. She just did her violent fit and went crazy on me again, this time the screaming was just ridiculous but then she ended up having the police called on us because she was just that loud. I mean, we didn't even live in an apartment complex and the neighbors still heard the next door over. We had no idea the police were on their way, I locked myself in a room to get away because she hurt me really bad, she threw a coffee mug at my head and it broke. I locked myself in and she just continued going crazy. Then, the police were actually stand-ing outside the whole time so after they had knocked a lot, during a lot of that violent outburst, they stormed in and saw her in there screaming, bloody knuckles and all from punching things and I of course came out of the room when I heard the police. I couldn't believe there was police inside our home. They were calming her down and asking me all sorts of questions like what was going on, what did I do to her and all that. Like, asking ME what I did when they came in she wasn't the one in the room hiding but I mean, they asked her what was going on too but I just got the feeling that they were just ready to go after me.

While police eventually helped John, he described a painful process in which police were reluctant to see him as the victim. I asked John, "Why do you think that was?," regarding how the police responded. He stated,

I have no idea. I mean maybe they saw her and saw me and then expected that I was the one starting things. She had just gotten off work so she was all in a business skirt and pretty and all but they don't know what she had just done. I bet they thought it was just like a common heterosexuals couple fight and so they were just ready to blame me because I was more mas-culine or just looked stronger or something I don't know. Instead of just like evaluating the situation they were quick to jump to conclusions about things. They asked her about her bloody knuckles and they saw my bruises and then they saw my head bleeding and the cup smashed on the floor, it was obvious they had it wrong. They arrested her and not me at least but if there had been no physical evidence, I bet you they would've arrested me or at least the both of us because, like most the other times, there was no real physical evidence. I got hurt several times but it wasn't the majority of the time. The other times were just the words, and verbal abuses.

In these accounts, the police represented a genderist help avenue that likely did more damage than good. Even for Jessica, who had local police swing by her car repair shop frequently for coffee and snacks, described that after her transition, the police and local community distanced themselves. When I asked Jessica about her relationship with local law enforcement, she told me, "In our neighborhood, for fifteen years, the police were at my house every day, my door was never locked, I ran my business from home, they would often come into the house for coffee and then call me in from the shop and say we got coffee ready and sometimes it would be one cop in there some days it was five cops in there and they were coming and going between six AM to ten and eleven PM at night and when I was arrested not one of the cops cared so, um, yeah." When she was arrested in one of many domestic disputes, Jessica stated, "Not one of them treated me as if they knew me, in fact I had asked for a female officer to do the search on me and they refused to do that and they didn't allow me to call a lawyer." Jessica described what seemed like years of legal manipulations by her abuser. While she acknowledged some mutual violence or at least retaliation, Jessica described a situation during which the relationship was coming to an end:

> Not only did I lose my friends and family she went as far to have me arrested. You know, charged with seven charges that really are just normal things that happen in marriage but if you shine them under a certain light—uh I had other judges look at the case, they said there's nothing here there's no evidence but the county police arrested me and I was convicted but they were not able to provide me a lawyer so I had no legal defense.

Jessica told me that the charges against her "were three assaults, one uttering threat, one destruction of property under five thousand dollars and then there was harassment." Maintaining her innocence, Jessica remained hopeful that the proceedings would clear her, but instead she found transphobic responses from the system:

> I was disrespected by the attorney. She constantly referred to me as Mister and the judge, until I called the judge out on it. I knew that the courts up there had sensitivity training and at a certain point I stopped the trail and said to the judge that "I've never been disrespectful to you have I?" and he said "no." "So explain to me why everyone here and your staff and yourself constantly is disrespectful to me. Have you or have you not received sensitivity training?" And he refused to answer the question. And I said "I wouldn't be surprised if you told me you didn't which you did—obviously you didn't apply what you learned and if you didn't receive it than you are lying because I know the people who trained you." And the next time I came to court all the posters they give out at training were put up all over the courthouse. So they did receive the training and ironically the Crown Attorney she was very bad at using the wrong pronouns and names and ironically for my sentencing I was given a lawyer and in front of that lawyer she wanted jail time for me and she said to him "your honor the trans stuff is not an issue here and in fact I volunteered for fifteen years with the trans community" and I said well thank you your honor for saying that because now I know its discrimination because the first thing you learn when you work with trans people is to get the pronoun right and I think we got about ten thousand examples of her using the wrong pronouns with me over the last ten months . . . it's in the transcripts. The very last thing she said was that she was a volunteer for fifteen years with trans people so obviously she says whatever pops into her head to try and win the trial and doesn't care about professionalism.

While Jessica was the sole respondent who survived intimate partner violence outside the United States (she was in Canada), negative experiences with legal systems remained a consistent thread throughout the accounts.

I asked Rebecca about one of her experiences with calling the police. She described her interactions with police but also the overall thought process behind deciding not have them involved. She stated, "It wasn't the first time he had hurt me physically but it was just one that was really out of control. I did fight back every time at least to block hits and defend myself. I never just sat there or something. But I gave him one big shove and used a chair to hit him and run. I had my cell phone so I locked myself in the bathroom and called the police. They came pretty quickly." I asked her if she had considered calling the police before this incident and she replied,

> No, not really. I'd rather not have any interaction with the police. It was never really an option I just don't like the police. I guess I've just, I just don't like strangers and maybe especially the police. I've had bad experiences with them in the past like just having to explain myself all of the time and I think they're just immediately suspicious of me. I mean I lived life as a black teenage boy and I know what it feels like to be judged by them but then being trans in addition and then being in the transition state, it was just all just never good with the police. . . . I had two cops before just refuse to call me by my girl name before. I had everything changed and they still called me "he." They kind of exchanged glances at each other and stuff. I mean I don't know, maybe I'm just paranoid and expected that but then again it's something I think about. How will they see me, will that play a role in how they treat me or believe me or something? Like if I have to explain myself before I can even explain my being a victim?

As victims navigated potential options, this was a common process in the evaluation of help-seeking avenues. The perception and actual experience of transphobia by police structured and limited legal recourse for these survivors. Notably in Rebecca's account and for other trans survivors of color, the idea of police interaction took on an added dimension that included perceptions of racism. While white respondents still echoed similar perceptions of genderism and transphobia by the criminal justice system, respondents of color shared experiences of racism and fear of racial bias. Importantly, Rebecca openly noted her uncertainty with how to read police interactions; steeped in the realities of well-documented racial biases against civilians of color, trans people of color often can't afford to give the systemic response the benefit of the doubt.

In a conversation on the police, I asked Laura why she felt calling the police was not an option when she was severely beaten (see chapter 3). She replied,

I didn't wanna call the police cuz that's just a mess. That would be awful. Oh god, can you imagine though? I mean I was in mid transition with new breasts, bleeding from them. I am still a man on record and my ID and stuff and I'm black. I'm black in [southern state]. It's like first, they're going to see I'm this black dude that got beat up by a white man, think that we're gay, then see that I'm trans and that I'm in mid transition and it would be a disaster having to explain all of that and you know the police have a certain way of looking at trans people. You know I got a ticket one time in women's clothes and I was just on my way home from work and he [the police] was like "you on your way from a club?" "you work at a club or something?" and he kept calling me "sir," I even asked to be called ma'am and he tried as much as he could to say my assigned name and call me sir. They just don't get it, they don't get us and it would just be a mess. Plus I can only imagine the court process. Being called sir and the assigned name all day long for a long period of time and then just everyone in there lookin' at me like I'm on display or a freak of nature or something.

For Anna, her immigrant status came up in her discussion of the police. When I asked her specifically if she considered the police an option, she stated,

Definitely, no. I would have never called the police. I mean like what are they going to do? I am a transsexual woman and I'm an immigrant and also I mean, I was doing illegal things like the hormone sharing and I don't think they would've believed that my ex was forcing me to have sex for money. I mean they would've been seen me like a stereotype like what he used to say you know. I think that's true they would've just gotten me into trouble too. . . . I just would rather avoid following through [with legal avenues] like in general like dealing with the courts and I just think they won't believe me. They're going to think I'm a drama tranny and like, just, they're not going to be nice to me. If my own friends and coworkers wouldn't help, imagine a total stranger. Especially like, in those jobs like they there to ask questions and they're suspicious of everyone and shit.

Anna's concerns with reaching out for help are grounded in the reality of what many trans migrant victims of intimate partner violence face. In February 2017, Ms. Gonzalez was detained by ICE agents in a courtroom while she was seeking a protective order against her abusive boyfriend.[22] Not only is this reportedly a violation of the confidentiality protection for undocumented survivors as described in the Violence Against Women Act (2005 reauthorization), but it was believed that ICE was tipped off by her abuser. Across my conversations, trans survivors of color faced specific circumstances that involved racial discrimination and bias at the intersections of gender identity and expression. For these survivors, the structural realities and oppressive dynamics manifested into more negative experiences and perceptions of the police.

As conversations turned to life after leaving, very few survivors discussed domestic violence shelters as an option, and only one had utilized this resource. While only four survivors mentioned this avenue, it is important to note the processes described that constructed this option as inaccessible. As John discussed how he processed his victimization and attempted to leave, he debated the idea of seeking help from the police and also a shelter. John's abuser owned the home they shared, and he had very few options for housing. He described,

> I kept everything secret. I was afraid of even hanging out with people just because I thought they might find out what was happening. I didn't really think to do anything about it but, um, I don't know, I didn't really see options. I mean what was I going to do? Call up the police? And then what? For them to see this man, that they think might've been a woman, who's being beat up by a woman? I mean I don't know, I should've now that I think about it, but I just, I didn't think to do that. I had the family close but we had lost touch really after I came out as trans and all and they're there, I know they are but I was ashamed because, here I was gonna go groveling back for help? I don't think so. And then I thought well, the first thing that came to mind is well, where am I gonna go. She's right, I don't have much without her. Everything we had was mostly cuz she could get it and I couldn't. So where am I gonna live? I made okay money but I needed savings to get out. So, for a while I thought well maybe like, I don't know, maybe a shelter will take me but then, you think these things through and when you're like thinking about it, it's just like, "really!?" Like what am I gonna do inside a women's shelter? Like, they don't let men in there for a reason and I look like a man, and I mean, like, I am a

man. So then I thought a homeless shelter maybe for a little bit but then, no, I can't really, I don't look homeless, I mean, I don't know how that works and it just, I don't know, what if someone found out I was in a homeless shelter, like my work or something?

Given limited opportunities, John saw no resource that he would fit neatly in. His fear of sex-classified shelters is echoed by many who do not conform to traditional constructs of gender, and the idea of a shelter for the homeless didn't fit what he thought he was experiencing. Several factors played into this thought process, but central to this discussion was the assumption that only ciswomen were victims and that help avenues were strictly gendered. These sentiments were echoed by Sam, who wrote,

> I have generally limited my access to formal systems because I work in the victim assistance field in a high profile position at a large nonprofit that runs a good portion of the services available in my city. I have had to be very careful because of that, and it has prevented me from accessing services. In addition, gender-segregated services have also prevented me from seeking supportive services (esp. support groups, which years later feel the most relevant), as most are not available to trans people. I have not found that system to be helpful; it just escalated the harassment (#1) and abuse (#2) and the system did nothing to help.

While many shelters now accept and place cismen, there is still a strong perception that these avenues are strictly for women. This is largely informed by the gendered narrative of victimization.

Recall that Anna had endured patterned sexual and physical abuse by a partner that she felt at least partially dependent on. She was the only respondent who briefly lived in a domestic violence shelter. After telling me that she made plans to leave with a friend, I asked her how she left. Anna said, "I left a note and I said why I was leaving and I went to her place." I replied asking, "How did that go?" She responded, "It was bad actually. She was nice and all but I just couldn't stay there. I barely knew her and she expected that I was going to be gone in like a matter of days and she made me feel like I was taking a long time to leave even though I was only there like two weeks." She described needing shelter regardless of whether it had domestic violence resources. With that in mind, she first contemplated a homeless shelter before then seeking out the domestic violence shelter:

> Well, I knew that I couldn't go to a homeless shelter. The homeless shelters are mostly full of men and I learned it wasn't safe for me there. Plus years ago when I needed them, I looked too much like a woman then that the staff was saying I needed to go a woman's homeless shelter that the men there may threaten me or something. But I remember the woman's shelter didn't want me either they said they only allow women there and they have children there and that I would cause like a scene or something I don't know they were just weird about it. I think if I would've pressed, they would've let me in but because they were so unwelcoming from the start I just couldn't. But the woman I was living with as a hint for me to get out she actually said I could go to a woman's domestic violence shelter and that at those shelters you don't have to leave during the day time you can stay like a couple months.

Here, Anna's account represented the challenge of navigating resources that were sex-classified. She described being "too woman" for the men's shelter and "too man" for the women's shelter. Eventually, she pursued a domestic violence shelter that accepted her. However, this came with its own issues:

> I tried to [go to a domestic violence shelter]. I went to one in the city but you see it was issues from the start like it was I couldn't have my own room because everyone was kind of crowded in there like sometimes there were like families living in one room. The staff said that they wanted to keep a calm place and that I would be likely to make others feel uncomfortable. . . . They wanted to help but they made a big fuss about my trans status. I overheard the staff say "the other residents are going to be scared and the children are going to be scared and it's not going to be the environment that we want here" and then told me they didn't have a room for a single person. So they put me in another room that housed four women in two bunk beds and I had one bunk. . . . I couldn't wait to get out, I mean the women were not violent to me but they were just not welcoming. Like they were just like, they'd stare at me

and when we tried to do the first group counseling like, the women just stared at me or just whispered or something. Even the staff was a little off because I knew from the start they weren't even on the same page about having me there.

While Anna's account serves as only one experience, it highlights the many dimensions involved in seeking formal help from a rigidly gendered structured resource. Likely as a result of many of these experiences, the majority of survivors managed to leave abusive relationships through supportive friends and/or family. Chris stated that for her

it was pretty easy once I came to just realize and accept what happened. I was able to just leave after the lease was up, I didn't re-sign, I just went back home to my family. They know what happened and I was able to kind of get new start. . . . I'd have to say the most helpful thing was family. I talked to my parents a lot. I feel like I can talk about just anything and finally one day I just started sobbing on the phone and they just told me not to re-sign the lease and get out. I didn't get out right then but I did eventually and they pestered me like, they, they would call frequently and ask if I had left yet. They wanted me out of there.

For David, the abuse he experienced brought him closer to his family, in spite of his abuser: "She would cut me away from family and try to get me as mad at my family as much as possible . . . I started actually talking to my family a lot more and my sister got me a job so I was like, I'm done." While most survivors did not have supportive family structures, many did have supportive friends and coworkers. For Joe, it was an online friend who helped him through the process of seeing that he was victimized and needing help: "She was a friend online for the longest time and I just sort of, I just sort of asked her some vague questions and I just sort of basically told her everything I told you up until that point." Joe added, "I had to have someone verbally tell me . . . this is what's happening to you. You can't just sit there in denial because you'll get hurt, you'll get even more hurt if that continues. I had to have someone from outside tell me what was going on. I was in denial." Similarly, Rebecca described that she left when she "realized it wasn't stability. This wasn't stability." She added,

I can't say there was just some grand awakening. I just figured, this is it, this has to end. So actually, I broke down and told a coworker. I was afraid of mixing this in with work but I knew I was valued at work. I was a top sales person and I was about to be promoted and I knew that they were interested in keeping me. I got closer to one coworker and I told her what was happening. She immediately told me that I need to move in with her and just not tell him. So I packed what I could in one bag, I didn't have much and while he was at work I left a note. I said I was done there and that was that.

Friendships and informal avenues were very crucial to these survivors, as many of them had lost familial ties and relationships due to their trans status. Early on Anna told me, "I don't have much family that talk to me anymore." Similarly, Tom stated, "My family doesn't talk all that much and I definitely didn't want to talk about this because they may just side with her and be like 'yeah, it's just too much, this trans thing.'" Rebecca too described, "I don't really have family connections anymore. I sometimes talk to a cousin just to keep up with them." Friendships took on a crucial role for many survivors left with few options. Casey wrote how they were able to leave their abuser by first reaching out to a friend:

A friend of mine was an intimate partner violence counselor during the relationship, and one day I finally said "hey, maybe we should talk about what's going on and you can tell me if my girlfriend's behavior seems weird to you." Up till then I had been mostly avoiding that friend because my girlfriend didn't like me to see her very often. I shut all the windows and locked all the doors before we sat down to have the conversation. I didn't even notice I had done that until my friend pointed it out. She had me describe our relationship and mapped it out visually—it ended up looking like a downward spiral that was getting tighter and tighter. I came out of that talk with a pretty clear feeling that the relationship was abusive. It took me awhile to do anything about it because I was scared my girlfriend would kill herself. We were on a temporary break from each other at one point and decided to have lunch as "friends." At the end of the date she handed me some printed information on coping with grief after a loved one commits suicide, and then walked away. It felt like fire in my hand. I felt so sure that I would be trapped in this cycle forever if I didn't do something, and I felt furious at her for playing off of my worst fears. I ran after her and broke up with her. I remember feeling so betrayed, that this person I loved would put me in a position where I felt like I had to choose between her life and my sanity. I asked her if she felt she was abusive towards me and she said yes. I told her it had to stop and I begged her not to harm herself. I gave her an emergency hotline phone number before I left, and planned to call several friend when I got home to ask them to keep an eye on her and offer her support in the next few days. As soon as I got home my phone rang and a friend of mine said they had just found a suicide note. It took many hours, many cops and paramedics, and many friends to finally find her and get her hospitalized. She had not hurt herself but did have hypothermia. My friend who was the counselor came and sat with me all night while I waited to find out if she was alive. I was catatonic with fear and sorrow. I threw up when they finally found her. That was the first time I didn't show up at the hospital to patch things back up and make sure she would be okay. It was terrible. I couldn't function. I remember crawling under my desk at work a few days later because I was having a panic attack and I was equally terrified that she would show up at my office to mess with me, or that she would never show up anywhere every again because she would be dead. It was completely horrible.

Living through the constant emotional manipulation of their abuser, Casey had reached a breaking point. Their abuser had regularly threatened to kill herself to "punish" Casey and on more than once occasion landed herself in the hospital. Empowered by a friend, Casey made the crucial decision to leave. However, for survivors like Owen, support from friends only went but so far:

Close to the end of the relationship (and the second time I had to take the morning after pill after being forced into vaginal sex), I knew it had to end. I was being held down, and it was not fair. I needed to take care of myself, not an overgrown brat. I was afraid to end the relationship, because he was physically stronger than me and could hurt me or my loved ones if I really set him off. I tried to end it in person, with friends to back me up, but couldn't. Finally, I had a mental breakdown and ended the relationship over the internet and that was that. The experiences were horrifying and I still have flashbacks regarding them.

For Owen, multiple attempts to leave had not proven successful. While he wrote that he depended on friends, ultimately he had only himself to rely on.

Some survivors had been isolated from both family and even most friends. While some survivors had informal ties with coworkers, most described a fear of bringing their personal issues into the workplace. Fatima described the importance of having a friend who would be supportive. She told me about how she made plans to leave:

> I was afraid of him [abuser] now, because I knew he was capable of hurting me physically like the way he grabbed me many times and that he would just have his way and do what he wanted with me, um, he could do anything I thought. I had to do everything like in secret, like the planning of leaving. Um, so, then first, I'm thinking like okay, I need a place of course that's the first thing but I also need money if I'm going to leave this job I need money or at least a job. I don't have any family and I was not really like familiar with the community, I didn't have connections to family anymore or that community at all, so um that was not an option. But I did have the, the friends back home and it was two hours away but I, I knew that was the only way. To call a friend. The bad thing was that, I was like "well, ugh, damn, um, I haven't talk to this person in so long" my depression put me away like from anyone. But I finally just decided no, I need to give them a call. I try to explain everything and she [friend] told me to call the police if I needed to and that she's going to tell her husband that I need to stay in the living room at least for a couple of weeks. Um, if it wasn't for her, I don't know what I would've done.

Her account emphasizes that without this connection, she may have had no better way out. When structural and formal resources are inaccessible, unwelcoming, and discriminatory, families and friendships become much more important.

Conclusion

As survivors recounted their experiences and how they managed to leave abusive relationships, the unique realities of those who live outside the gender binary emerged as they processed their victimization and navigated genderist help resources. The larger cultural narratives constructed a gendered discourse behind victimization that left survivors rejecting their realities. In the broader research literature, it is common to find evidence of survivors struggling with seeing themselves as victims and then subsequently with their limited ability to seek help. However, as these accounts illustrate, there are distinct processes that play out for transgender survivors.

A significant factor in understanding help-seeking behaviors for survivors of intimate partner violence is to explore how individuals come to see themselves as victims. While for cisgender and heterosexual survivors this struggle may include feelings of embarrassment, denial, or in some cases religious devotion to marriage or gender subservience, the transgender survivors I spoke with struggled with the gendered constructs of victimization and the genderist response system. Recalling Erbaugh's critique of dominant theorization in intimate partner violence, the genderist assumptions in the victim-perpetrator binary contribute to the silencing of LGBTQ victims. She argued that these approaches were largely representative of the cultural assumptions of "victim" as feminine or always female. As noted throughout the stories, most of the survivors invoked some form of gendered discourse when describing their process of identifying as a victim of intimate partner violence. Specifically, they struggled with perceiving victims of intimate partner violence as "helpless housewives" or passive and nonresistant. Regardless of a survivor's own gender identification, many of them described what it meant to be a victim of intimate partner violence in this way. Of particular interest was the role that the perceptions of others played in how respondents struggled to see themselves as victims.

Because of the gendered assumptions behind victimization, many survivors described feelings of not being believed because they were "too butch" or were "once a man," among other reasons. The role of the perceptions of others was prominent in how survivors described navigating various help resources. While most turned to friends and family, many accessed more formal resources. Survivors experienced a range of various genderist barriers to help. In a world where the rigid gender binary structured these resources, survivors described not fitting into the services or spaces provided. The findings in the stories have various applied implications for domestic violence response organizations and

LGBTQ-serving programs. A stronger effort should be made to ensure that services and community education programs are trans inclusive and approachable. Trans inclusivity requires that service providers acknowledge the unique realities faced by transgender survivors. Davis identifies many of the experiences that trans people encounter with rigidly gendered help structures as sex-identity discrimination rooted in the administration of sex.[23] If trans inclusivity is the goal, these avenues (e.g., shelters) require a reframing in how they define and manage sex. The following chapter reviews some of the ways in which the accounts of these survivors inform potential new directions in how our society responds to trans victims of intimate partner violence.

6

Conclusion

Moving toward Trans Inclusivity

One of the final questions I asked in the research interviews that provide the data for this study was purposefully open-ended: I asked the survivors if there were any other points they wanted to make that had not already been covered in our conversations. For those who opted to write their stories, they were also asked if there were any other aspects to their experiences that they wanted to highlight. This was often when survivors described what happened after the abuse or where they filled in more detail to their stories. Sam wrote a pointed and legitimate response to the free-write option some survivors took: the fact that I did not spend more time on life after the abuse. They wrote,

> You didn't ask about the impact of the abuse, and I'm not sure why. I figured that would be a big part of the interview, but it wasn't even part of the story you asked about. The first abusive relationship had an intense impact on my physical and mental health, as did the second one. So much of my life has been impacted by these relationship experiences. That's where I think survivors share experience, is in the impact and in the ways we cope. You asked about formal/[informal] systems but did not ask about coping with the abuse and the aftermath of the abuse.

While all survivors spoke about the impact of abuse, Sam offered an important critique: what happens when it is all over?

David was one survivor who described some aspects of abuse that were linked to his transition. Despite this, David emphasized that he did not really know for sure whether his trans status had anything to do with the abuse he experienced. As my conversation with David came to a close, he told me a bit about how things were going for him after leaving his abuser:

I'm in therapy right now, I actually, this is only the fourth time I've talked about this. . . . I had a really hard time for a long time, well, specifically, some of it had to do with dysphoria but a good portion of it had to do with trust in general and even though my ex never stated she didn't want to be with me because I was trans, *that's what I felt anyway* and *I'm pretty sure it was a reason* and so when I started dating this [other] girl, like she was identified as lesbian so for a really long time I had a really hard time believing that she could actually be attracted to me as a male. So it took me a really long time to be like, okay that's okay. I mean, I don't think it carries a weight anymore, it did for years after, I was really depressed, I had really hard time getting confidence back and I still kind of do a little bit, um. It took me some time to just go out in the world.

Despite the fact that David told me his abuser never mentioned his trans status, he described feeling as though that was an issue. The subsequent impact was a deteriorated sense of self, one that impacted his future dating and his confidence. The consequences and outcomes of the abuse on David's life and trans identity were echoed by others. In his final remarks, Joe shared words for trans-identified individuals who may be experiencing intimate partner violence:

If you don't have a clear idea of your boundaries, step back and think about it. If you see anything that does not fit well with you, do not, don't engage, [don't] take the unnecessary risk if you feel. You can't change a person, if they make these comments, they will not suddenly accept you. You can't make them suddenly accept you as any less of a threat. Just like, you know, don't rush, don't be so desperate to find some sort of human contact. Take it easy. You'll find better people if you do it that way, I guess. Like, just don't give in to feeling lonely and desperate because you open yourself up to something much worse.

Depending on the flow of our conversation, I did have the opportunity to ask some survivors what has affected them in the long term. Fatima told me, "The self-confidence, the paranoia is there. Like, I do want to live life as a woman. I would rather just pass like a woman and I think I do that but he made me feel like I wasn't doing something right, or that I was just like, um not desirable in any way as a woman. But I'm working, I'm, working on that now." Similarly, Laura told me,

> I mean, well it's a lot. I mean I was depressed for months. I even just questioned if it was worth finishing the transition. I really took to heart all of those things and I just wasn't even sure any more if I could be a woman if my own boyfriend couldn't love me, who will? Therapy, the counselor . . . I went like every week for a long time and it was free. I could only do an hour a week but I did it all the time and it helped, she helped me think things through. If it wasn't for her and that building I wouldn't be around I don't think.

Surprisingly for Sam, their three abusers all left before they had a chance to leave the relationship. They wrote,

> Interestingly enough, all three of these people broke up with me after I made a significant stand that challenged their control, and then tried to resume relationship with me afterwards. 1. Part of the psychological abuse included gaslighting, and as an abusive technique the abuser told me to engage in therapy and called me crazy a lot. My journaling helped me parse what was happening, though it took a long time. So, when I called my old therapist I was ready to tell her what was going on and to see it as a problem. She helped me think through a plan for trying to change the relationship, and an emergency escape backup plan if that didn't work. It didn't work, so I immediately used the backup plan. I had already packed bags, and when he refused to engage in any of the changes I requested, I called someone I knew (who he had introduced me to and exchanged me for services with, in fact) to ask if they could come get me and I could stay as I gave notice at my job and moved away. When he realized I was leaving immediately, he raged and yelled and manipulated and threw things and made threats for a few hours until they arrived to get me and then I left. My mother and godmother got me a ticked to leave the state, and then after realizing I could not find employment where I went, I moved back to my city of origin and stayed with my mother for a few months until I found work and an apartment. He engaged in abusive dynamics when I came to get my belongings and continued to harass me and financially abuse me after I left. 2. I realized (through therapy, journaling,

and discussions with my tiny support system) that the abusive dynamics (esp. the sexual and psychological abuse) had damaged the relationship so much that first I needed a physical separation (separate rooms) and then when it continued, I asked her to move out, but was willing to consider some continuance of the relationship. She ended the relationship. She took a long time to move out, and then moved back because the housing she found was not suitable for the child we were co-parenting (it was also a bid to get me back that did not work). It took her a long time to find another place to live. After she moved out, I continued to parent the child with her and her ex for 6 months, and then they cut me off from the child. 6 months later, they offered renewed contact with the child but I refused, for the child's sake as well as my own. I needed a clean complete break. 3. The sexual abuse incident with the husband damaged our relationship and my efforts to safety plan around it for my own safety led to arguments and more intense psychological abuse, which led me to cancelling an important visit (he was going to come down for an award I got from work). My cancelling the visit led him to break up with me immediately. He then tried to continue the relationship and when I refused, there was a very bad incident of psychological and spiritual abuse, and harassment for a few weeks.

While Casey's written account had few specific details of the abuses she experienced, she wrote at length about her feelings after the relationship ended:

After we broke up, I was a hot mess for a really long time. I was so scared and heartbroken that I could barely function and almost lost my job. After a while of being broken up, things started getting weird again. She would disappear for a while then come back, wreak some sort of havoc in my life, and then disappear again. She would show up at my office (even though I had told her not to), or suddenly become best friends with one of my roommates and start showing up at my house unannounced, or she would cause a scene yelling at my friends in public, and things like that. I never knew where she was and when she would show up next. . . . Our friends really tried to help us. That was years and years ago. I still periodically wonder if she is dead or alive, and worry about her. She feels like a ghost in my heart. When I think of her I feel a wave of sorrow and fear.

I can't breathe when I get on a bus and see someone who looks a lot like her. My heart just stops. I worry that people will judge me for thinking that our relationship was abusive, because she never physically harmed me, and because there are disparities of privilege between us. I still wonder if I am making it up somehow, or if she will come back and convince everyone I love that I am a liar or a terrible person. I really hope she has gotten the help she needs and found balance and wellness and love in her life. But I still have a burst of fear every once in a while that she's just around the corner, waiting for the right moment to come fuck up my life again. I know that it sounds really self-important for me to say that; it sounds like she has nothing better to do than mess with me. I'm sure that that's not true, that she has a full life of her own and has gotten over me. But I feel haunted.

For Casey and others, the end of the abuse was an ending only to the physical presence of the relationship but not to its lasting effects. The psychological impacts of intimate partner violence are well documented across the heterosexual, cisgender literature as well as for same-gender relationships.[1] Depression, anxiety, posttraumatic stress disorder, and even physiological effects like migraines are commonly reported among survivors of abuse.[2] However, less is known about how an intimate partner violence experience affects transgender people.

Some research has indicated that transgender individuals suffer from higher rates of anxiety and posttraumatic stress disorder as a result of hostile societal conditions, which produce more traumatic events in their lives compared to cisgender people.[3] Scholars have identified themes in how transgender people of color cope with traumatic events by taking pride in their identities while also seeking community, health, and financial resources, activist connections, family acceptance, and spirituality.[4] It is logical to assume that some of the same outcomes exist across gender identities; given some of the details shared by the survivors, there are clear similarities across the mental health consequences. Despite these similarities, trans survivors echo how much the abuse impacted their trans identity and transition, something distinct from the consequences of abuse experienced by cisgender survivors. While across the board abuse undermines self-concept and identity, trans people may be at unique risk for deterioration of identity as they work toward living authentic lives.

Understanding the dynamics of abuse as experienced by transgender survivors of intimate partner violence is crucial in illustrating the unique realities faced by the community. Throughout the stories, survivors emphasized the central aspect of transphobic and genderist attacks in their relationships. Scholars have pointed to the notion that abusers of transgender individuals may utilize these tactics, as gay and lesbian abusers have often utilized homophobia and heterosexism; however, in the US context, rarely have they relied on data to demonstrate how this is manifested among transgender victims.[5] Nonprofit studies outside of the United States have provided data. The 2015 Transgender People's Experiences of Domestic Abuse study from the Scottish Transgender Alliance showed that 73 percent of their respondents had experienced at least one transphobic attack from a current or former intimate partner.[6]

While the survivors I spoke with and surveyed had experienced a wide array of abuse in the context of an intimate relationship, many of the accounts focused on these emotional and psychological torments, which abusers directed toward their trans status or ability to "pass." These experiences illustrated the significant role that hostile social contexts play in the construction of power and control in these relationships. Merrill and others have shown how intimate relationships do not exist separate from social influence, but rather the interactional power dynamics of any relationship are informed and shaped by the larger context in which they occur. This not only is a starting point toward explaining the high rates of intimate partner violence reported by transgender people, but also expands theoretical understandings of the types of abuse experienced.

As evidenced by the stories here, the abusers of transgender people utilized attacks that would shame and isolate on the basis of gender nonconformity. Essentially, these attacks represented more than putdowns from the abuser as victims experienced the attacks as continued reflections of the external hostile social environment they live in daily. The continued marginalization and oppression of the transgender community provides an opportunity for abusers to manipulate, control, and shame. Significantly, power differentials need not be rooted in identity, as these stories showed that some abusers were not cisgender themselves but that the opportunity to abuse and direct attacks toward trans identities exists regardless of their own gender identities.

The stories of abuse that emerged in my research provided a more comprehensive understanding of how survivors of abuse understand the motives of their abusers and how they explain why the abuse occurred. Through these discussions, survivors attributed meaning and interpretation to their victimization. Specifically, they addressed, from their own perspective, why abusers acted in the ways that they did. These narratives were of particular significance as they offered a deeper glimpse into the dynamics of abuse as described by transgender victims than had been previously available in research.

In some conversations, I asked about the survivor's transition and potential role it played in the abuse. For others, the issue made of their transition emerged as they told their stories of abuse. Overall, the most salient meaning constructed behind victimization was the overarching pattern of abusers controlling the gender transition. This finding expands what is known about power dynamics in abusive relationships in which the victim is transgender. Survivors explained how strong and consistent their abusers' desires were to control their transitional development. Among the aspects of controlling transition, abusers intervened in personal medical decisions, ridiculed the transition process, and micromanaged victims' gendered presentations. Trans vulnerability set the stage for these broader patterns of control as they manifested in the discrediting of identity work by the transgender survivors. While most survivors either had already started transitioning before they entered these relationships or were open about their transition goals with abusers, they described the abusers as wanting to control the process. Survivors saw this as a time in their life during which an abuser could more easily manipulate them. Even survivors who had transitioned long before this abusive relationship described abusers as latching on to past insecurities and bringing them to the forefront. According to many of the stories, trans vulnerability meant that they longed for stability and love and to be wanted in return. Abusers used trans vulnerability to ensnare victims in a pattern of violence. Some survivors described feeling that this was what they deserved or that it was the best they could do given their trans status. As a result, for many of the survivors trans vulnerability was a motivation to stay in their abusive relationship. Returning to Walker and the Scottish study referenced above, it shows the specific stages of vulnerability to abuse for transgender people:

Trans people's vulnerability to IPV/A is intensified at three key stages: first, periods of reassignment whereby the victim is considering gender reassignment surgery or starting a course of medications to aid transformation; second, publicly dressing as their preferred gender identity such as wearing make-up, changing hairstyles, or using a name more commonly associated with their new identity; and third, when considering "coming out" to family and friends. It can be inferred from analysis of the narratives provided to Roch and Morton by trans women who had experienced IPV/A that the aggressor is challenging the trans person's identity. It would appear that although the aggressors in these cases were aware of their partners' transgender identity, the suggestion of a more public and/or permanent transformation triggered abusive situations.[7]

The proposed stages of trans vulnerability are exemplified across many of the stories here. The present accounts echo these theoretical arguments as relevant within the US context. Further, the identity work perspective presented here supports the theoretical language to specify the ways in which abusers of trans people target identities. Many survivors described their transition as becoming more like their "true self" or gaining self-confidence. Throughout the stories, abuser motives involved keeping victims feeling isolated and ashamed or unwanted, centrally around their trans status. Survivors described that the abuser's desire to control transition was rooted in the intent to cripple their self-confidence and gain power over as many aspects of their lives as possible.

Finally, survivors explained grappling with their victimization and how they managed the abuse and recovery process. Our conversations revealed a key aspect in the processing of victim identity that involved the use of a gendered discourse on the meaning behind victimization. As survivors discussed how they struggled with viewing the relationship as problematic and then finally began to see themselves as victims, they often contrasted what happened to them with their cultural assumptions about intimate partner violence. Many survivors described struggling with labeling their experiences as intimate partner violence, as domestic violence, or even as abusive. The survivors distanced themselves from what they perceived an intimate partner violence victim was; this involved the construct of victim as feminine and "helpless." They often rejected the notion that they were either passive or helpless. Indeed, this contributed to their perception that others would not believe their stories. Because many of the survivors grappled with not being what they thought was a typical victim, they felt as if others would not validate their experiences as abuse. For some, these feelings were confirmed as others would advise them to "handle it themselves." The acceptance of others becomes significantly important as most of the survivors found help through friends and families more so than formal resources. Survivors who attempted to access more formal avenues found themselves navigating genderist services that were either not welcoming or not suited to their needs. The law enforcement, legal, and shelter resources were described by most as non-options; for some who utilized these avenues, they evaluated them as providing mixed outcomes. Trans survivors of color reported institutionalized resources as most out of reach and perceived them as unhelpful. The complicated interactions and experiences revealed the pattern of systemic marginalization from legal recourses.

Taken as a whole, the stories of these eighteen transgender survivors of intimate partner violence yield several implications in moving toward trans-inclusivity in theory, research, and the real world. First, the accounts show a need to destabilize the rigid ways in which scholars approach gender in the field of intimate partner violence. They also inform how research can better capture the trans experience to more holistically reflect lived realities. Last, the stories highlight potential new directions in how we respond to survivors across shelter, policing, and legal avenues of help. Additionally, they bolster arguments for the continued inclusion of trans experiences in order to devise useful resources for victims of intimate partner abuse.

Trans-Inclusive Theory

At the onset of this book, I noted that no singular theory guided my inquiry, but rather multiple complementary perspectives offered some context for the investigation. I argued that postmodern feminism, queer criminology, and symbolic interactionism (i.e., identity work perspectives) provided the most relevant theoretical backdrop from which to think about the trans experience of intimate partner violence. The research data, together with my analysis of the survivors' stories, argue for a trans-inclusive way of understanding intimate partner violence that starts with destabilizing the centrality of gender in broader victimological thought and theorization.

While queer criminology has begun to destabilize the ways in which we think about queer offenders by developing new theories or queering existing theories, significantly less has been done to queer victimological approaches to gender in intimate partner violence.[8] Overall, victimology is focused on definitions of victimization, how the criminal justice system applies these definitions, and how our society responds to victims. As a subfield, especially in the US context, it has generally lacked a critical examination of the power and inequality that contextualize the victimization experience. Critical scholars have previously noted the conservative bias in victimology that largely takes definitions of crime for granted, looks toward a punitive system for retribution, focuses on street crime, and misses key aspects of powerful currents of injustices in our society that frame victimization.[9] While gender has been central to how victimologists understand intimate partner violence, less has been done to complicate gender in a way that is trans-inclusive. Moving beyond Johnson's argument that family violence and feminist scholars examined two different types of intimate partner violence (i.e., common couple versus intimate terrorism), I echo the call from other scholars to move toward theorization that examines gender discursively and situationally. As researchers Clare Cannon, Katie Lauve-Moon, and Fred Buttell argue, "Deconstructing gender and power binaries creates new opportunities to re-conceptualize intimate partner violence for male and female perpetrators in heteronormative couples as well as LGBTQ couples."[10] Parallel to their analysis, I argue that the stories of trans survivors of intimate partner violence show how gendered power is constructed interactionally rather than merely by structure. This stands in contrast to some traditional feminist models that still dominate intimate partner violence theorization and research; rather than think of gendered power as rigidly structured by culture and maintained by institutions in which one person has *all* of the predetermined power while the other has none, trans inclusivity in theorization begins with acknowledging how all social beings have differential access to power that can be situationally defined.

Structural power should not be ignored; the order and design of social hierarchies are historically ingrained and foster inherent power differentials between groups. The structure of patriarchal power is useful in explaining men's violence against women: it highlights economic disparities and cultural motivations of role. However, queering the centrality of gendered power in intimate partner violence could serve several functions. First, thinking of gendered power as emerging not just from structure but also from situation and interaction captures a wider range of intimate partner violence (i.e., women's, same-gender, and trans perpetration). Cannon and colleagues state, "People, based on their social location, use tactics and strategies available to them to negotiate dynamics of power."[11] This rings true across the stories I heard as seven of the abusers were described by survivors as non-cisgender. Regardless of the gender identity of the abusers (their social location), power can be constructed within the dyad. In my research, much of that power came from the distinct vulnerability in which trans people may be placed. At least in part, the utilization of transphobic and genderist attacks serves as a mechanism for the manipulation of power. A trans-antagonistic culture fosters increased trans vulnerability in intimate relationships. Abusers may rely on this broader hostility to entrap victims, making them feel they have less of an ability to choose to leave. As regularly cited across the accounts, transphobic and genderist attacks eroded the survivors' sense of self. Second, queering gendered power also takes into account intersecting realities. Trans migrants and people of color face multiplicative factors of marginalization that contribute to vulnerability while also rigidly restricting their help avenues. This was evident throughout the stories I heard from trans people of color and was most prominent for survivors when they related leaving the abuse. Finally, queering gendered power in intimate partner violence theorization leaves room for bidirectional violence.[12] Queering challenges the categorization of social life into neat, binary categories such as victim and abuser. This means that victims of intimate partner violence can also be perpetrators of reciprocal violence. As some of the survivors noted, the idea of being perceived as helpless was rejected. Leaving room for agency acknowledges that victimization does not have to be a linear experience where abusers (default cismen) have all the power and victims (default ciswomen) have none. Instead of a unilateral, one-size-fits-all approach to thinking about power in abusive relationships, queering disrupts the static categories of abuser and victim by recognizing that agency can be exercised by those experiencing violence: they might fight back and might even initiate violence. This is not to undermine violent victimization experiences but to more accurately reflect potential dynamics in some abusive relationships in which there is not one sole receiver and perpetrator of violence.

Beyond more representative theorization, intimate partner violence research must also advance toward trans inclusion. To start, large-scale surveys should offer more options for gender categories. Given the potentially limitless options for gender identification, methodological challenges are likely. Offering broad questions that may capture all trans identities could be a simpler solution. As one example, the 2015 US Transgender Survey opened with broad questions on trans identities. While their focus was not exclusively on intimate partner violence, they did dedicate a section of the survey to these experiences:

1.10 Do you think of yourself as transgender? [Must answer to continue.]
    No
    Yes

1.11 Do you identify as more than one gender or as no gender (such as genderqueer or non-binary)? [Must answer to continue.]
    No
    Yes

1.12 Do you currently live full-time in a gender that is different from the one assigned to you at birth? [Must answer to continue.]
    No [Skip to 1.14]
    Yes

Additionally, they offered questions about assigned sex at birth and a list of terms with which transgender individuals may identify with (e.g., agender, androgynous, bi-gender, etc.). In section 2 of their survey, they offered more specific options to measure trans identities including perceived gender.

2.3 If you had to choose only one of the following terms, which best describes your current gender identity? (Please choose only one answer.)

Cross-dresser

Woman

Man

Trans woman (MTF)

Non-binary/Genderqueer [Respondents who selected this answer received questions 2.3_1, 2.3_2, and 2.3_3.]

2.3_1 For people in your life who don't know that you're non-binary/genderqueer, what gender do they usually think you are? [Only respondents who selected "Non-binary/Genderqueer" in response to 2.3 received this question.]

Man

Woman

Trans Man

Trans Woman

Non-Binary/Genderqueer

They can't tell

It varies

The Williams Institute offers a "gender-related measures overview" document that reviews several methods for more successfully capturing transgender identities.[13] In their document, they highlight four methods of capturing more diverse gender identities, which range from two-step gender identity and assigned sex questions to single-question options that list various trans identities. Finally, while the present stories and the scant literature available on trans intimate partner violence show that there are distinct types of violence experienced, existing measures generally fail to capture them. Measures of prevalence for trans-specific abuses like transphobic and genderist manipulation, controlling transition, and attacks that discredit identity work are needed.

Achieving the goal of representativeness in samples for quantitative trans-inclusive research presents unique challenges. Probability-based, generalizable samples often still lack enough gender diversity to make any claims about trans populations. Consequently, the existing literature on same-gender intimate partner violence commonly cites the insufficiency of transgender responses to surveys. I have encountered this same problem in a couple of my own quantitative studies that failed to reach a sufficient number of trans respondents. Recent research has identified ways in which probability-based sampling frames could work to capture a more representative pool of LGBTQ-identified respondents. Graham and colleagues illustrate how various probability and non-probability techniques can improve LGBTQ research, especially for small populations like transgender individuals.[14] While probability-based frameworks are often expensive and require long-term commitments, they recommend (1) disproportionate stratification, (2) respondent-driven sampling, and (3) time-location sampling. Each of these strategies utilizes a targeted model for locating (respectively) concentrations of the population, a chain-referral method, or multiple stages of data collection that increase the chances of obtaining a more representative pool. Non-probability-based samples are most common in trans-inclusive research and can be improved with larger samples and more purposive techniques that recruit trans respondents. Likewise, quota sampling would focus on obtaining a set number of transgender respondents in order to make more representative claims.

Policy and Help Structures

As evidenced throughout the stories, survivors left their abusive relationships through a variety of help structures—mainly informal avenues like friends. The implications for both cultural and systemic responses are far-reaching. Importantly, there is a broader cultural implication about transphobia and genderism: while trans activists have advanced the national dialogue on gender identity issues, the broader culture remains rigidly transphobic. In late 2017, the Pew Research Center found that a third of Americans believe that society has gone too far in accepting transgender people; a quarter more think that the progress has been "about right."[15] Despite this, they also found that almost four in ten Americans now say they know someone who is transgender—a higher number than in previous years.[16] Much of what the survivors related that made them vulnerable to abuse was cultural transphobia and genderism; this is further sustained by how our society has rigidly codified sex and gender. Arguably, reducing and eliminating cultural transphobia and genderism would have an impact on reducing transgender intimate partner violence. No clear answer exists on how to reduce cultural transphobia and genderism; however, trans scholars have proposed ideas for dismantling the systems that promote sex-identity discrimination. Davis refers to this as a "specific subcategory of sexism . . . judgments about who does and does not belong in the sex categories of male or female."[17] The proposal is to interrogate the assumed necessity of the administration and identification of sex by institutions (e.g., birth certificates, driver's licenses, bathrooms). The process would involve explicit definitions of what is meant by sex and why/how it serves a logical purpose in classification. Davis argues that through this open and honest inquiry, many institutions would find it unnecessary to manage and regulate sex. Structural changes have great influence on individual interactions and perceptions of problems: in this case, they would move society away from rigid policing of sex identity, which could arguably not only improve quality of life for all gender-nonconforming individuals but maybe also reduce pervasive cultural transphobia and genderism. Because friends and family played such a critical role in help seeking for many of the survivors here, cultural progress in this sphere would be influential even if it simply lessened the broader hostility that exists in the public.

While many survivors did not access formal help avenues, the primary systemic resources that survivors utilized were mental health and medical professionals, law enforcement, and domestic violence shelters. Across the mental health and medical professions, trans-inclusive perspectives and practices are growing. Despite this, many transgender people report negative interactions with both mental health and medical professionals including refusal of care, harassment and violence, and, most commonly, lack of provider knowledge.[18] Barrett and Sheridan note of particular concern the fact that most trained psychologists do not report familiarity with transgender issues.[19] Additionally, they report that recent surveys of mental health professionals who serve LGBTQ survivors of intimate partner violence show that most believed their educational training had not prepared them well enough to address this type of violence.

Intimate partner violence against transgender people should be seen as a major public health care problem. Both mental and medical professionals who serve transgender populations should screen for intimate partner violence and talk to clients about the risks. These screenings are now common across practices, but an emphasis on violence prevention during and after transition should be central to the services provided. Transgender mental health providers often cite fears of violence and finding partners among clients, and therefore discussing the high risk of partner abuse should be crucial to the journey toward self-authenticity.[20] In particular, as evidenced in the present stories but also echoed across trans intimate partner violence literature, there may be particular stages of transition that increase risk (e.g., early stages; see chapter 5). Trans-specific safety plans should also become part of the knowledge base for those working with trans survivors of intimate partner violence. For example, Cook-Daniels declares that "get away kits" for trans survivors exiting abusive relationships should include any relevant and necessary identity documents, medications and equipment, and multiple options for gender-affirming clothing.[21]

The few survivors who interacted with law enforcement during their abusive relationships largely reported negative experiences; most did not rely on law enforcement for any help in preventing or escaping the abuse. I have two rather conflicting arguments about how to think about law enforcement responses to transgender intimate partner violence. My first point takes a critical approach to the system, its role, and overreliance on the idea that this is a helpful avenue to transgender victims of intimate partner violence. The very nature of law enforcement presents multiple conflicts in how it responds to transgender intimate partner violence. As a rigidly gendered institution, policing may innately attract and cultivate homophobic, transphobic, and genderist attitudes. The long-standing history of racial bias and discrimination in American law enforcement is well documented across the criminological literature and continues to be a central political argument. Generally, many studies find that law enforcement interactions with domestic violence victims are unhelpful and often lead to revictimization. Additional evidence shows that legal intervention may not be what victims desire, could isolate survivors in the process, and removes their agency.[22]

Given the problematic nature of the system, some scholars and activists openly question its role in responding to intimate partner violence victimization. Domestic violence statutes across the country generally focus entirely on physical abuse, more specifically the type of physical abuse that leaves evidence. A largely punitive system that is set up to respond to one type of abuse with a narrow focus with a standard of physical evidence may not be the best recourse for a lot of transgender victims of intimate partner violence. Legal scholars have also openly questioned whether domestic violence should be decriminalized given its ties to mass incarceration and the "tough-on-crime" era of the 1980s and 1990s.[23] Considering the historical problems with the criminal justice system, some alternative suggestions have been made in the past, achieving little popularity. These interventions have generally fit under the broader restorative justice umbrella, while some more creative alternatives suggest breaking from the justice system entirely. Most restorative justice approaches to domestic violence violations work in tandem with the criminal justice system. With diversion from incarceration as the focus, alternatives are offered to victims and perpetrators that include court-sponsored mediation, community conferencing, peacemaking groups, and batterer intervention programs. The common goal throughout these alternatives is to center victims' needs while making offenders fully understand their violation of both the victim's rights and the entire community affected. Ultimately, while end results would vary, repairing harm to the victim and community would be the conclusion. These alternatives are typically monitored by the courts, overseen by judges or other magistrates.

While there are many critiques, central among them are concerns for victim safety and well-being; additionally, activists and scholars alike fear that these alternatives would signal a "soft" approach to very serious acts of violence. Scholars have noted several shortcomings to these alternatives, including the argument that apologies and remorse discourses could mean different things to victims, offenders, and the community.[24] Importantly, the gendered nature of apology discourse and the notion that men, women, and trans folks may interpret intimate partner violence very differently make it difficult or impossible to achieve reconciliation. Kim offers a call for more creative solutions to address violence that merge social justice with an antiviolence focus.[25] She cites a call from Incite! that states, "It is critical that we develop responses to gender violence that do not depend on a sexist, racist, classist, and homophobic criminal justice system." As one solution, Kim established the Creative Interventions organization in Oakland, California. Broadly, the group focuses on centering stories of violence that inform community-based responses to intimate partner and sexual violence. At its core, the idea is that those who are most impacted by violence (i.e., the community at large) have the most motivation and strongest answers to enforce accountability, promote healing, and prevent violence. Of particular significance, the movement has provided creative intervention toolkits to communities curious to see if the model works for them.[26]

A second broader point turns toward reforming the existing system and perhaps improving the ways in which it responds to marginalized survivors of intimate partner violence. While these approaches acknowledge the inherent biases and historical problems within the system, they also emphasize that historically oppressed and marginalized survivors of intimate partner violence are entitled to equal protections and access to those resources (i.e., adequate police response, due process). Walker notes that "a point made by Moran and Sharpe is that the lack of acknowledgment of trans people within the justice system adds to their marginalized status and preserves trans people's lack of trust and confidence in law enforcement agencies."[27] One of the central arguments of the reform approach focuses on training for law enforcement and court officials. This includes training for basic knowledge on gender identity and expression and proper use of gendered pronouns and names. Beyond the basics, law enforcement should also be trained in stereotype-reduction strategies that help identify internalized biases against gender-nonconforming people and how that affects their ability to evaluate situations. Organizations like the Network/La Red offer technical assistance and training to agencies working with LGBTQ survivors of violence. One such training is titled "Working with Transgender and Non-Binary Survivors of Partner Abuse" and features an interactive workshop model that is aimed at reducing transphobia, utilizing respectful language, and best supporting trans and/or gender-nonconforming survivors. The few survivors in the present stories who reported interactions with law enforcement cited problems with disrespect, transphobia, and the undermining of their experiences based on their trans status. These problems were often compounded by other racialized and gendered responses to their victimization.

Recall that Anna was the sole survivor who utilized a domestic violence shelter. While it is not known whether trans survivors frequent shelters as a common resource, significant improvements to many spaces could serve to reach more trans and other gender-nonconforming victims. As a rigidly gendered space, shelters have historically been constructed around the needs of ciswomen. While this is not inherently problematic, as ciswomen face distinct types of intimate partner violence like intimate terrorism that may make them more likely to need shelter, spaces that do not actively benefit from gender segregation should be reconsidered. Anna's experience with the shelter she accessed exemplifies some of the central concerns for trans survivors. Being misgendered or made to feel like they are the cause of disruption may keep many trans survivors away from shelters.

Importantly, the most recent version of the Violence Against Women Act (VAWA) mandates that shelter services receiving VAWA funds cannot discriminate on the basis of sex, gender identity, and/or sexual orientation among protected statuses. Gender segregation is permitted only when it is demonstrated that doing so more effectively serves survivors. This means that VAWA-funded shelters must already be trans-inclusive. Despite this, many trans survivors may experience hostility or illegal rejection from shelters. Given the increasingly volatile political climate, the future of VAWA in general has been jeopardized. Since VAWA is tied to larger federal budget battles, the law expired as a result of the partial government shutdown that began in late December 2018.[28] The National Center for Transgender Equality provides a resource on "Knowing Your Rights" as a trans survivor of intimate partner, sexual, or stalking violence that offers resources to victims who may be experiencing shelter discrimination.[29] Since shelters often work in collaboration with law enforcement and are staffed by mental health professionals, the aforementioned reforms for training are just as relevant for domestic violence program staff.

The Queer Response

Todd was the only survivor I interviewed who currently lived in a community in which I had previously lived for several years, although we did not have any mutual friends. Like other survivors, he regularly mentioned how others perceived the violence; he spoke of his friends and other acquaintances in the small and tight-knit LGBTQ community: "I haven't really felt like I was able to talk about it with anyone specifically because I felt like my experiences would be, I guess not validated. Like, I have had other experiences with abuse and I have always found that I am most afraid of other people just telling me it's not true because it's hard enough to just accept it anyway and I am not really sure if anyone knows about it but definitely . . . I feel pretty isolated from a large part of the community."

Holistically, the movement toward a trans-inclusive approach to intimate partner violence starts within our queer community, as friends, chosen family members, community members, activists, and scholars. The call to end violence requires the interrogation of normative politics that have suggested a one-size-fits-all approach to social justice. For too long, trans voices have been undermined in the mainstream gay and lesbian movement, excluded from dominant feminist thought, and forced to the margins of antiracist progress. As more people transgress the boundaries of gender and live their most authentic truths, the queer response must be to disrupt business as usual. Echoing the call of Creative Interventions, community accountability starts with the recognition that violence among and against LGBTQ people is not an individual problem but rather a systemic one that affects all of us linked by a shared experience. As Sam wrote, "I feel like lots of times we talk about abuse as an individual experience, but I think that in many situations—including mine—it is a community experience, and we need to look at how it impacts not just the individuals involved but the people that love them, live with them, etc. . . . . I feel like I don't really know how to navigate these complicated realities." Expanding the focus of responsibility and blame from a sole offender to the community takes us all to task, the task to acknowledge that too often the community has ignored or perpetuated these forms of violence, marginalizing or silencing the voices of the most marginalized.

ACKNOWLEDGMENTS

This book is the product of years' worth of mentoring, love, and support from many people. First, I'd like to thank the survivors of intimate partner violence who took time out of their busy lives to talk or write to a total stranger about their most personal stories. Without their contributions, none of the insights at the core of this book would have been possible. Our conversations will always remain with me, and I hope they continue to make an impact on how readers think about this form of abuse.

Over the years I've been fortunate enough to receive some of the best scholarly and personal mentoring. The journey began with my first undergraduate violence against women course with professor Gay Cutchin at Virginia Commonwealth University, who first inspired me to pursue my interests in same-gender intimate partner violence. That course connected me to other students and organizations doing antiviolence, social justice work that changed my life forever. It was during my first two years of graduate school that Dr. Sarah Jane Brubaker motivated me to work more closely with these organizations and challenged me to anchor my scholarship within the community. At the University of Central Florida, Dr. Jana Jasinski quickly picked up on my desire to engage in community-based scholarship and pushed my work to the next level. Her close mentoring, attention to detail, and personal encouragement for my ideas led me to the development of the central data for this book. I must thank Drs. Heili Pals, Liz Grauerholz, and Libby Mustaine, all of whom contributed to many aspects of my development as a scholar. The identity work background that so heavily influenced how I interpreted the data in this book was inspired by my then coauthor, Dr. Amanda Koontz, who so eagerly taught me the immense relevancy of this subfield to understanding transgender intimate partner violence.

I have had continued fortune in receiving exceptional mentorship from my colleagues at Framingham State University. Drs. Virginia Rutter, Vin Ferraro, Patricia Sánchez-Connally, Sue Dargan, Ben Alberti, and Beth Whalley, among many others, have all supported so many aspects of this project and my overall work life. Whether you provided feedback, support for course releases, research strategies, and so much more, I am thankful to you all. I am thankful to Ilene Kalish at NYU Press for her enthusiastic support of this project. I'm paraphrasing here, but Ilene told me early on in this process that "good books aren't written, they're rewritten and rewritten." A similar sentiment was echoed by my amazing colleagues, neighbors, friends, and writing coaches Drs. Sandy Hartwiger and Belinda Walzer, who were instrumental in the development of my writing for this project. I am thankful to these folks and the anonymous peer reviewers who all contributed to the improvement of my work.

I am eternally grateful for the support of my loving husband (Brien Sink) who was and still is with me every single day to hear out my ideas, problems, and feelings. His contagious wit, endless compassion, and clever thinking have gotten me through many struggles. Like him, I couldn't ask for more a supportive father- and mother-in-law (Joe and Tona Sink), who are always eager to hear about my work and cheer me on. I am thankful to all of my friends and my broader scholarly community for distracting me when it was much needed but also giving me the clarity I needed moving forward. Finally, I wouldn't be here without two great parents (Lizbeth and Luciano) who instilled an endless curiosity that guides me through to this day. Many thanks to my brother and sister-in-law (Emanuel and Yhanni) and sister ("Lizzy"), Tití Vanessa and Jose, and Tío Harry and Margaret, all of whom have been major sources of love and support.

Obtaining a sample of transgender-identified survivors of intimate partner violence was a major methodological challenge. After working a few years in antiviolence organizations and programs that focused on LGBTQ populations, I did, however, have a significant advantage going into this endeavor. My strategy for recruitment involved reaching out to some of my existing contacts while branching out to new ones. I primarily relied on e-mails and social media to spread the word about the study. On social media, I created and paid for advertisements on Facebook and shared images of the study call. For the duration of recruitment, I also created a Facebook page for the study. Various LGBTQ and domestic violence organizations circulated my study call and contact information via e-mail listservs and printed and electronic flyers. Whenever I got the chance, I handed out flyers at LGBTQ nonprofits and businesses.

During the early stages of recruitment, I was fortunate enough to reach a member of the Trans Latin@ Coalition who agreed to meet with me to discuss my plans. In this meeting, I was able to discuss the scope of the project and ways to improve my outreach. I received invaluable feedback on my line of questioning, how to maximize a potential sample, and overall how to approach my interactions in the best way possible.

ETHICS

Securing a sample of transgender survivors of intimate partner violence came with a host of ethical concerns. These concerns revolved around how to market the study, how to approach questioning in a way that would avoid triggering traumatic memories, and the storing of the data. As previously mentioned, a flyer that circulated via e-mail, social media, and LGBTQ events/organizations was a primary recruitment tool. The top of the flyer stated the name of the study: "Transgender Intimate Partner Violence and Abuse Study." I wanted the purpose of the study to be clear and up-front. Underneath the study name was an image of a transgender pride symbol. My hope was to communicate that the study was trans-affirmative and that the central focus was not about questioning participants' gender identity or expression. Two questions were placed directly below the trans pride symbol: "Do you identify as transgender?" and "Have you ever experienced violence or abuse by an intimate or romantic partner?" I wanted to reach those who *had* experienced intimate partner violence in the past but were not currently in abusive relationships. The description of the study further required a "yes" response to those two questions and required that potential participants be at least eighteen years of age. The call listed five potential options for interview format: in person, by phone, via online chat, by Skype, or through an online questionnaire version of the interview. The flyer advertised my e-mail address and cell phone number and listed two potential locations for in-person interviews.

The study proposal was reviewed by the institutional review board (IRB) of the University of Central Florida and was found exempt from regulation. Those who viewed the study call self-selected to participate in research that would require them to volunteer whatever details about their personal life and experience with abuse they felt comfortable sharing. Before each interview began, I provided an electronic copy of the consent form. The IRB did not require that these be signed before interviewing. The consent form reiterated the purpose of the study and what was being asked of the participants. Further, the consent form stated, "Some of the questions in this survey require you reflect upon previous experiences with violence. You are not required to finish the survey or answer every question. If at any point you feel uncomfortable or distressed you may exit the survey." Additionally, I provided a list of trans-inclusive domestic and sexual violence resources including local and national hotlines. At the beginning of each interview, I reviewed the purpose of the study and reminded participants that they could end the interview at any time or pass on any question that was asked. Participants knew ahead of time, via the consent form, that the interviews would be audio-recorded. After these interviews were transcribed from the audio recording, the audio file itself was deleted. Interview data and free-write questionnaire responses were stored on a password-protected USB drive.

It was impossible to avoid a line of questioning that would prompt the recall of traumatic experiences. As a result, I ensured that participants knew that I had competent resources to direct them toward, and the aforementioned consent form listed these options. I decided that after initial introductions and background discussions simply asking the respondents very openly to share their story (or stories) that made them reach out would give them control on where to start and what to include. I hope that this made participants feel like they had the reins at all times and were free to tell the story they wanted to.

Initially, I had proposed that in-depth interviews be semistructured. While loosely structured, these questions were broad and open, allowing for the participant to speak more freely. The follow-up questions listed were there as ideas to further the conversation if needed. After the first couple of interviews, I found the best results when I let participants speak more openly, with less prescribed probes, simply using follow-up questions that emerged from their stories. Essentially, the probing questions that emerged more naturally related to the stories they were actively telling and served to gather richer detail on the directions they were taking. Below is the original structure of my inquiry and a sample of the types of questions I asked respondents.

PART I: PARTICIPANT BACKGROUND
1. Could you tell me a little bit about yourself . . . ?
    a. *Potential prompts*
        i. Where you're from or grew up?
        ii. What is your racial or ethnic background?
        iii. How old are you?
2. How would you describe your gender identity and sexual orientation?
3. Could you describe your experiences with transitioning? How did that play out in your life?

PART II: RELATIONSHIPS
1. How would you describe your relationship status now? Are you seeing / dating someone?
    a. *Potential prompts*
        i. What do you consider "seeing" or "dating"?
        ii. Are you currently living together?
        iii. How long have you been together?

PART III: INTIMATE PARTNER VIOLENCE, AND ABUSE

1. As I mentioned a little earlier, the central aspect of this study is focused on experiences with intimate partner violence; have you experienced some form of violence or abuse by an intimate or romantic partner . . . ? Could you please share your story with me?
   a. *Potential Probes*
      i. What was the sexual orientation and gender identity of your abuser?
      ii. Were you of the same racial or ethnic background?
      iii. Had you transitioned before or after this began?
2. Do you think transitioning made it more difficult for you?
3. Did you think transitioning or trans-status played any role in your abuse?
      i. How long did the abuse last? Are you still with this person?
4. Do you see yourself as a victim? Why / why not?

PART IV: HELP-SEEKING

1. (If still with abuser) Have you ever thought about leaving the relationship? Why / why not?
2. (If not with abuser) At what point did you decide to leave? Or at what point did the abuser leave (if abuser left and not the participant)? What did you do? What were those experiences like?
   a. *Potential probes*:
      i. Where did you go for help? Was that/were they helpful to you? Why / why not?
      ii. Did you ever need to call the police or seek legal help? If yes, how did that process go?

PART V: CLOSING

1. Is there anything else that you wanted to talk about that we didn't get a chance to address?

Those who opted to free-write their stories anonymously did so via a Qualtrics survey link. The following open-ended questions were asked of those participants:

1. How would you describe your racial and/or ethnic background? Where are you from?

2. What is your age?

3. How would you describe your gender identity and sexual orientation?

4. If this applies, could you describe your experiences with transitioning? How did that play out in your life?

5. How would you describe your relationship status now? Are you seeing / dating someone?
   a. Describe the living situation with your partner. How long have you been together?

6. As mentioned earlier, the central aspect of this study is focused on experiences with intimate partner violence; have you experienced some form of violence or abuse by an intimate or romantic partner . . . ? Could you please share your story with me?

7. How would you describe the race, gender, and sexual orientation of the abuser?

8. If this applies, had you transitioned before or after the abuse began?
   a. Do you think transitioning or trans-status played any role in your abuse?

9. How long did the abuse last? Are you still with this person?
   a. Do you think of yourself as a victim? Why or why not?

10. (If still with abuser) Have you ever thought about leaving the relationship? Why / why not? (If not with abuser) At what point did you decide to leave? Or at what point did the abuser leave (if abuser left and not you)? What did you do? What were those experiences like?

11. Where did you go for help? Was that/were they helpful to you? Why / why not? Did you ever need to call the police or seek legal help? If yes, how did that process go?

12. Is there anything else that you wanted to talk about that we didn't get a chance to address? Use this space to free write any other aspect of your story that was not addressed by the questions.

During the interviews, some participants paused at difficult moments in their stories. I would also ask participants if they needed a break when I sensed some emotion or difficulty. While all interviewees finished their story, the length of discussion and pace were ultimately set by their telling of the account. Retelling stories of survival can retraumatize survivors or trigger posttraumatic stress disorder, among other mental health consequences of having endured intimate partner violence. Since none of these interviews were conducted in person, I did not have bodily or nonverbal cues to rely on. Instead, I had to rely on my subjective interpretation of the distress levels in their voice or the manner in which the story was told. To my knowledge, no participant cried on the phone or had a disruptive emotional moment. Instead, I more commonly heard quivers in their voice or pauses and deep breaths. In those moments, I made sure to ask if we could continue or if we needed a break.

Recording traumatic accounts also took a toll on me as the researcher. As an empathetic listener and someone vested in the LGBTQ community and the advancement of survivors' needs, I struggled to have these conversations. It was a bit of an isolating experience. Not only was I the only one listening to the accounts as they were being told, but I also had to listen to the recordings many, many times before deleting the original audio files. In addition to listening to their voices again and again, I also typed out their words. I felt a bit helpless and also deeply disturbed by the stories. An instinctual reaction sometimes is to want to help someone or at least find someone or something helpful for them. However, I wasn't in any capacity (beyond sharing resources on the consent form) to help out in a more substantial way. Many of these survivors were already resilient and thriving; they all had left their abusers and were seemingly in varying stages of recovery. For my own well-being, I took many breaks away from transcription and spent more time outdoors. Sometimes I would vent to my dissertation advisor, husband, and some fellow researchers about the injustices survivors faced while ensuring to never expose identifiable details. Ultimately, I found the process to be fulfilling; it was important to me to share the accounts and findings with other scholars and the broader community.

DATA ANALYSIS

In the first chapter, I mentioned that I utilized a modified grounded theory approach to data collection. Grounded theory was initially developed by Glaser and Strauss as a "systematic, inductive, and comparative approach for conducting inquiry for the purpose of constructing theory."[1] Through this approach, I moved from the specific to the more general as I continuously engaged in the analysis of the data. Charmaz explains that grounded theorists study their "early data and begin to separate, sort, and synthesize these data through qualitative coding."[2] This coding process attempts to summarize parts of the data utilizing a researcher-defined label that constructs emerging categories. These codes ultimately represent the meanings behind stories of violence. The coding scheme then directs the analytical framework that serves as the foundation for further analysis. Together, these codes were analytically integrated into categories that emerged through repeated close looks at the data and defining what they meant. I then merged these categories into concepts that Corbin and Strauss explain "represent an analyst's impressionistic understandings of what is being described in the experiences, spoken words, actions, interactions, problems and issues expressed by participants."[3]

While this grounded method was the overarching analytic strategy I employed, I acknowledge that I approached the analyses with a solid understanding of the intimate partner violence literature and theoretical frameworks. My perspectives were influenced by theories of violence and queer, feminist, and identity perspectives in criminology and sociology. This background informed my curiosities and some of my questions and analyses of the data. For example, as previously discussed, prominent aspects of the literature involve understandings of the dynamics of abuse, help-seeking behaviors, and victim identities. This subsequently shaped some of my own curiosities as they related to the trans experience. However, while prior knowledge enters the realm of analyses, I worked actively to remain open to new directions and stayed close to the data. Through this process, I avoided "imposing a forced framework" and allowed for the opportunity for emerging directions in the data.[4]

CODING STRATEGY

All interviews were transcribed and stored in a text file format. Further, the five online questionnaires were also downloaded as text files. To begin, I utilized an initial line-by-line coding technique that assigned a code to each line of data. Examples of my early codes include "sexual violence," "transition attack," "genderism," "identity manipulation," and "informal help." These initial codes were open and useful in moving through the data quickly while remaining open and close to the data; codes were kept short, simple, and precise. Line-by-line coding effectively fueled the discovery of implicit and explicit concerns that survivors raised during the interview process. Utilizing this strategy familiarized me with the data and started the process of illuminating themes, patterns, and particular points of interest in participants' accounts. As Charmaz explains, "Line-by-line coding gives you leads to pursue."[5] This was particularly important in the initial stages of analysis as I sought to understand the meanings behind reported experiences. Crucial to the development of grounded analyses are analytic memos. After each interview was conducted or each questionnaire was read, I utilized these analytic memos as a form of journaling my internal discussion about what I was hearing and reading. Throughout my brief memos, I thought about what was being done and why and challenged potential assumptions.

For this initial wave of coding and memoing, interviews and online questionnaires were analyzed separately to examine any potential differences in the accounts as they were collected through different methods. The only significant difference between interviews and online questionnaires was that interviews were far more detailed. I don't want to understate the fact that interviews revealed much more nuance to the stories. The ability to follow-up on points made and the fact that it's more efficient to talk through than it is to write out experiences contributed to the differences in quality. The content of the accounts did not differ in any other way, and therefore all accounts were analyzed as one body for the second wave of analyses.

After initial line-by-line coding, I progressed to focused coding. In this second wave of coding I sifted through the data for the most frequent or significant codes found in the initial line-by-line stage. Through this process, the initial open codes were read through and conceptually arranged into emerging categories. Throughout this process, new codes were compared with existing codes to examine how they related to each other or if unexpected findings emerged. Comparing data to data helped the development of focused codes and ultimately refined the larger concepts they define. Here, my analytic memos became essential as they served as a focused "code and category-generating method."[6] The linking of codes and categories within the stories became systematically integrated and built the theoretical concepts that explained or described the patterns of abuse, meanings, and outcomes.

LIMITATIONS

Every study contains a range of limitations to its design, analysis, and implications. First, while the patterns of abuse that are highlighted throughout the book offer a significant glimpse into the dynamics of violence experienced by trans survivors, they are not generalizable to the entire transgender community and were offered with a reliance on participant memory. While generalizability was never a goal of this study, it should be mentioned that the themes represent findings from a sample of eighteen participants who were not randomly selected. The findings provide strong evidence and support for these themes but are not necessarily representative of all or even most experiences with intimate partner violence in the transgender community. Additionally, by chance, most participants were in very similar stages of transition, with few who had started transitioning well before the abusive relationship. Every participant had undergone some form of hormone therapy, transition care, or other medical interventions, which is not necessarily representative of all transgender experiences. Many trans-identified, gender-nonconforming, and gender-nonbinary individuals do not seek medical interventions either by choice or because they cannot afford the care.

While rigorous recruitment techniques were utilized to maximize the size and diversity of the sample, it was rather limited in both aspects. Given the constraints of conducting a study of this nature, the diversity of the sample was still robust, with seven of the eighteen participants identifying as nonwhite. However, it is apparent that this may not have been sufficient, as few (but significant) differences emerged between white respondents and those of color. This is not to declare that differences must necessarily exist, but it does call into question whether the sample was diverse enough to provide a stronger picture of these narratives.

The method in which the data were collected may also present several limitations. As I made the decision to provide both a personal interview option and an online free-write questionnaire, the latter option resulted in significantly shorter accounts. I noted that the online free-write responses were significantly less detailed and thus limited the ability to gather richer data. However, the accounts differed not in content but in length and detail. Providing this more anonymous method of participation allowed for a greater number of respondents to feel comfortable in sharing their stories.

While there is really no specific number that is "enough" for qualitative research, a sample of eighteen is quite small. A couple of important methodological considerations justify the sample size. First, the study required that participants identify as both transgender and a survivor of intimate partner violence, culling those with experiences with a crime (intimate partner violence) from an already small sector of the population. As previously mentioned, part of the reason transgender accounts have been largely left out of studies on intimate partner violence is because of the difficulty in recruiting samples. Second, and more important, my goal was to achieve data saturation. This means that once I began to hear similar patterns and developed no new themes or codes in the analysis, I had enough information to make grounded claims. Scholars have argued that for some studies, data saturation can be reached in as few as six participants.[7] Just as a larger sample size does not guarantee rich, in-depth data, a smaller sample size does not necessarily mean there is not enough there to arrive at definitive conclusions.

Table A.1 Participant Characteristics

Description of Sample

Pseudonym	Gender Identity*	Race/Ethnicity	Age
Todd	Transmasculine/genderqueer	White	22
Jessica	Transwoman	White	49
Brittany	Transwoman	White	34
Anna	MTF transgender	Latina	30
Laura	Transwoman	Black	33
Tom	Transman	Black	24
David	FTM transgender	White	23
Joe	Transgender male	White/Latino	18
Rebecca	Transwoman	Black	38
Chris	Transfeminine/genderqueer	White	22
John	FTM, transmale	Multiracial/Latino	29
Fatima	Transwoman	Latina	30
Audrey	Transfemale	White	42
Jim	FTM transgender	White	21
Sam	Transgender stone butch	White	38
Casey	Genderqueer	White	32
William	Male, transmale	White	35
Owen	Transsexual man	Latino	19

*Transmasculine and transfeminine identities fall more masculine or more feminine of center on the gender spectrum; genderqueer identities are fluid or overlap and may include gender-nonbinary identities. Stone butch typically describes a hypermasculine lesbian woman; this respondent also identifies as transgender (Feinberg, *Trans Liberation*).

Reflexive statements allow space for researchers to discuss the interplay between the subject, the investigator, and the data. While objectivity and neutrality are often the standard for positivist research, all inquiry is subjective and filtered through the human experience. Here I take time to discuss my role as researcher in the broader context of this topic. Additionally, I discuss some of the strategies I employed throughout this exploration not only to improve the quality of the data but also to ensure that participants felt comfortable and empowered to share their stories.

While adhering to a modified grounded approach (see Appendix A), I recognize that any form of research in which one is interpreting and constructing the meanings behind the lived experiences of others requires reflection on the part of the researcher. Before, during, and after conducting interviews and analyses, I needed to continuously stay mindful of how my own experiences and standpoints may frame conversations and findings. By remaining honest and open about myself as a researcher, I made a concerted effort to avoid assumptions. In chapter 1, I discussed how I arrived at this topic after studying violence and working with LGBTQ advocacy organizations. As I am a Puerto Rican and gay, queer-identified man, the topics of social justice were not merely academic or activist but also personal. I noted in the first chapter that in my studies and advocacy, I continued to notice the absence of transgender community members and a lack of information on how the issues of violence we were addressing affected folks who were gender-nonconforming. In one experience that jump-started this idea, I partnered with local agencies in gathering data on LGBTQ and experiences with same-gender intimate partner violence. While we made a rigorous effort to obtain a diverse sample, we were able to reach only eight transgender respondents over the course of several months, despite reaching hundreds of cisgender LGBQ folks. After several years of this glaring absence of trans experiences and voices in both my own work and the academic literature on intimate partner violence, I arrived at the decision to undertake this exploration.

While I have a strong personal connection to the advancement and advocacy of issues affecting the transgender community, I do not identify as transgender. For some researchers and activists, this may be seen as a weakness. Further, some activists may also feel that it is not the place for cisgender academics to make subjects out of the transgender community. These sentiments are at least partially rooted in the thought that those without this standpoint or lived experience cannot adequately interpret, construct meaning of, or understand secondhand accounts. As a queer brown man, I do empathize with the notion that "outside" researchers may not be best at constructing knowledge on otherwise marginalized or underrepresented communities. However, I argue that researchers who do not have similar or identical experiences to subjects offer many useful perspectives in conjunction with work that comes from those more closely linked to the problem in a personal way. When I approached this project, I did so with the intention of staying close to the voices featured and advancing the development of knowledge on violence as experienced by trans folks. It is my hope that I made clear the purpose of this project was not to make the transgender community the center of curiosity but rather to expand the knowledge on intimate partner violence to include those voices that have been otherwise largely excluded from the conversation. The project was rooted in a social justice perspective that aimed to string together prominent themes in intimate partner violence victimization and provide deeper context into the unique realities faced by the transgender community. It is my firm belief that social research is strengthened by the incorporation of diverse perspectives regardless of the identities of the researcher(s) and the subject(s).

Finally, establishing rapport with participants is a common challenge in social research projects. In particular, the current project presented unique challenges as it dealt with highly sensitive topics of violent victimization and gender identity. A common interview strategy is to engage in warm-up conversations that initially establishes some kind of trust between the researcher and the participant. I found it particularly helpful to start a conversation about how the participant found out about the study. Because the study was marketed through outlets that serve the trans community, whether they be private businesses or social services, I could first engage participants in conversations about their community resources. I believe that these informal conversations helped establish that I was familiar with the needs and services of the transgender community or at the very least that I cared about the over- all well-being of the community. After discussing the mandatory con- sent information and providing participants with resources, another small portion of the conversation was devoted to their experiences with coming out as trans and the transition process. In these initial con- versations, while not the focal point of this study, participants spent some time openly describing their gender identities as well as their de- velopment and processes in transition. Through these conversations, I learned more from the participants about what terminologies or lan- guage to use when referencing them, their abuser, or some other part of their life and identity.

Ultimately, the goal was to remain open in our conversations and avoid making any rushed assumptions or filtering the discussion through my own experiences and knowledge. I approached the participants' nar- ratives grounded and open to finding the most salient themes in their experiences. By staying close to the data, through constant comparisons and conversations with myself on how I was piecing together this larger story, I was best able to construct descriptions, processes, and meanings according to the participants' own words. The data here were analyzed multiple times at different stages. The first rounds of analyses occurred earlier in my career. Importantly, I went back to the data again for the publication of two articles on identity work and help-seeking, respec- tively. Parts of those works are featured in this book (chapters 4 and 5): Xavier L. Guadalupe-Diaz and Amanda Koontz Anthony, "Discrediting Identity Work: Understandings of Intimate Partner Violence by Trans- gender Survivors," *Deviant Behavior* 38, no. 1 (2017): 1–16 and Xavier L. Guadalupe-Diaz and Jana Jasinski, "'I Wasn't a Priority, I Wasn't a Vic- tim': Challenges in Help Seeking for Transgender Survivors of Intimate Partner Violence," *Violence Against Women* 23, no. 6 (2017): 772–792. My coauthor Amanda Koontz was central in developing my identity per- spective as it related to my early analyses relevant to that chapter.

NOTES

CHAPTER 1. INTIMATE PARTNER VIOLENCE OUTSIDE THE BINARY

1 The bill is "an act to provide for single-sex multiple occupancy bathroom and changing facilities in schools and public agencies and to create statewide consistency in regulation of employment and public accommodations." The act prohibits transgender individuals from utilizing public accommodations of the gender they identify with. A binary refers to a system of two categories; in the case of the gender binary, it means male and female.

2 Bornstein et al., "Understanding the Experiences"; Feinberg, *Trans Liberation.*

3 Schilt and Westbrook, "Doing Gender, Doing Heteronormativity."

4 Centers for Disease Control and Prevention, "Violence Prevention."

5 Smith et al., "National Intimate Partner and Sexual Violence Survey (NISVS)."

6 Kimmel, "'Gender Symmetry' in Domestic Violence."

7 Campbell, "Health Consequences of Intimate Partner Violence."

8 Petrosky et al., "Racial and Ethnic Differences."

9 American Psychological Association, "Intimate Partner Violence Facts & Resources."

10 Girshick, *Woman-to-Woman Sexual Violence,* 7.

11 Ristock, *Intimate Partner Violence in LGBTQ Lives.*

12 NCAVP, "Lesbian, Gay, Bisexual, Transgender, Queer, and HIV-Affected Intimate Partner Violence in 2015."

13 Martin and Ruble, "Patterns of Gender Development."

14 Johnson, *Typology of Domestic Violence.*

15 Bilodeau, "Genderism," ii.

16 Bilodeau, "Genderism."

17 Hill and Willoughby, "Development and Validation."

18 Tebbe, Moradi, and Ege, "Revised and Abbreviated Forms."

19 Martin, *Battered Wives*; Dobash and Dobash, *Violence Against Wives*; Dobash et al., "Myth of Sexual Symmetry."

20 Martin, *Battered Wives,* xxi.

21 Hart, "Lesbian Battering"; Island and Letellier, *Men Who Beat the Men Who Love Them.*

22 Messinger, *LGBTQ Intimate Partner Violence.*

23 Walters, Chen, and Breiding, "National Intimate Partner and Sexual Violence Survey (NISVS)."

24 Courvant and Cook-Daniels, "Trans and Intersex Survivors of Domestic Violence."

25 National Coalition of Anti-Violence Programs (NCAVP), "Lesbian, Gay, Bisexual, Transgender, Queer, and HIV-Affected Intimate Partner Violence in 2011."

26 NCAVP, "Media Release."

27 Brown and Herman, "Intimate Partner Violence and Sexual Abuse among LGBTQ People."

28 Dobash and Dobash, *Violence Against Wives.*

29 Collins, *Black Feminist Thought.*

30 Crenshaw, "Mapping the Margins."

31 Potter, *Intersectionality and Criminology*, 3.

32 Moyer, "Caitlyn Jenner."

33 *Advocate*, "Ted Cruz Responds to Caitlyn Jenner."

34 Grinberg, "Caitlyn Jenner Doesn't Regret Voting for Trump."

35 Bograd, "Strengthening Domestic Violence Theories."

36 Bograd, "Strengthening Domestic Violence Theories," 276.

37 Bograd, "Strengthening Domestic Violence Theories," 29.

38 Island and Letellier, *Men Who Beat the Men Who Love Them*, 2.

39 Merrill, "Ruling the Exceptions."

40 Erbaugh, "Queering Approaches to Intimate Partner Violence."

41 Browne and Nash, "Queer Methods and Methodologies," 4.

42 West and Zimmerman, "Doing Gender."

43 Anderson, "Theorizing Gender in Intimate Partner Violence Research," 856.

44 Foucault, *Order of Things.*

45 Milovanovic, *Primer in the Sociology of Law.*

46 Foucault, *Power/Knowledge.*

47 Butler, *Gender Trouble.*

48 Butler, *Gender Trouble*, xv.

49 Jeffreys, *Unpacking Queer Politics.*

50 Grosz, *Volatile Bodies.*

51 Greer, *Whole Woman*; Grosz, *Volatile Bodies.*

52 Johnson, "Being Transsexual," 606.

53 Johnson, "Being Transsexual," 613–615.

54 Bernard, Snipes, and Gerould, *Vold's Theoretical Criminology*, 278.

55 Arrigo and Bernard, "Postmodern Criminology," 44.

56 Davis and Glass, "Reframing the Heteronormative Constructions," 18.

57 Arrigo and Bernard, "Postmodern Criminology," 42.

58 Peterson and Panfil, *Handbook of LGBT Communities, Crime, and Justice.*

59 Panfil, *Gang's All Queer.*

60 Buist and Lenning, *Queer Criminology*; Ball, "Queer Criminology."

61 Herman, "Interactionist Research Methods," 93.

62 Browne and Nash, "Queer Methods and Methodologies."

63 Ezzy, *Qualitative Research*, 22.

64 See Table A.1 in Appendix A for gender identity descriptions.

CHAPTER 2. THE CONTEXTS OF ABUSE FOR TRANSGENDER SURVIVORS

1 Ard and Makadon, "Addressing Intimate Partner Violence."
2 McClennen, "Domestic Violence between Same-Gender Partners"; Guadalupe-Diaz and Yglesias, "'Who's Protected?'"; Burke and Follingstad, "Violence in Lesbian and Gay Relationships."
3 Bornstein et al., "Understanding the Experiences," 163.
4 Hobson, *Are All the Women Still White?*
5 Barrett and Sheridan, "Partner Violence in Transgender Communities."
6 Walker, "Investigating Trans People's Vulnerabilities."
7 Lombardi et al., "Gender Violence."
8 Girshick, *Woman-to-Woman Sexual Violence.*
9 Davis, *Contesting Intersex.*
10 Connell, *Gender and Power.*
11 T is short for testosterone, which is typically taken as a hormonal supplement for those who seek more masculine physical markers.
12 GLAAD, "New Report Reveals Rampant Discrimination."
13 GLAAD, "End Healthcare Discrimination."
14 Kodjak, "Trump Admin Will Protect Health Workers."
15 I assume that David's use of "gay" here was a catchall for non-heterosexuals.
16 Vogue and Lee, "Meet Gavin Grimm."
17 Garcia, "Colorado's Transgender Students."
18 Balingit, "Education Department No Longer Investigating."
19 Human Rights Campaign, "Discrimination Against Transgender Workers."
20 Greenwood, "Sessions Reverses DOJ Policy."
21 Vogue and Cohen, "Supreme Court Allows Transgender Military Ban."
22 Movement Advancement Project and Center for American Progress, "Paying an Unfair Price."
23 "Fish" is commonly used as an adjective in the drag and queer scene to describe someone who passes as a ciswoman. Someone who is "fish" has a very effeminate and womanly presentation.
24 National Center for Transgender Equality, "National Transgender Discrimination Survey."
25 National Center for Transgender Equality, "Housing & Homelessness."
26 Lewis et al., "Stressors for Gay Men and Lesbians."
27 Lewis et al., "Minority Stress," 249.
28 Balsam and Szymanski, "Relationship Quality and Domestic Violence."
29 US Department of Justice, "Matthew Shepard and James Byrd, Jr."
30 O'Hara, "Trans Women of Color."
31 *Out*, "7 Trans Women of Color Have Been Murdered in 2017."
32 Flores, "Attitudes toward Transgender Rights."
33 Norton and Herek, "Heterosexuals' Attitudes toward Transgender People."

34 Lorde, "Learning from the 60s," 136.

35 GLAAD, "Honoring Known Cases."

36 Federal Bureau of Investigation (FBI), "About Hate Crime Statistics 2015." According to FBI reports, hate-motivated crimes based on gender identity increased from 31 incidents in 2013 to 114 in 2015. Arguably, the recording of gender-identity-based hate crimes has improved, which may have resulted in the documented increase.

37 Walker, "Here Are Some of Mike Pence's Most Controversial Stances."

38 Wierks, "Indiana Schools."

39 Cis-heteropatriarchy characterizes a culture in which genderism, heteronormativity, and patriarchy construct rigid notions of gender and sexuality, effectively marginalizing gender diversity beyond the binary and subjugating women or feminine people.

40 Essence, "Laverne Cox Explains."

41 Malo, "In First, U.S. Man Sentenced for Transgender Hate Crime."

42 Phillips, "10 Things to Know"; Stack, "U.S. Hate Crime Law."

43 Wilson, "US Prison Population Falling."

44 Meisner, "Federal Charges Net Dozens." Prior to the Trump administration, gangs like the Latin Kings had been unraveling due in part to large federal crackdowns.

45 Saavedra, "Latin Kings Member Gets 50 Years."

46 Neoliberalism refers to a broader market, economic, and political structure that emphasizes individual responsibility, reductions in social safety nets, and deregulated capitalism.

47 Meyer, "Resisting Hate Crime Discourse."

48 Spade, *Normal Life.*

CHAPTER 3. "NO MAN IS GOING TO SEE YOU AS A WOMAN"

1 A drag mother typically denotes an individual performer who has started a "drag family" or a close-knit group of drag performers.

2 Anna was saving for gender confirmation surgery.

3 Referring to the repeat and forced sex work and rape.

4 Courvant and Cook-Daniels, "Trans and Intersex Survivors of Domestic Violence"; Munson and Cook-Daniels, "Transgender/SOFFA."

5 Brown, "Holding Tensions of Victimization and Perpetration," 162.

6 Bockting, Robinson, and Rosser, "Transgender HIV Prevention."

7 National Coalition of Anti-Violence Programs (NCAVP), "Hate Violence Against Transgender Communities."

8 NCAVP, "Our Reports."

9 Sharpe, "Criminalising Sexual Intimacy."

10 Sharpe, "Criminalising Sexual Intimacy."

11 Spade, *Normal Life.*

12 Stotzer, "Violence Against Transgender People."

13 Loseke, "Study of Identity."

14 Schilt and Westbrook, "Doing Gender, Doing Heteronormativity."

15 Iantaffi and Bockting, "Views from Both Sides of the Bridge?"

16 Iantaffi and Bockting, "Views from Both Sides of the Bridge?"

17 "Zie" is a gender-neutral pronoun used in place of she or he.

18 OkCupid is an online dating site.

19 PlentyOfFish is an online dating site that is mainly popular in Canada but is used in the United States as well.

20 Breiding et al., "Intimate Partner Violence Surveillance," 15.

21 Follingstad and Edmundson, "Is Psychological Abuse Reciprocal in Intimate Relationships?"

22 NCAVP, "Lesbian, Gay, Bisexual, Transgender, Queer, and HIV-Affected Intimate Partner Violence in 2016."

23 Sims, "Invisible Wounds, Invisible Abuse."

24 Hannem, Langan, and Stewart, "'Every Couple Has Their Fights. . . .'"

25 Messinger, *LGBTQ Intimate Partner Violence.*

26 Stotzer, "Violence Against Transgender People."

27 Brittany described the relationship as open and not polyamorous. I interpret this to mean that they were not romantically involved with mutual partners but rather were sexually involved with others outside of their own dyadic relationship.

28 Bilodeau, "Genderism."

29 Munson and Cook-Daniels, "Transgender/SOFFA."

30 Brown, "Holding Tensions of Victimization and Perpetration."

CHAPTER 4. MEANINGS OF VIOLENCE

1 Edwards-Leeper, Leibowitz, and Sangganjanavanich, "Affirmative Practice with Transgender and Gender Nonconforming Youth."

2 Davis, *Beyond Trans.*

3 Budge, Adelson, and Howard, "Anxiety and Depression in Transgender Individuals."

4 Goffman, *Presentation of Self in Everyday Life.*

5 Mason-Schrock, "Transsexuals' Narrative Construction"; Schwalbe and Mason-Schrock, "Identity Work as Group Process"; Snow and Anderson, "Identity Work among the Homeless."

6 Blumer, *Symbolic Interactionism.*

7 Guadalupe-Diaz and Koontz Anthony, "Discrediting Identity Work."

8 Leisenring, "Confronting 'Victim' Discourses."

9 Weinstein and Deutschberger, "Some Dimensions of Altercasting."

10 Thoits, "Resisting the Stigma of Mental Illness."

11 Cast and Burke, "Theory of Self-Esteem."

12 Felson and Messner, "Control Motive in Intimate Partner Violence."

13 Stark, *Coercive Control.*

14 Snow and Anderson, "Identity Work among the Homeless," 1348.

15 Owens, Robinson, and Smith-Lovin, "Three Faces of Identity," 479.

16 Zhao, Grasmuck, and Martin, "Identity Construction on Facebook."

17 Perinbanayagam, *Presence of Self*, 223.

18 Crawley, Foley, and Shehan, *Gendering Bodies*.

19 Cerulo, "Identity Construction."

20 Goffman, *Presentation of Self in Everyday Life*, 4.

21 Goffman, *Presentation of Self in Everyday Life*, 4.

22 Stets and Burke, "Identity Verification."

23 Burke and Stets, "Trust and Commitment through Self-Verification."

24 Goffman, *Interaction Ritual*, 27.

25 Goffman, *Interaction Ritual*, 23–26.

26 Weinstein and Deutschberger, "Some Dimensions of Altercasting."

27 McCall and Simmons, *Identities and Interactions*.

28 Tracy, "Discourse and Identity."

29 Loseke, "Lived Realities."

30 Loseke, "Lived Realities," 231.

31 Leisenring, "'Whoa! They Could've Arrested Me!'"

32 Leisenring, "'Whoa! They Could've Arrested Me!,'" 362.

33 Cooley, *Human Nature and the Social Order*.

34 Valenta, "Immigrants' Identity Negotiations."

35 Mason-Schrock, "Transsexuals' Narrative Construction," 177.

36 Brown, "Holding Tensions of Victimization and Perpetration."

37 Valenta, "Immigrants' Identity Negotiations," 366.

38 Weinstein and Deutschberger, "Some Dimensions of Altercasting," 458.

39 Stark and Flitcraft, *Women at Risk*.

40 Allen-Collinson, "Assault on Self."

41 Ebaugh, *Becoming an Ex*.

42 Miller and Caughlin, "'We're Going to Be Survivors,'" 78.

43 Walker, "Investigating Trans People's Vulnerabilities," 119.

CHAPTER 5. PROCESSING VICTIM IDENTITY

1 Penner et al., "Aversive Racism and Medical Interactions."

2 Grant et al., "National Transgender Discrimination Survey Report on Health and Health Care."

3 Kelly, Burton, and Regan, "Beyond Victim or Survivor."

4 Tehrani, "Victim to Survivor."

5 Tehrani, "Victim to Survivor," 43.

6 Liang et al., "Theoretical Framework for Understanding Help-Seeking Processes."

7 Logan et al., "Barriers to Services."

8 Renzetti, *Violent Betrayal*.

9 McLaughlin and Rozee, "Knowledge about Heterosexual versus Lesbian Battering among Lesbians."

10 McLaughlin and Rozee, "Knowledge about Heterosexual versus Lesbian Battering among Lesbians," 44.

11 Ristock, *No More Secrets.*

12 Cruz, "'Why Doesn't He Just Leave?'"

13 Renzetti, *Violent Betrayal.*

14 Renzetti, *Violent Betrayal*, 91.

15 McClennen, "Domestic Violence between Same-Gender Partners"; Guadalupe-Diaz, "Disclosure of Same-Sex Intimate Partner Violence."

16 National Coalition of Anti-Violence Programs (NCAVP), "Lesbian, Gay, Bisexual, Transgender, Queer, and HIV-Affected Intimate Partner Violence in 2010."

17 McClennen, Summers, and Vaughan, "Gay Men's Domestic Violence."

18 Brown, "Holding Tensions of Victimization and Perpetration."

19 Erbaugh, "Queering Approaches to Intimate Partner Violence," 454.

20 National Center for Transgender Equality, "National Transgender Discrimination Survey."

21 NCAVP, "Lesbian, Gay, Bisexual, Transgender, Queer, and HIV-Affected Intimate Partner Violence in 2016."

22 Transgender Law Center, "Undocumented Trans Woman and Survivor of Domestic Violence."

23 Davis, *Beyond Trans.*

CHAPTER 6. CONCLUSION

1 Lagdon, Armour, and Stringer, "Adult Experience of Mental Health Outcomes."

2 Gelaye et al., "Childhood Abuse."

3 Mizock and Lewis, "Trauma in Transgender Populations."

4 Singh and McKleroy, "'Just Getting Out of Bed Is a Revolutionary Act.'"

5 Brown, "Holding Tensions of Victimization and Perpetration."

6 Roch, Ritchie, and Morton, "Out of Sight, Out of Mind?"

7 Walker, "Investigating Trans People's Vulnerabilities," 116.

8 Panfil, *Gang's All Queer.*

9 Myers, "Positivist Victimology."

10 Cannon, Lauve-Moon, and Buttell, "Re-theorizing Intimate Partner Violence," 681.

11 Cannon, Lauve-Moon, and Buttell, "Re-theorizing Intimate Partner Violence," 670.

12 Cannon and Buttell, "Social Construction of Roles in Intimate Partner Violence."

13 Williams Institute, "Gender-Related Measures Overview."

14 Graham et al., "Health of Lesbian, Gay, Bisexual, and Transgender People."

15 Kent, "About a Third of Americans."

16 Kent, "Nearly Four-in-Ten Americans."

17 Davis, *Beyond Trans*, 10–11.

18 National Center for Transgender Equality, "National Transgender Discrimination Survey."

19 Barrett and Sheridan, "Partner Violence in Transgender Communities."

20 Kaplan, "Basic Issues in Transgender Mental Health."

21 Cook-Daniels, "Intimate Partner Violence in Transgender Couples."

22 Stubbs, "Domestic Violence and Women's Safety."

23 Goodmark, "Should Domestic Violence Be Decriminalized."

24 Stubbs, "Domestic Violence and Women's Safety."

25 Kim, "Alternative Interventions to Violence."

26 Creative Interventions, "Toolkits."

27 Walker, "Investigating Trans People's Vulnerabilities," 116.

28 Gathright, "Violence Against Women Act Expires."

29 National Center for Transgender Equality, "Survivors of Violence."

APPENDIX A

1 Bryant and Charmaz, *Sage Handbook of Grounded Theory*.

2 Charmaz, *Constructing Grounded Theory*, 3.

3 Corbin and Strauss, *Basics of Qualitative Research*, 51.

4 Charmaz, *Constructing Grounded Theory*, 66.

5 Charmaz, *Constructing Grounded Theory*, 53.

6 Saldaña, *Coding Manual for Qualitative Researchers*, 157.

7 Guest, Bunce, and Johnson, "How Many Interviews Are Enough?"

BIBLIOGRAPHY

Advocate. "Ted Cruz Responds to Caitlyn Jenner with Transphobic Fear Mongering." May 1, 2016. www.advocate.com.

Allen-Collinson, Jacquelyn. "Assault on Self: Intimate Partner Abuse and the Contestation of Identity." *Symbolic Interaction* 34, no. 1 (2011): 108–127.

American Psychological Association. "Intimate Partner Violence Facts & Resources." 2017. www.apa.org.

Anderson, Kristin L. "Theorizing Gender in Intimate Partner Violence Research." *Sex Roles* 52, nos. 11–12 (2005): 853–865.

Ard, Kevin L., and Harvey J. Makadon. "Addressing Intimate Partner Violence in Lesbian, Gay, Bisexual, and Transgender Patients." *Journal of General Internal Medicine* 26, no. 8 (2011): 930–933.

Arrigo, Bruce A., and Thomas J. Bernard. "Postmodern Criminology in Relation to Radical and Conflict Criminology." *Critical Criminology* 8, no. 2 (1997): 39–60.

Balingit, Moriah. "Education Department No Longer Investigating Transgender Bathroom Complaints." *Washington Post*, February 12, 2018. www.washingtonpost.com.

Ball, Matthew. "Queer Criminology, Critique, and the 'Art of Not Being Governed.'" *Critical Criminology* 22, no. 1 (2014): 21–34.

Balsam, Kimberly F., and Dawn M. Szymanski. "Relationship Quality and Domestic Violence in Women's Same-Sex Relationships: The Role of Minority Stress." *Psychology of Women Quarterly* 29, no. 3 (2005): 258–269.

Barrett, Betty Jo, and Daphne Vanessa Sheridan. "Partner Violence in Transgender Communities: What Helping Professionals Need to Know." *Journal of GLBT Family Studies* 13, no. 2 (2017): 137–162.

Bernard, Thomas J., Jeffrey B. Snipes, and Alexander L. Gerould. *Vold's Theoretical Criminology*. New York: Oxford University Press, 2010.

Bilodeau, Brent Laurence. "Genderism: Transgender Students, Binary Systems and Higher Education." PhD dissertation, Michigan State University, 2007.

Blumer, Herbert. *Symbolic Interactionism*. Berkeley: University of California Press, 1986.

Bockting, Walter O., B. E. Robinson, and B. R. S. Rosser. "Transgender HIV Prevention: A Qualitative Needs Assessment." *AIDS Care* 10, no. 4 (1998): 505–525.

Bograd, Michele. "Strengthening Domestic Violence Theories: Intersections of Race, Class, Sexual Orientation, and Gender." *Journal of Marital and Family Therapy* 25, no. 3 (1999): 275–289.

———. "Strengthening Domestic Violence Theories: Intersections of Race, Class, Sexual Orientation, and Gender." In Sokoloff and Pratt, *Domestic Violence at the Margins*, 25–38.

Bornstein, Danica R., Jake Fawcett, Marianne Sullivan, Kirsten D. Senturia, and Sharyne Shiu Thornton. "Understanding the Experiences of Lesbian, Bisexual and Trans Survivors of Domestic Violence: A Qualitative Study." *Journal of Homosexuality* 51, no. 1 (2006): 159–181.

Breiding, Matthew, Kathleen C. Basile, Sharon G. Smith, Michele C. Black, and Reshma R. Mahendra. "Intimate Partner Violence Surveillance: Uniform Definitions and Recommended Data Elements. Version 2.0." Atlanta: Centers for Disease Control and Prevention, 2015.

Brown, Nicola. "Holding Tensions of Victimization and Perpetration." In Ristock, *Intimate Partner Violence in LGBTQ Lives*, 153–168.

Brown, Taylor N. T., and Jody L. Herman. "Intimate Partner Violence and Sexual Abuse among LGBTQ People: A Review of Existing Research." 2015. https://williamsinstitute.law.ucla.edu.

Browne, Kath, and Catherine Nash. "Queer Methods and Methodologies: An Introduction." In *Queer Methods and Methodologies: Intersecting Queer Theories and Social Research*, ed. Browne and Nash, 1–24. Farnham: Ashgate, 2010.

Brownmiller, Susan. *Against Our Will: Men, Women and Rape*. New York: Simon & Schuster, 1976.

Bryant, Antony, and Kathy Charmaz, eds. *The Sage Handbook of Grounded Theory*. Thousand Oaks, CA: Sage, 2007.

Budge, Stephanie L., Jill L. Adelson, and Kimberly A. S. Howard. "Anxiety and Depression in Transgender Individuals: The Roles of Transition Status, Loss, Social Support, and Coping." *Journal of Consulting and Clinical Psychology* 81, no. 3 (2013): 545–547.

Buist, Carrie, and Emily Lenning. *Queer Criminology*. Abingdon: Routledge, 2015.

Burke, Leslie K., and Diane R. Follingstad. "Violence in Lesbian and Gay Relationships: Theory, Prevalence, and Correlational Factors." *Clinical Psychology Review* 19, no. 5 (1999): 487–512.

Burke, Peter J., and Jan E. Stets. "Trust and Commitment through Self-Verification." *Social Psychology Quarterly* 62 (1999): 347–366.

Butler, Judith. *Gender Trouble: Feminism and the Subversion of Identity*. New York: Routledge, 2011.

Campbell, Jacquelyn C. "Health Consequences of Intimate Partner Violence." *Lancet* 359, no. 9314 (2002): 1331–1336.

Cannon, Clare, and F. P. Buttell. "The Social Construction of Roles in Intimate Partner Violence: Is the Victim/Perpetrator Model the Only Viable One?" *Journal of Family Violence* 31, no. 8 (2016): 967–971.

Cannon, Clare, Katie Lauve-Moon, and Fred Buttell. "Re-theorizing Intimate Partner Violence through Post-structural Feminism, Queer Theory, and the Sociology of Gender." *Social Sciences* 4, no. 3 (2015): 668–687.

Cast, Alicia D., and Peter J. Burke. "A Theory of Self-Esteem." *Social Forces* 80, no. 3 (2002): 1041–1068.

Centers for Disease Control and Prevention. "Violence Prevention." August 22, 2017. www.cdc.gov.

Cerulo, Karen A. "Identity Construction: New Issues, New Directions." *Annual Review of Sociology* 23, no. 1 (1997): 385–409.

Charmaz, Kathy. *Constructing Grounded Theory: A Practical Guide through Qualitative Research.* London: Sage, 2006.

Collins, Patricia Hill. *Black Feminist Thought: Knowledge, Consciousness, and the Politics of Empowerment.* New York: Routledge, 2002.

Connell, Raewyn. *Gender and Power.* Cambridge, MA: Polity Press, 2003.

Cook-Daniels, Loree. "Intimate Partner Violence in Transgender Couples: 'Power and Control' in a Specific Cultural Context." *Partner Abuse* 6, no. 1 (2015): 126.

Cooley, Charles Horton. *Human Nature and the Social Order.* New York: Shocken Books, 1902.

Corbin, Julliett, and Anselm Strauss. *Basics of Qualitative Research.* Thousand Oaks, CA: Sage, 2008.

Courvant, Diana, and Loree Cook-Daniels. "Trans and Intersex Survivors of Domestic Violence: Defining Terms, Barriers and Responsibilities." National Coalition of Domestic Violence, 1998. www.survivorproject.org.

Crawley, Sara L., Lara J. Foley, and Constance L. Shehan. *Gendering Bodies.* Lanham, MD: Rowman & Littlefield, 2007.

Creative Interventions. "Toolkit." 2018. www.creativeinterventions.org.

Crenshaw, Kimberlé. "Mapping the Margins: Intersectionality, Identity Politics, and Violence Against Women of Color." *Stanford Law Review* 43 (1991): 1241–1299.

Cruz, J. Michael. "'Why Doesn't He Just Leave?' Gay Male Domestic Violence and the Reasons Victims Stay." *Journal of Men's Studies* 11, no. 3 (2003): 309–323.

Davis, Georgiann. *Contesting Intersex: The Dubious Diagnosis.* New York: New York University Press, 2015.

Davis, Heath Fogg. *Beyond Trans: Does Gender Matter?* New York: New York University Press, 2017.

Davis, Kierrynn, and Nel Glass. "Reframing the Heteronormative Constructions of Lesbian Partner Violence." In Ristock, *Intimate Partner Violence in LGBTQ Lives,* 13–37.

Dobash, R. Emerson, and Russell Dobash. *Violence Against Wives: A Case Against the Patriarchy.* New York: Free Press, 1979.

Dobash, Russell P., R. Emerson Dobash, Margo Wilson, and Martin Daly. "The Myth of Sexual Symmetry in Marital Violence." *Social Problems* 39, no. 1 (1992): 71–91.

Ebaugh, Helen Rose Fuchs. *Becoming an Ex: The Process of Role Exit.* Chicago: University of Chicago Press, 1988.

Edwards-Leeper, Laura, Scott Leibowitz, and Varunee Faii Sangganjanavanich. "Affirmative Practice with Transgender and Gender Nonconforming Youth: Expanding the Model." *Psychology of Sexual Orientation and Gender Diversity* 3, no. 2 (2016): 165–172.

Erbaugh, Elizabeth B. "Queering Approaches to Intimate Partner Violence." In *Gender Violence: Interdisciplinary Perspectives*, edited by Laura L. O'Toole, Jessica R. Schiffman, and Margie L. Kiter Edwards, 451–459. New York: New York University Press, 2007.

Essence, Leon Bennett. "Laverne Cox Explains What Anti-trans Bathroom Legislation Is Really About." *The Cut*, February 24, 2017. www.thecut.com.

Ezzy, Douglas. *Qualitative Analysis: Practice and Innovation*. New York: Routledge, 2002.

Federal Bureau of Investigation. "About Hate Crime Statistics 2015." October 18, 2016. https://ucr.fbi.gov.

Feinberg, Leslie. *Trans Liberation: Beyond Pink or Blue*. Boston: Beacon Press, 1998.

Felson, Richard B., and Steven F. Messner. "The Control Motive in Intimate Partner Violence." *Social Psychology Quarterly* 63 (2000): 86–94.

Flores, Andrew R. "Attitudes toward Transgender Rights: Perceived Knowledge and Secondary Interpersonal Contact." *Politics, Groups, and Identities* 3, no. 3 (2015): 398–416.

Follingstad, Diane R., and Maryanne Edmundson. "Is Psychological Abuse Reciprocal in Intimate Relationships? Data from a National Sample of American Adults." *Journal of Family Violence* 25, no. 5 (2010): 495–508.

Foucault, Michel. *The Order of Things: An Archaeology of the Human Sciences*. New York: Pantheon, 2002.

———. *Power/Knowledge: Selected Interviews and Other Writings, 1972–1977*. New York: Pantheon, 1980.

Garcia, Nicholas. "Colorado's Transgender Students Will Still Get to Use the Bathrooms They Choose Despite Trump's Order. Here's Why." *Denver Post*, February 23, 2017. www.denverpost.com.

Gathright, Jenny. "Violence Against Women Act Expires Because of Government Shutdown." National Public Radio, December 24, 2018. www.npr.org.

Gay & Lesbian Alliance Against Defamation (GLAAD). "End Healthcare Discrimination for Transgender People." July 11, 2014. www.glaad.org.

———. "Honoring Known Cases of Deadly Anti-trans Violence in 2017." January 8, 2018. www.glaad.org.

———. "New Report Reveals Rampant Discrimination Against Transgender People by Health Providers, High HIV Rates and Widespread Lack of Access to Necessary Care." National LGBTQ Task Force, October 13, 2010. www.thetaskforce.org.

Gelaye, Bizu, Ngan Do, Samantha Avila, Juan Carlos Velez, Qiu-Yue Zhong, Sixto E. Sanchez, B. Lee Peterlin, and Michelle A. Williams. "Childhood Abuse, Intimate Partner Violence and Risk of Migraine among Pregnant Women: An Epidemiologic Study." *Headache: The Journal of Head and Face Pain* 56, no. 6 (2016): 976–986.

Gilbert, Louisa, Paula Poorman, and Sandra Simmons. "Guidelines for Mental Health Systems Response to Lesbian Battering." In *Confronting Lesbian Battering: A Manual for the Battered Women's Movement*, edited by Pam Elliot, 105–117. Saint Paul: Minnesota Coalition for Battered Women, 1990.

Girshick, Lori B. *Woman-to-Woman Sexual Violence: Does She Call It Rape?* Lebanon, NH: University Press of New England, 2002.

Goffman, Erving. *Interaction Ritual: Essays in Face-to-Face Behavior.* New Brunswick, NJ: Aldine Transaction, 2005.

———. *The Presentation of Self in Everyday Life.* New York: Anchor, 1959.

Goodmark, Leigh. "Should Domestic Violence Be Decriminalized?" *Harvard Women's Law Journal* 40 (2017): 53–113.

Graham, Robert, Bobbie Berkowitz, Robert Blum, Walter Bockting, Judith Bradford, Brian de Vries, and Harvey Makadon. "The Health of Lesbian, Gay, Bisexual, and Transgender People: Building a Foundation for Better Understanding." Washington, DC: Institute of Medicine, 2011.

Grant, Jaime M., Lisa A. Mottet, Justin Tanis, Jody L. Herman, Jack Harrison, and Mara Keisling. "National Transgender Discrimination Survey Report on Health and Health Care." Washington, DC: National Center for Transgender Equality and the National Gay and Lesbian Task Force, 2010.

Greenwood, Max. "Sessions Reverses DOJ Policy on Transgender Employee Protections." *The Hill*, October 5, 2017. www.thehill.com.

Greer, Germaine. *The Whole Woman.* London: Doubleday, 1999.

Grinberg, Emanuella. "Caitlyn Jenner Doesn't Regret Voting for Trump." *CNN*, April 26, 2017. www.cnn.com.

Grosz, Elizabeth A. *Volatile Bodies: Toward a Corporeal Feminism.* Bloomington: Indiana University Press, 1994.

Guadalupe-Diaz, Xavier. "Disclosure of Same-Sex Intimate Partner Violence to Police among Lesbians, Gays, and Bisexuals." *Social Currents* 3, no. 2 (2016): 160–171.

Guadalupe-Diaz, Xavier L., and Amanda Koontz Anthony. "Discrediting Identity Work: Understandings of Intimate Partner Violence by Transgender Survivors." *Deviant Behavior* 38, no. 1 (2017): 1–16.

Guadalupe-Diaz, Xavier L., and Jana Jasinski. "'I Wasn't a Priority, I Wasn't a Victim': Challenges in Help Seeking for Transgender Survivors of Intimate Partner Violence." *Violence Against Women* 23, no. 6 (2017): 772–792.

Guadalupe-Diaz, Xavier L., and Jonathan Yglesias. "'Who's Protected?' Exploring Perceptions of Domestic Violence Law by Lesbians, Gays, and Bisexuals." *Journal of Gay & Lesbian Social Services* 25, no. 4 (2013): 465–485.

Guest, Greg, Arwen Bunce, and Laura Johnson. "How Many Interviews Are Enough? An Experiment with Data Saturation and Variability." *Field Methods* 18, no. 1 (2006): 59–82.

Hannem, Stacey, Debra Langan, and Catherine Stewart. "'Every Couple Has Their Fights . . .': Stigma and Subjective Narratives of Verbal Violence." *Deviant Behavior* 36, no. 5 (2015): 388–404.

Hart, Barbara. "Lesbian Battering: An Examination." In *Naming the Violence: Speaking Out about Lesbian Battering*, edited by Kerry Lobel, 173–189. Seattle: Seal Press, 1986.

Herman, Nancy J. "Interactionist Research Methods: An Overview." In *Symbolic Interaction: An Introduction to Social Psychology*, edited by Nancy J. Herman and Larry T. Reynolds, 90–111. Lanham, MD: AltaMira, 1994.

Hill, Darryl B., and Brian L. B. Willoughby. "The Development and Validation of the Genderism and Transphobia Scale." *Sex Roles* 53, nos. 7–8 (2005): 531–544.

Hobson, Janell, ed. *Are All the Women Still White? Rethinking Race, Expanding Feminisms*. Albany: State University of New York Press, 2016.

Human Rights Campaign. "Discrimination Against Transgender Workers." 2019. www.hrc.org.

Iantaffi, Alex, and Walter O. Bockting. "Views from Both Sides of the Bridge? Gender, Sexual Legitimacy and Transgender People's Experiences of Relationships." *Culture, Health & Sexuality* 13, no. 3 (2011): 355–370.

Island, David, and Patrick Letellier. *Men Who Beat the Men Who Love Them: Battered Gay Men and Domestic Violence*. New York: Psychology Press, 1991.

Jeffreys, Sheila. *Unpacking Queer Politics*. Cambridge, MA: Polity Press, 2002.

Johnson, Katherine. "Being Transsexual: Self, Identity and Embodied Subjectivity." PhD dissertation, Middlesex University, 2001.

Johnson, Michael P. *A Typology of Domestic Violence: Intimate Terrorism, Violent Resistance, and Situational Couple Violence*. Lebanon, NH: University Press of New England, 2010.

Kaplan, Ami. "Basic Issues in Transgender Mental Health." Transgender Mental Health, April 8, 2015. https://tgmentalhealth.com.

Kelly, Liz, Sheila Burton, and Linda Regan. "Beyond Victim or Survivor: Sexual Violence, Identity and Feminist Theory and Practice." In *Sexualizing the Social: Power and the Organization of Sexuality*, edited by Lisa Adkins and Vicki Merchant, 77–101. Basingstoke: Palgrave Macmillan, 1996.

Kent, David. "About a Third of Americans Say Society Has Gone Too Far in Accepting Transgender People." Pew Research Center, November 6, 2017. www.pewresearch.org.

———. "Nearly Four-in-Ten Americans Say They Know Someone Who Is Transgender." Pew Research Center, November 6, 2017. www.pewresearch.org.

Kim, Mimi. "Alternative Interventions to Violence: Creative Interventions." *International Journal of Narrative Therapy and Community Work* 2006, no. 4 (2006): 45–52.

———. "Creative Interventions." 2018. www.creativeinterventions.org.

Kimmel, Michael S. "'Gender Symmetry' in Domestic Violence: A Substantive and Methodological Research Review." *Violence Against Women* 8, no. 11 (2002): 1332–1363.

Kodjak, Alison. "Trump Admin Will Protect Health Workers Who Refuse Services on Religious Grounds." NPR, January 18, 2018. www.npr.org.

Lagdon, Susan, Cherie Armour, and Maurice Stringer. "Adult Experience of Mental Health Outcomes as a Result of Intimate Partner Violence Victimisation: A Systematic Review." *European Journal of Psychotraumatology* 5, no. 1 (2014): 24794.

Leisenring, Amy. "Confronting 'Victim' Discourses: The Identity Work of Battered Women." *Symbolic Interaction* 29, no. 3 (2006): 307–330.

———. "'Whoa! They Could've Arrested Me!' Unsuccessful Identity Claims of Women during Police Response to Intimate Partner Violence." *Qualitative Sociology* 34, no. 2 (2011): 353–370.

Lewis, Robin J., Valerian J. Derlega, Jessica L. Griffin, and Alison C. Krowinski. "Stressors for Gay Men and Lesbians: Life Stress, Gay-Related Stress, Stigma Consciousness, and Depressive Symptoms." *Journal of Social and Clinical Psychology* 22, no. 6 (2003): 716–729.

Lewis, Robin J., Robert J. Milletich, Michelle L. Kelley, and Alex Woody. "Minority Stress, Substance Use, and Intimate Partner Violence among Sexual Minority Women." *Aggression and Violent Behavior* 17, no. 3 (2012): 247–256.

Liang, Belle, Lisa Goodman, Pratyusha Tummala-Narra, and Sarah Weintraub. "A Theoretical Framework for Understanding Help-Seeking Processes among Survivors of Intimate Partner Violence." *American Journal of Community Psychology* 36, nos. 1–2 (2005): 71–84.

Logan, T. K., Lucy Evans, Erin Stevenson, and Carol E. Jordan. "Barriers to Services for Rural and Urban Survivors of Rape." *Journal of Interpersonal Violence* 20, no. 5 (2005): 591–616.

Lombardi, Emilia L., Riki Anne Wilchins, Dana Priesing, and Diana Malouf. "Gender Violence: Transgender Experiences with Violence and Discrimination." *Journal of Homosexuality* 42, no. 1 (2002): 89–101.

Lorde, Audre. "Learning from the 60s." In *Sister Outsider: Essays & Speeches by Audre Lorde*, 134–144. Berkeley, CA: Crossing Press, 2007.

Loseke, Donileen R. "Lived Realities and the Construction of Social Problems: The Case of Wife Abuse." *Symbolic Interaction* 10, no. 2 (1987): 229–243.

———. "The Study of Identity as Cultural, Institutional, Organizational, and Personal Narratives: Theoretical and Empirical Integrations." *Sociological Quarterly* 48, no. 4 (2007): 661–688.

Malo, Sebastien. "In First, U.S. Man Sentenced for Transgender Hate Crime." Reuters, May 17, 2017. www.reuters.com.

Martin, Carol Lynn, and Diane N. Ruble. "Patterns of Gender Development." *Annual Review of Psychology* 61 (2010): 353–381.

Martin, Del. *Battered Wives*. Volcano, CA: Volcano Press, 1981.

Mason-Schrock, Douglas. "Transsexuals' Narrative Construction of the 'True Self.'" *Social Psychology Quarterly* 59 (1996): 176–192.

McCall, George J., and Jerry Laird Simmons. *Identities and Interactions*. Chicago: University of Chicago Press, 1966.

McClennen, Joan C. "Domestic Violence between Same-Gender Partners: Recent Findings and Future Research." *Journal of Interpersonal Violence* 20, no. 2 (2005): 149–154.

McClennen, Joan C., Anne B. Summers, and Charles Vaughan. "Gay Men's Domestic Violence: Dynamics, Help-Seeking Behaviors, and Correlates." *Journal of Gay & Lesbian Social Services* 14, no. 1 (2002): 23–49.

McLaughlin, Erin M., and Patricia D. Rozee. "Knowledge about Heterosexual versus Lesbian Battering among Lesbians." *Women & Therapy* 23, no. 3 (2001): 39–58.

Meisner, Jason. "Federal Charges Net Dozens of Alleged Latin Kings in Sweeping Conspiracy." *Chicago Tribune*, July 27, 2016. www.chicagotribune.com.

Merrill, Gregory S. "Ruling the Exceptions: Same-Sex Battering and Domestic Violence Theory." *Journal of Gay & Lesbian Social Services* 4, no. 1 (1996): 9–22.

Messinger, Adam M. *LGBTQ Intimate Partner Violence: Lessons for Policy, Practice, and Research*. Berkeley: University of California Press, 2017.

Meyer, Doug. "Resisting Hate Crime Discourse: Queer and Intersectional Challenges to Neoliberal Hate Crime Laws." *Critical Criminology* 22, no. 1 (2014): 113–125.

Miller, Laura E., and John P. Caughlin. "'We're Going to Be Survivors': Couples' Identity Challenges during and after Cancer Treatment." *Communication Monographs* 80, no. 1 (2013): 63–82.

Milovanovic, Dragan. *A Primer in the Sociology of Law*. Albany, NY: Harrow and Heston, 1994.

Mizock, Lauren, and Thomas K. Lewis. "Trauma in Transgender Populations: Risk, Resilience, and Clinical Care." *Journal of Emotional Abuse* 8, no. 3 (2008): 335–354.

Movement Advancement Project and Center for American Progress. "Paying an Unfair Price: The Financial Penalty for Being Transgender in America." 2014. www.lgbtmap.org.

Moyer, Justin Wm. "Caitlyn Jenner: 'I like Ted Cruz.'" *Washington Post*, March 4, 2016. www.washingtonpost.com.

Munson, Michael, and Loree Cook-Daniels. "Transgender/SOFFA: Domestic Violence/Sexual Assault Resource Sheet." FORGE. 2007.

Myers, David. "Positivist Victimology: A Critique Part 2: Critical Victimology." *International Review of Victimology* 1, no. 3 (1990): 219–230.

National Center for Transgender Equality. "Housing & Homelessness." 2018. https://transequality.org.

———. "National Transgender Discrimination Survey." 2016. https://transequality.org.

———. "Survivors of Violence." 2018. https://transequality.org.

National Coalition of Anti-Violence Programs (NCAVP). "Hate Violence Against Transgender Communities." 2014. https://avp.org.

———. "Lesbian, Gay, Bisexual, Transgender, Queer, and HIV-Affected Intimate Partner Violence in 2010: A Report from the National Coalition of Anti-Violence Programs." 2011. https://avp.org.

———. "Lesbian, Gay, Bisexual, Transgender, Queer, and HIV-Affected Intimate Partner Violence in 2011: A Report from the National Coalition of Anti-Violence Programs." 2012. https://avp.org.

———. "Lesbian, Gay, Bisexual, Transgender, Queer, and HIV-Affected Intimate Partner Violence in 2015: A Report from the National Coalition of Anti-Violence Programs." 2016. https://avp.org.

———. "Lesbian, Gay, Bisexual, Transgender, Queer, and HIV-Affected Intimate Partner Violence in 2016." 2017. https://avp.org.

———. "Media Release: 2013 Report on Intimate Partner Violence in Lesbian, Gay, Bisexual, Transgender, Queer and HIV-Affected Communities in the U.S." 2014. https://avp.org.

———. "Our Reports." NYC Anti-Violence Project. 2018. https://avp.org.

Norton, Aaron T., and Gregory M. Herek. "Heterosexuals' Attitudes toward Transgender People: Findings from a National Probability Sample of US Adults." *Sex Roles* 68, nos. 11–12 (2013): 738–753.

O'Hara, Mary Emily. "Trans Women of Color Face an Epidemic of Violence and Murder." *Vice*, November 20, 2014. www.vice.com.

Out. "7 Trans Women of Color Have Been Murdered in 2017." March 6, 2017. www.out.com.

Owens, Timothy J., Dawn T. Robinson, and Lynn Smith-Lovin. "Three Faces of Identity." *Annual Review of Sociology* 36 (2010): 477–499.

Panfil, Vanessa R. *The Gang's All Queer: The Lives of Gay Gang Members.* New York: New York University Press, 2017.

Penner, Louis A., John F. Dovidio, Tessa V. West, Samuel L. Gaertner, Terrance L. Albrecht, Rhonda K. Dailey, and Tsveti Markova. "Aversive Racism and Medical Interactions with Black Patients: A Field Study." *Journal of Experimental Social Psychology* 46, no. 2 (2010): 436–440.

Perinbanayagam, Robert S. *The Presence of Self.* Lanham, MD: Rowman & Littlefield, 2000.

Peterson, Dana, and Vanessa Panfil. *Handbook of LGBT Communities, Crime, and Justice.* New York: Springer, 2014.

Petrosky, Emiko, Janet M. Blair, Carter J. Betz, Katherine A. Fowler, Shane P. D. Jack, and Bridget H. Lyons. "Racial and Ethnic Differences in Homicides of Adult Women and the Role of Intimate Partner Violence—United States, 2003–2014." *Morbidity and Mortality Weekly Report* 66 (2017): 741–746. www.cdc.gov.

Phillips, Amber. "10 Things to Know about Sen. Jeff Sessions, Donald Trump's Pick for Attorney General." *Washington Post*, January 10, 2017. www.washingtonpost.com.

Potter, Hillary. *Intersectionality and Criminology: Disrupting and Revolutionizing Studies of Crime.* New York: Routledge, 2015.

Renzetti, Claire M. *Violent Betrayal: Partner Abuse in Lesbian Relationships.* Thousand Oaks, CA: Sage, 1992.

Ristock, Janice L., ed. *Intimate Partner Violence in LGBTQ Lives.* New York: Routledge, 2011.

———. *No More Secrets: Violence in Lesbian Relationships.* New York: Routledge, 2002.

Roch, Amy, Graham Ritchie, and James Morton. "Out of Sight, Out of Mind? Transgender People's Experiences of Domestic Abuse." Edinburgh: Scottish Transgender Alliance, 2010.

Saavedra, Ryan. "Latin Kings Member Gets 50 Years for Killing Trans Girlfriend." *Breitbart*, May 17, 2017. www.breitbart.com.

Saldaña, Johnny. *The Coding Manual for Qualitative Researchers.* Thousand Oaks, CA: Sage, 2015.

Schilt, Kristen, and Laurel Westbrook. "Doing Gender, Doing Heteronormativity: 'Gender Normals,' Transgender People, and the Social Maintenance of Heterosexuality." *Gender & Society* 23, no. 4 (2009): 440–464.

Schwalbe, Michael L., and Douglas Mason-Schrock. "Identity Work as Group Process." *Advances in Group Processes* 13, no. 113 (1996): 47.

Sharpe, Alex. "Criminalising Sexual Intimacy: Transgender Defendants and the Legal Construction of Non-consent." *Criminal Law Review* 3 (2014): 207–223.

Sims, Christy-Dale L. "Invisible Wounds, Invisible Abuse: The Exclusion of Emotional Abuse in Newspaper Articles." *Journal of Emotional Abuse* 8, no. 4 (2008): 375–402.

Singh, Anneliese A., and Vel S. McKleroy. "'Just Getting Out of Bed Is a Revolutionary Act': The Resilience of Transgender People of Color Who Have Survived Traumatic Life Events." *Traumatology* 17, no. 2 (2011): 34–44.

Smith, Sharon G., Kathleen C. Basile, Leah K. Gilbert, Melissa T. Merrick, Nimesh Patel, Margie Walling, and Anurag Jain. "National Intimate Partner and Sexual Violence Survey (NISVS): 2010–2012 State Report." Atlanta: Centers for Disease Control and Prevention, 2017.

Snow, David A., and Leon Anderson. "Identity Work among the Homeless: The Verbal Construction and Avowal of Personal Identities." *American Journal of Sociology* 92, no. 6 (1987): 1336–1371.

Sokoloff, Natalie J., and Christina Pratt, eds. *Domestic Violence at the Margins: Readings on Race, Class, Gender, and Culture.* New Brunswick, NJ: Rutgers University Press, 2005.

Spade, Dean. *Normal Life: Administrative Violence, Critical Trans Politics, and the Limits of Law.* Durham, NC: Duke University Press, 2015.

———. "Transformation—Three Myths Regarding Transgender Identity Have Led to Conflicting Laws and Policies That Adversely Affect Transgender People." *Los Angeles Lawyer* 31 (2008): 34–41.

Stack, Liam. "U.S. Hate Crime Law Punishes Transgender Woman's Killer, in a First." *New York Times*, May 16, 2017. www.nytimes.com.

Stark, Evan. *Coercive Control: The Entrapment of Women in Personal Life.* New York: Oxford University Press, 2009.

Stark, Evan, and Anne Flitcraft. *Women at Risk.* Thousand Oaks, CA: Sage, 1996.

Stets, Jan E., and Peter J. Burke. "Identity Verification, Control, and Aggression in Marriage." *Social Psychology Quarterly* 68, no. 2 (2005): 160–178.

Stotzer, Rebecca L. "Violence Against Transgender People: A Review of United States Data." *Aggression and Violent Behavior* 14, no. 3 (2009): 170–179.

Stubbs, Julie. "Domestic Violence and Women's Safety: Feminist Challenges to Restorative Justice." In *Restorative Justice and Family Violence*, edited by Heather Strang and John Braithwaite, 42–61. Cambridge: Cambridge University Press.

Tebbe, Elliot A., Bonnie Moradi, and Engin Ege. "Revised and Abbreviated Forms of the Genderism and Transphobia Scale: Tools for Assessing Anti-trans* Prejudice." *Journal of Counseling Psychology* 61, no. 4 (2014): 581–592.

Tehrani, Noreen. "Victim to Survivor." In *Building a Culture of Respect: Managing Bullying at Work*, edited by Noreen Tehrani, 43–58. London: Taylor & Francis, 2001.

Thoits, Peggy A. "Resisting the Stigma of Mental Illness." *Social Psychology Quarterly* 74, no. 1 (2011): 6–28.

Tracy, Karen. "Discourse and Identity: Language or Talk." In *Explaining Communication: Contemporary Theories and Exemplars*, edited by Brian B. Whaley and Wendy Samter, 15–38. New York: Routledge, 2006.

Transgender Law Center. "Undocumented Trans Woman and Survivor of Domestic Violence Arrested while Seeking Safety." 2017. https://transgenderlawcenter.org.

US Department of Justice. "The Matthew Shepard and James Byrd, Jr., Hate Crimes Prevention Act of 2009." 2010. www.justice.gov.

Valenta, Marko. "Immigrants' Identity Negotiations and Coping with Stigma in Different Relational Frames." *Symbolic Interaction* 32, no. 4 (2009): 351–371.

Vogue, Ariane De, and Zachary Cohen. "Supreme Court Allows Transgender Military Ban to Go into Effect." *CNN*, January 22, 2019. www.cnn.com.

Vogue, Ariane De, and Alex Lee. "Meet Gavin Grimm, the Transgender Student at the Center of Bathroom Debate." *CNN*, September 8, 2016. www.cnn.com.

Walker, Chris. "Here Are Some of Mike Pence's Most Controversial Stances on Gay Rights, Abortion, and Smoking." *Business Insider*, November 14, 2016. www.businessinsider.com.

Walker, Julia K. "Investigating Trans People's Vulnerabilities to Intimate Partner Violence/Abuse." *Partner Abuse* 6, no. 1 (2015): 107–125.

Walters, Mikel L., Jieru Chen, and Matthew J. Breiding. "The National Intimate Partner and Sexual Violence Survey (NISVS): 2010 Findings on Victimization by Sexual Orientation." Atlanta: National Center for Injury Prevention and Control, Centers for Disease Control and Prevention, 2013.

Weinstein, Eugene A., and Paul Deutschberger. "Some Dimensions of Altercasting." *Sociometry* 26 (1963): 454–466.

Weitzman, Lenore J. "To Love, Honor, and Obey? Traditional Legal Marriage and Alternative Family Forms." *Family Coordinator* 24 (1975): 531–548.

West, Candace, and Don H. Zimmerman. "Doing Gender." *Gender & Society* 1, no. 2 (1987): 125–151.

Wierks, Kylee. "Indiana Schools, Gov. Pence React to Obama Administration's Directive on Transgender Access to School Bathrooms." FOX59, May 13, 2016. https://fox59.com.

Williams Institute. "Gender-Related Measures Overview." February 22, 2013. https://williamsinstitute.law.ucla.edu.

Wilson, Reid. "US Prison Population Falling as Crime Rates Stay Low." *The Hill*, January 3, 2017. http://thehill.com.

Zemsky, Beth. "Screening for Survivor Services: Or Are We Serving the Right Woman?" In *Confronting Lesbian Battering: A Manual for the Battered Women's Movement*, edited by Pam Elliot, 88–90. Saint Paul: Minnesota Coalition for Battered Women, 1990.

Zhao, Shanyang, Sherri Grasmuck, and Jason Martin. "Identity Construction on Facebook: Digital Empowerment in Anchored Relationships." *Computers in Human Behavior* 24, no. 5 (2008): 1816–1836.

INDEX

abuse. *See specific types*

abuse identification complexities, 70, 74–75

abusers: Brown on tactics of, 56–57; as cisgender, in transgender survivors study, 61; dating of, 63–67; gender expression and, 87; gifting by, 107; jealousy and attacks from, 103–4; medicalization manipulation by, 34, 108; power and control of, 7, 13; thoughts on goodness of, 62–68; as transgender partners, 83–84. *See also* genderist attacks; transphobic attacks; *specific topics*

Adichie, Chimamanda Ngozi, 17

altercasting, 109; controlling transition and, 91–92, 94–101; insecurities and, 98–99, 111; IPV and, 110; long-term relationships and, 95; Miller and Caughlin on, 110; power plays and, 101; process of, 95; romantic narratives in, 95; self-identities and, 95; Weinstein and Deutschberger on, 92

Anderson, Leon, 88, 90

Anna, as trans-Latina, 31; abuse frequency increase for, 73; abuser and help-seeking, 121; abuser of, 52–54; abuser sexual exploitation of, 54–56; as drag performer, 38, 51–52; family rejection of, 40, 46, 51; friends and informal supports for, 137; genderist attacks of, 78; homelessness of, 37, 40, 51; increased isolation of, 53–54; law enforcement and, 132; people of color violence threat for, 57; religiosity and, 45; social prac-

tice of, 32; student discrimination of, 34; survival sex of, 37–38, 51–54, 73–74; transphobic attack of, 79–80, 82; victim identity of, 120–21

anxiety, of trans victims, 146

Arrigo, Bruce A., 18

Audrey, as white transwoman, 73; abuser use of emotional manipulation, 71, 99, 100–101; altercasting and, 99; genderist attacks of, 77; genderqueer abuser of, 83; polyamorous relationship with, 67–68; sex work of, 71; transition and employment loss of, 36–37; victim identity of, 123–24

Barrett, Betty Jo, 156

bathroom debates: Cox on, 47–48; gender identity and, 35; in student discrimination, 34–35; Title IX policies and sex discrimination for, 35, 46–47

beauty and attractiveness perspective, of cisgender, 25

Bernard, Thomas J., 18

black women: social stigmatization of, 12; social theory and, 10

Bono, Chaz, 44

Bornstein, Danica, 1

Breitbart news blog, on Williamson hate crime, 48–49

Brittany, as white transwoman: dating of abuser and, 63; on family support, 41; genderist attacks of, 76; polyamorous relationship of, 60–61, 68, 185n27

Brown, Taylor N. T., 8, 56–57, 118–19

in, 13; social and political climate and LGBTQ issues, 46. *See also specific Departments*

Vallum, Joshua: gender identity hate crime conviction of, 42–43; sentencing of, 48–49
VAWA. *See* Violence Against Women Act
victim identity, 93; exiting and, 109, 113–19; gendered language and, 116, 119, 140, 149–50; processing of, 112–41; research on, 88
victimization, 157–58; criminal justice system and, 151; trans victims exit and, 116, 119–24. *See also* transgender victims
victim-perpetrator gendered binary, Erbaugh on, 14, 140
violence: anti-trans cultural and social climates impact on, 57; hate-motivated, 27, 46, 48, 184n36; intersecting systems and, 46, 47; Island and Letellier on learned, 12–13; LGBTQ victimization by, 2; as masculinity act, 9, 14, 15; at trans people, 1; United States culture facilitation of, 26
Violence Against Women Act (VAWA), 133; on domestic violence shelters, 160
violence and abuse accounts, in transgender survivors study, 51–57;

abusers as cisgender in, 61; descriptive violent accounts of, 68–75; genderism and transphobia power and social context, 82–85; genderist attacks in, 58, 75–78; on relationships, 60–61; thoughts of goodness in abuser, 62–68; transphobic attacks in, 58, 79–82

Walker, Julia K., 27, 111, 148, 159
Weinstein, Eugene A., 88, 91, 92
West, Candace, 15
Westbrook, Laurel, 62
white supremacy, 49
William, as white transman, abuse types of, 71
Williams Institute, 8, 154
Williamson, Mercedes, 42–43, 48
Woman-to-Woman Sexual Violence: Does She Call it Rape? (Girshick), 2
women: black, 10, 12; Butler on meaning of, 16; help-seeking structures for cisgender, 8, 117, 160; IPV against, 1–2, 6; Leisenring on identity work and, 92–93; subordination of, 58, 78; victim cultural construct for, 14. *See also* transwomen

Zimmerman, Don, 15

ABOUT THE AUTHOR

Xavier L. Guadalupe-Diaz is Assistant Professor of Sociology and Criminology at Framingham State University in Massachusetts.